647- 888-

Exploring Leadership and Ethical Practice through Professional Inquiry

Déirdre Smith, Editor

Patricia Goldblatt , Editor

Exploring Leadership
and Ethical Practice through
Professional Inquiry

Ontario
College of
Teachers

THE CATHOLIC
PRINCIPALS' COUNCIL
OF ONTARIO

LES PRESSES DE L'UNIVERSITÉ LAVAL

Les Presses de l'Université Laval receives funding each year from the Société de développement des entreprises culturelles du Québec for its entire publishing program.

We wish to acknowledge funding from the Government of Canada through the Book Publishing Industry Development Program for our publishing activities.

Design and computer graphics: Mariette Montambault

Cover: iStockphoto

ISBN 978-2-7637-8666-7

2e tirage 2010

Les Presses de l'Université Laval
Pavillon Pollack, bureau 3103
2305, rue de l'Université
Université Laval, Québec
Canada, G1V 0A6

www.pulaval.com

To current and future school and system leaders.

Lou Rocha
Executive Director
The Catholic Principals' Council of Ontario

For the highly committed and dedicated educational leaders in Ontario.

Brian McGowan
Registrar and Chief Executive Officer
Ontario College of Teachers

Table of Contents

Foreword

Robert J. STARRATT
Professor of Education, Boston College

Case studies provide useful learning opportunities for those preparing to become teachers and administrators, as well as for those already on the job who are seeking to advance the quality of their leadership practice. Case studies allow participants to imaginatively enter into the dramas that emerge amidst the realities of life in schools. These dramas involve students, teachers and parents in relationships of conflict, in situations of unequal power and status, in circumstances charged with moral consequences, in the pulls and tugs of personalities, clashing assumptions and beliefs, over-lapping areas of responsibilities, and exceptional circumstances with few policy guidelines – all of which call for professional judgment, diverse perspective taking, value prioritizing, and a search for reasonable short-term and goal focused long-term responses.

Case studies often reveal that life in schools is not the rational process school leaders would like the public to think it is. In order to garner public support and confidence, schools present themselves to their communities as places where teachers are all in agreement over what should be taught and in what sequence, using what specific pedagogies, as places where all children are treated fairly and with respect and care, where values of the community are taught and upheld, and where those in charge know what they are doing and act rationally and decisively within clear policies and procedures. While the staff in all schools, in their own way, want to believe that this picture of their school is the ideal they all desire, they would readily admit that the reality falls far short of the ideal on most days.

Rather, considering the realities of their students' home situations, their students' readiness to successfully engage in the learning tasks put before them varies enormously from student to student and from class period to class period. Given limited resources for smaller classes, the steady flow of new curriculum materials, and the finite hours in the school day and week, some teachers will inevitably feel shortchanged and frustrated. Given the variability among teaching staff, some parents will feel that their children have not been placed with the better teachers. Given the pressures that administrators face every day to respond to every problem situation that arises in the building, criticisms of their leadership, their decisiveness, and their sensitivity will arise.

In other words, schools in contemporary societies are places where messes occur on a daily basis. Preparing for their professional careers and sustaining their professional practice require that educators continue to learn, both in university programs and on the job, how to respond to the immediacy of situations that arise every day in the practice of teaching and administering schools. Some of these situations clearly involve ethical issues or dilemmas requiring ethical deliberation and reflection. Some of these situations involve misunderstandings over professional responsibilities that require more direct, pragmatic responses. Some involve challenges to authority or institutional legitimacy and require both policy clarification and political compromise.

Case studies, therefore, provide opportunities to engage the drama of school problems, conflicts, disagreements and challenges in a safe learning environment where the players in the drama can adopt the role of one of the protagonists, discuss with others their perceptions of the problem or issue, and explore several alternative responses and their probable consequences. Through multiple rehearsals of the messy drama of everyday life in schools, educators can develop greater professional flexibility and adaptability in their responses, can become more reflective about the assumptions they and others bring to conflict situations, can develop a deeper sense of compassion toward the human propensity to unintentionally create messes, can clarify the core values they will stand by, can explore policy issues behind decisions, and finally, can grow in their capacity to deal with the short-term symptoms of problems while looking toward the more effective long-range preventive measures required to forestall similar problems in the future.

The cases presented in this text offer a wide variety of situations that may very well crop up next week in any given school. Engaging the issues in these cases will help develop the pragmatic responses and value-laden considerations required not only for survival on the job, but also for developing a sense of leadership that can turn many of these situations into opportunities for the growth of those involved.

Acknowledgements

Exploring Leadership and Ethical Practice through Professional Inquiry has been a collaborative provincial project between the Ontario College of Teachers and the Catholic Principals' Council of Ontario. This partnership was realized through the work of the editors Déirdre Smith, Patricia Goldblatt and principals Denis Maika, Nelly Kelders and Barbara McMorrow. The development, structure and content of this book honour and reflect the important role of dialogue, inquiry and community within educational leadership practices.

The principals and vice-principals who wrote the cases presented in this book are committed to supporting leadership formation. They reflected on their professional practice within diverse education contexts and offered their lived experiences as curriculum for the enhancement of ethical practice and leadership development. Their experiences serve as educative resources for the teaching profession and teacher education.

James Moloney, Jerry Wheeler, and Carson Allard supported the validation of the written cases and the professional inquiry processes included in this text. Thousands of aspiring and practising principals and vice-principals engaged with these cases in both online and face-to-face leadership courses. Their feedback affirmed the importance of these written case experiences as meaningful and relevant leadership curriculum. The case commentary writers generously offered their wisdom and insight to help extend professional dialogue and inquiry regarding the complex nature of educational leadership in our ever-changing society.

The College's Standards of Practice and Education Committee also significantly contributed to the realization of this text. Committee members include Ted Coulson, Suzanne DeFroy, Brian Doubleday, Nick Forte,

Gary Humphreys, Nancy Hutcheson, Peter Joong, Bill Matheson, Ruth Ann Penny, Jennifer Pitt, Susan Robertson, Patrick Slack, Tianna Travaglini-Babic and Don Watson.

The assistance provided by Kristine Egli, Suzanne Baril, Carmen Dragnea and the Ontario College of Teacher's Communications staff helped this book to become a reality through their careful research, formatting, editing and translation.

This text has been a collaborative endeavour from inception to completion. It illustrates an approach to shared professional inquiry that includes the voices of practitioners, academics, researchers and policy makers.

Introduction

Ethical professional practice is the hallmark of effective educational leadership. To be an exemplary educational leader it is imperative to have a deeply developed and integrated level of ethical knowledge and awareness. This essential form of professional knowledge enables educational leaders to respond to the complex and multi-faceted ethical dimensions inherent in the challenges, tensions, issues and dilemmas that are consistently encountered in professional practice.

An unwavering commitment to fostering the collective ethical knowledge and consciousness of all members of the school learning community is a necessary prerequisite for educational leaders today. The joint development of ethical understanding, sensitivity and agency can enable all members of an educational community to respond to moral issues and challenges with critical awareness, transparency and integrity.

Exploring Leadership and Ethical Practice through Professional Inquiry is a collaborative collection of practices, commentaries and educative pedagogies designed to support the development and enhancement of ethical professional practice in education. This text was created by integrating the experiences and insights of practising educational leaders and academic scholars. School principals and vice-principals write about the dilemmas they have encountered as educational leaders in the province of Ontario. Teaching in the province of Ontario is shaped by the existence of an established set of ethical standards for the teaching profession. These standards were developed by educators and members of the public. The ethics of *Care, Respect, Trust* and *Integrity* (Ontario College of Teachers, 2006a) that comprise these standards serve as principles to inspire, inform and support educators' ethical practice. The presence of these public principles is intended to provide collective ethical guidance for educational leaders and school communities.

This collection of narratives and commentaries has been developed as a curriculum and pedagogical resource for leadership formation, teacher education and professional learning. It honours the voices, perspectives and experiences of educational leaders. It respects the insights and role of academic scholars in helping to explicate the lived knowledge and ethical wisdom of practitioners. This text illuminates processes for the integration of theory and practice through activities that will foster meaningful and useful educative applications. Most importantly, it illustrates that the lived experiences of educators can be effectively used to advance educational leadership and ethical practice. In this text, the professional practice of educators provides effective sources of pedagogy for exploring leadership dimensions and the ethical nature of professional knowledge and action.

ETHICAL LEADERSHIP DEVELOPMENT

The ongoing ethical formation and consciousness of educational leaders resides at the foundational core of authentic and effective ethical leadership. The ongoing development of ethical awareness and knowledge are moral imperatives for contemporary educational leaders. The authenticity, presence (Starratt, 2004) and critical consciousness (Freire, 2005; Giroux, 2001) of leaders is central to the facilitation of learning communities that are socially just, inclusive and honour diversity. These leaders, as agents of ethical change, possess strong conviction as they strive to honour the dignity of the individual, demonstrate courage to act justly, maintain dedication to social justice, sustain a deep desire to collaboratively develop the ethical leadership capabilities of all members of the school community and model an unwavering commitment to the common good.

Presence, according to Starratt (2004), can be understood as an ethic of educational leadership that underpins all actions and decisions. Educational leaders who practise the ethic of presence engage with learners, teachers, parents and others in ways that convey deep sensitivity, attention, honesty, empathy and a form of listening that communicates to others that they are genuinely being heard and understood (Tschannen-Moran, 2004; Miller, 2000). This form of listening is devoid of judgment or distraction. It involves being fully present in body and mind to others. Embodying the ethic of presence can be transformational in relationships and interactions as "our presence activates our authenticity and the authenticity of others" (Starratt, 2004, p. 91). Presence, as explained by O'Donohue (1999), is a core dimension of *being* that encompasses the spirit surrounding and emanating through a person. To possess "integrity of presence" an individual must recognize and revere the presence of oneself and others. Presence is illuminated in the embodied compassion, empathy, respect, acceptance and attention individuals unconditionally offer to others in relational encounters (Buber, 1970). Buber's relational philosophy identifies presence as life-transforming. This vision of relation and presence is enacted when people respond to others with all of their being (Ladson-Billings and Tate, 2006).

Authenticity is also an important dimension of ethical practice (Duignan, 2007; Starratt, 2004; Langlois, 2004; Tschannen-Moran, 2004; Miller, 2000, 1994). Authenticity involves responding in ways that are truthful and have integrity. Authentic leaders possess a high level of congruence between their lived actions and espoused values. These educators are genuine and trustworthy. Their openness and self-knowledge inform their practices, actions and decisions.

Aware of the need for the qualities of presence and authenticity in developing leaders, the writers of this book offer a variety of reflective inquiry processes to help educators develop their own professional practices from places of presence, authenticity and consciousness. At the core of this text is an exploration of the complex dimensions associated with educational leadership practices. The cases, commentaries and professional inquiry components herein invite readers to explore leadership practices through multiple perspectives. Personal professional investigations (Connelly and Clandinin, 1988) support the ongoing construction of professional knowledge through collegial reflection and dialogue. Concepts that are critical to the development of ethical leadership, ethical capacity and ethical school cultures are interwoven into the inquiry methods presented in this text: student learning, social justice, democracy, ethical knowledge, presence, authenticity, decision making, pedagogy, *Care*, *Respect*, *Trust*, *Integrity*, efficacy, vision, commitment to the common good, equity, justice and a belief in a collaborative approach to teaching and learning.

CASES FROM PROFESSIONAL PRACTICE

Encapsulating and representing the lived experiences of educators through the narrative genre of a written case makes visible the actions and thoughts of school leaders. The written record of these leadership scenarios enables educators' practices to be revisited, analyzed and used for professional learning. Having available, illustrative cases from professional practice enables the teaching profession to use them for both individual and collective enhancement. The effectiveness of case methods for advancing professional knowledge and skill has been well documented in education (Shapiro and Gross, 2008; Strike, 2007; Goldblatt and Smith, 2005; Strike, Haller and Soltis, 2005; Haynes, 2002; Darling-Hammond, 2002; Stake, 1995; Shulman, L. 1992; Shulman, J. 1992).

The use of case narratives is especially important in the study of ethical leadership. Cases are effective means for capturing the rich layers of meaning that are integrated within educational leadership experiences. Leadership cases offer rare windows into the often private and extremely complicated journeys of educational leaders. By looking into complex educational leadership practices, educators gain deeper insight into professional practice. Leadership cases provide a unique entrance into the experiences of individual practitioners. Reading, reflecting and discussing individual narratives can initiate a process of inviting colleagues into a dialogue, a critique or a shared experience of collaboration and focused professional inquiry.

A collection of 14 cases is presented in this text for the purpose of illustrating the challenges intrinsic in educational leadership. These cases, written by practising school leaders, reveal the diversity and complexity of leadership dilemmas, tensions and issues in a variety of contexts. Many of the challenges encountered by this group of contemporary educational leaders are ethical in nature. Recognizing, understanding, and responding to the ethical dimensions inherent in these challenges and issues is imperative for the enactment of forms of ethical leadership that will justly, fairly, equitably and compassionately serve students and the community.

The cases in this text provide rich lenses into the ethical thinking, values, commitments and actions of educational leaders in a range of different education settings. Their lived experiences, as depicted in these cases, serve as a professional learning text for principals, teachers and aspiring educational leaders. The cases provide explicit representations of practice that can be read, reflected on, discussed and critiqued in an attempt to extend professional knowledge and deepen ethical analysis.

PROFESSIONAL INQUIRY

A variety of inquiry methods is integrated into this text to facilitate investigation into the authentic leadership tensions, issues and dilemmas experienced by school vice-principals and principals. Examining professional practice by using illustrative scenarios provides a genuine context for educators to explore the meaning of individual and collective ethical leadership. Educators can gain additional insight and awareness regarding leadership and ethical practice by inquiring into dilemmas and issues that have actually occurred in practice.

Engaging in diverse inquiry processes helps educators to deepen ethical knowledge, consolidate ethical professional identity, strengthen sensitivity toward moral responsibilities and activate ethical action. The professional inquiry methods that are incorporated in this text include reflection, dialogue, collaboration, case analysis and commentary critique, along with ethical frameworks. These methods invite further investigation into ethical principles, concepts, pedagogies, processes, decisions and practices.

Each case narrative in this text is followed by a Professional Inquiry section that provides a series of reflective questions and ethical frameworks. These questions and frameworks are designed to guide readers through processes of reflection and analysis. Engaging in dialogue with colleagues regarding the dilemmas or ethical dimensions in each case will support ongoing professional learning and the co-construction of additional insights regarding leadership practices.

INQUIRY FRAMEWORKS

Ethically responsible educational leaders incorporate ethical analysis and critique as key components of their thinking and reasoning (Duignan, 2007). These educators are conscious of the impact and implications of their choices when confronted with ethical decisions. Their decisions can be significantly informed through the use of ethical frameworks (Shapiro and Gross, 2008; Duignan, 2007; Smith, 2003, 2007; Starratt, 2004; Langlois, 2004; Shapiro, 2006; Shapiro and Stefkovich, 2005; Haynes, 1998) that can assist them in identifying the issues, complexities, perspectives, impacts and dimensions involved in making ethical decisions.

Inquiry frameworks provide structures or lenses that can help educators distinguish the multi-layered nature of ethical challenges and action. These models or constructs can also support educational leaders in mediating and negotiating the difficult ethical terrain often found in the complex contexts of schools. A variety of practical-inquiry frameworks is offered in this text to assist educators in explicating the multi-faceted and complicated nature of leadership issues and dilemmas. These frameworks can help educators make sense of the complexities associated with leadership and ethical practice. Thinking about practice in different ways and using alternative frames of reference can contribute to additional insight and awareness.

CASE COMMENTARIES

A set of commentaries also accompanies each case scenario. The commentaries were written by educational scholars, teacher educators and practitioners. They provide a multiplicity of perspectives on the recounted lived experiences written by educational leaders. The commentaries offer alternative reflections, interpretations and critiques. Readers are invited, through the commentaries, to re-examine each case scenario from different viewpoints and to contemplate additional issues and implications they may not have considered on initial reading and discussion of the case. The alternative lens and voice provided by each commentator can help readers to explicate the complexities and issues inherent in educational leadership.

The commentaries may stretch and challenge a reader's initial responses to and assumptions about a given case. Or, they may affirm deeply rooted values and principles. A specific action or decision in the context of the case may evoke feelings of discomfort. The commentaries are catalysts for additional insight, reflection and understanding. They may function as educative and dialogic methods in revealing the deep complexity inherent in professional practice.

As well, the commentaries function as yet another inquiry process to explore dimensions of leadership practice. They invite ethical analysis and ethical dialogue (Duignan, 2007; Campbell, 2004) that may ultimately foster the construction of ethical knowledge (Ontario College of Teachers,

2003). In essence, each commentary encourages readers to enter the "room" depicted by the author of the case, but through a different "door." In this way, the reader can gain deeper awareness of the underlying issues associated with each case and acquire multiple perspectives. To support the process of exploring multiple perspectives, an analysis framework titled Case Commentary Critique has been developed. This framework provides a guided method for exploring the dimensions, issues and theoretical orientation suggested by the commentaries.

OVERVIEW OF TEXT

Exploring Leadership and Ethical Practice through Professional Inquiry is organized into five interrelated sections. Each section focuses on a different theme associated with educational leadership: Leaders as Ethical Decision Makers, Leaders as Facilitators of Community, Leaders as Reflective Practitioners, Leaders as Models of Professionalism and Leaders as Educational Partners.

Section I: Leaders as Ethical Decision Makers

Leaders as Ethical Decision Makers provides illustrative examples of the multi-faceted ethical decisions educational leaders are required to make. The tensions and responsibilities associated with these decisions are highlighted. Several ethical frameworks are provided to guide investigation of various concepts and highlight the dimensions associated with ethical leadership. The importance of a leader's professional judgment, ethical knowledge, ethical leadership and commitment to developing the ethical capacity of others provides focus for professional inquiry in this section.

Section II: Leaders as Facilitators of Community

Leaders as Facilitators of Community introduces three scenarios that emphasize the influence of school leaders as facilitators of professional communities in order to support a culture of inquiry. The complexities involved in forming, sustaining and leading a community committed to the pursuit of learning are explored in this section. Also considered are the significance of vision, democratic practices, authentic leadership, instructional knowledge, ethical assessment, professional efficacy, trust, presence, shared responsibility, moral purpose and school culture.

Section III: Leaders as Reflective Practitioners

Leaders as Reflective Practitioners presents three cases illuminating the importance of reflective practice for educational leaders. Educational leaders who do not pause to reflect on and inquire into their practices may lose the opportunity to benefit from the wealth of knowledge that can be culled from these processes. Professional insight and learning are significantly enhanced by critically reflecting on one's own practice. Professional identity, efficacy, school culture, commitment to the best interests of learners, the common good, professionalism, the impact of education change and an analysis of educational leadership styles are some of the topics examined in this section.

Section IV: Leaders as Models of Professionalism

Leaders as Models of Professionalism probes the meaning and influence of a leader's actions and decisions on a culture of professionalism in a learning community. Thus, the impact of a leader's lived and espoused values and practices on relationships and norms within a community are critiqued. The roles of trust and collaboration within schools is also highlighted in the leadership scenarios in this section. The individual responsibilities of educational leaders in relation to the shared responsibilities assumed by the collective teaching profession also become a focus for scrutiny.

Section V: Leaders as Educational Partners

Leaders as Educational Partners reveals the important role educational leaders play in developing authentic partnerships with families in support of student learning and development. The significance of presence, inclusion, advocacy, understanding, freedom and open communication are highlighted in this section. Authentic partnerships that include the voices and perspectives of all partners create spaces for democracy to occur. These covenants are based on mutual *Care, Respect, Trust* and *Integrity.*

CASE MATRIX

The following case-matrix chart has been developed as a pedagogical resource to support integration of the cases, commentaries and professional inquiry components of this text into courses for leadership formation, teacher education and professional learning. The matrix provides an at-a-glance overview of the sections of this text. It includes cases, commentaries, professional inquiry focus areas and concepts identified by the commentary writers. Course facilitators may choose to use it as a planning and instructional tool.

			Case Matrix		
Section	**Case**	**Case Overview**	**Processional Inquiry Focus**	**Commentary Writers**	**Concepts from Commentaries**
Section 1: Leaders as Ethical Decision Makers	Words of Destruction	A vice-principal is placed in the tenuous position of responding to a student's public criticism of a teacher while dealing with the disturbing instructional practice that led the student to such action.	• Values • Ethical responsibilities • Ethical school culture • Ethical pedagogy and identity • Culture of professionalism • Ethical decision making	• Rita L. Irwin • Patrick M. Jenlink • Peter McLaren, Dianna Moreno and Jean J. Ryoo	• Professional judgment • Ethical action • Discernment • Political awareness • Human dignity • Ethical responsibility • Trust • Ethical dilemmas • Purpose of school • Restorative justice • Empowerment
	An Emotional Friday Afternoon	A principal is confronted by several outraged staff members regarding the issues they have about working together and responding to the needs of a learner with unique needs.	• Ethical responsibility • Ethical leadership • Ethical awareness and knowledge • Ethical pedagogy • Ethical capacity building • Culture of professionalism • Care and respect for learners	• Julia O'Sullivan • Felicity Haynes • Elizabeth Campbell • Stefinee Pinnegar and Lynnette B. Erikson • Lyse Langlois • Craig E. Johnson	• Autonomy • Ethical practice • Fairness • Personal power • Positioning theory • Ethical decision making • Best interests of students • Care and safety • Human dignity • Special Education • Disrespect • Dehumanization of children • Power
	Initiated	A new vice-principal discovers a tradition of student initiation in the school community.	• Vision • Ethical practice • School culture • Leadership practice • School policy • Public trust • Reflective practice	• Jean Clandinin • Steven Jay Gross • Kay Johnston • Stéphane Thibodeau	• Ethical pedagogies • Communication • Community • Inclusive partners • Turbulence theory • Conformity versus leadership • Moral thinking • Care • Respect • Empowerment • Transparency • Accountability

Case Matrix					
Section	**Case**	**Case Overview**	**Processional Inquiry Focus**	**Commentary Writers**	**Concepts from Commentaries**
Section II: Leaders as Facilitators of Commu-nity	Striptease on Day Three	A principal new to the school uncovers a school culture, norms and issues that require strategic and transformative leadership.	• Vision • Leadership practice • Professional efficacy • Shared leadership • Ethical practice • Collaborative community of inquiry	• Pauline Leonard • Brenda Beatty • Andy Hargreaves and Pauline Hargreaves • Theresa Shanahan • Ulrika Bergmark	• School culture • Authenticity • Reflective thinking • Role of principal/ vice-principal • Entry plans • Staff relationships • Student safety • Student conduct and morale
	A School Divided	A vice-principal observes significant division among teachers and between parents and teachers. The lack of professional-ism and commit-ment to professional learning are issues the vice-principal identifies and attempts to respond to.	• Vision • Leadership practice • Leadership authenticity and presence • Instructional leadership • Culture of professionalism • Collaborative community of Inquiry • Professional learning	• Joan Poliner Shapiro • Patrick Duignan • Lorraine Savoie-Zajc • Ben Levin	• Ethic of justice • Ethic of critique • Ethic of care • Leadership presence • Trust • Professional responsibility • Moral leadership
	Growing Pains	A principal is confronted by resentful and vocal teachers regarding the school's professional learning plan. The teachers feel that the plan has been imposed on them during a time of extensive curriculum change.	• Instructional leadership • Collaborative community of inquiry • Leadership capacity • Democratic practices • Reflective practice • Professional learning • Curriculum change	• John M. Novak • Ann Lieberman • Jeanne Doucet • Ellie Drago-Severson	• Professional growth • Self-directed professional learning • Care • School culture • Professionalism • Teacher leadership • Ethical leadership

			Case Matrix		
Section	**Case**	**Case Overview**	**Processional Inquiry Focus**	**Commentary Writers**	**Concepts from Commentaries**
Section III: Leaders as Reflective Practitioners	A Staffing Hotspot	During the annual school staffing process, a principal must deal with angry and discontented teachers. Their perception is that a specific teacher is receiving preferential treatment with regard to staffing placement. This ultimately affects the school climate.	• Ethical leadership • Leadership in a collaborative community of inquiry • Staffing • School climate • Equity • Relationships	• John Loughran • Margaret Olson • Paul Axelrod • Jean Plante	• Curriculum change • Empathy • Staffing • Trust • Conflict • Teacher advisory committee • Personal agendas • Conflicts of interest • Organizational dysfunction • Participative management • Power and leadership
	Life Changes	A principal concerned with test scores and student learning faces a dilemma when a teacher is perceived as requiring significant support and guidance.	• Vision • Instructional leadership • Culture of professionalism • Leadership practice • Decision making • Professional efficacy • Reflective practice • Test scores	• Alice Collins • Pat Rogers and Lara Doan • Katherine Merseth	• Decision making • Parental rights • Care • Staffing
	The Principal in the Middle	A principal is compelled to deal with a custody issue involving a staff member and his spouse. The situation is exacerbated by the child's attendance at the school where her father teaches.	• Tensions • Ethical practice • Leadership practices • Implementing policy • Culture of professionalism • Reflective practice	• A.G. Rud • Julie Mueller • Denise E. Armstrong	• Students' rights • Fair and ethical treatment • Relationships • School culture • Trust • Political, legal and ethical challenges • Values • Administrative tension • Fragile leaders • School culture • Moral exemplar • Ethical and professional boundaries

Case Matrix					
Section	**Case**	**Case Overview**	**Processional Inquiry Focus**	**Commentary Writers**	**Concepts from Commentaries**
Section IV: Leaders as Models of Professiona-lism	Choosing Sides	The challenges experienced by a vice-principal include teacher leadership, teacher professionalism and strained staff relationships. These issues impact significantly on the culture of the school and the educational leadership.	• Vision and influence • Instructional leadership • Decision making • Professionalism • Professional identity • Ethical practice • Ethical knowledge • Trust • Teacher leadership	• John Wallace • Anthony H. Normore • John Lundy • Pierre Toussaint	• Accountability • Relationships • Role of vice-principal • Climate of trust • Responsibilities • Feedback • Best interests of students • School climate • Modelling • Turbulence and chaos • Toxicity • Unprofessional behaviour • Pedagogic duties • Ethical dilemma
	An Occasional Dilemma	A vice-principal responsible for supporting a beginning teacher encounters challenges related to induction, school culture, teacher professionalism, and his role as vice-principal.	• Values • Professional identity • Professional responsibilities • Relationships • Decision making • Ethical knowledge • Professional knowledge • Induction	• Lindy Zaretsky • James Heap • Jules Rocque	• Ethic of critique • Ethic of justice • Ethic of care • Ethic of the profession • Ethic of the community • Coaching • Reflective practice • Ethical standards • Responsibility • Professional obligation
	Samantha	A principal encounters dilemmas associated with teacher performance and professionalism.	• Professional identity • Responsibilities • Decision making • Relationships • Professionalism • Performance appraisal • Teacher supervision	• Richard Shields • Michel Saint-Germain • Tom Russell	• Professional community of practice • Ethical standards • Care • Respect • Trust • Integrity • Shared practice • Ethical leadership • Difficult resolutions • Integration • Communication • Responsibility

Case Matrix					
Section	**Case**	**Case Overview**	**Processional Inquiry Focus**	**Commentary Writers**	**Concepts from Commentaries**
Section V: Leaders as Educational Partners	Blindsided	A principal and the school faculty are taken off guard when a parent makes unexpected requests at the annual review meeting for a learner with diverse needs.	• Vision • Leadership practice • Instructional leadership • Professional knowledge • Ethical practice • Education partnerships	• Cheryl J. Craig • Carolyn Shields • Pam Bishop • Anne Phelan	• Student growth • Special Education • Decision making • Power • Powerlessness • Test scores • Purpose of education • Rights • Commitment • Funding • Responsibility
	The School Supper Club	Relationships between parents, teachers and the school principal suffer when the school council's expectations for teachers are not shared by the collective school faculty.	• School councils • Working conditions • Authentic partnerships • Principal responsibilities • School district responsibilities	• Robert Stake and A. Rae Clementz • Vivienne Collinson • Linda Grant • Laura C. Jones	• Principals • Norms • Work conditions • Relationships • Inquiry • Judgment

Section I

Leaders as Ethical Decision Makers

LEADERS AS ETHICAL DECISION MAKERS

Effective educational leaders are ethical decision makers. These leaders have developed a high level of ethical awareness and knowledge. They understand the ethical dimensions inherent in dilemmas, issues and practices encountered in education. Their highly developed ethical insight enables them to approach ethical dilemmas with an unwavering commitment to compassion, justice, fairness, equity and due process. The actions of these ethical decision makers embody and integrate trust, respect, inclusion, collaboration and communication.

The decision making approaches employed by school leaders can have a profound impact on the ethical culture of a school community. The words and actions of a school leader can serve as a positive catalyst for fostering a strong foundation of ethics that is consistently represented in the lived and espoused ethical practices of all members of a school community. The decision making processes utilized by the ethical leader serves as a model for all members of the community. As an ethical decision maker, the school leader consistently models the importance of reflection, inquiry, critical analysis and dialogue in mediating and responding to ethical dilemmas and issues that emerge in professional practice. The underlying values influencing the decisions of the ethical leader are visible, congruent and guide the decision making process. Integrity, presence and openness are qualities that the ethical leader employs to assist in rendering ethical decisions in each situation and context.

CASES FROM PROFESSIONAL PRACTICE

The three cases in this section of the book provide illustrative examples of the ethical tensions and issues encountered by educational leaders as they attempt to model effective ethical practices. These authentic examples from practice demonstrate the complex challenges educators experience as they consider ethical decisions. These challenges often include:

- mediating commitments toward the needs of the individual and pursuit of the common good

- acting in a professional arena in a manner that is congruent with one's personal values

- honouring moral responsibility toward learners, the school community and the public

- responding with openness, transparency, honesty, integrity and trust

- encouraging ethical pedagogies that are inclusive and just

- facilitating and maintaining ethical school cultures

- modelling authenticity, presence, care, justice and respect

- supporting inclusion, diversity and equity

- fostering the development of ethical knowledge and awareness with others

- employing consistent frameworks that support ethical decision making.

> ### Cases:
> *Words of Destruction*
> *An Emotional Friday Afternoon*
> *Initiated*

CASE COMMENTARIES

The commentaries associated with the three cases in this section were written by educational scholars in the fields of leadership, ethics, critical pedagogy, narrative, self-study, art and case methods. The commentary writers address issues of power, political awareness, moral action, professional judgment, relationships, ethical responsibility, positioning of individuals, communication, commitment to the best interests of learners and ethical decision making.

Commentaries

Words of Destruction
Rita L. Irwin
Patrick M. Jenlink
Peter McLaren, Dianna Moreno and Jean J. Ryoo

An Emotional Friday Afternoon
Julia O'Sullivan
Felicity Haynes
Elizabeth Campbell
Stefinee Pinnegar and Lynnette B. Erickson
Lyse Langlois
Craig E. Johnson

Initiated
Jean Clandinin
Steven Jay Gross
Kay Johnston
Stéphane Thibodeau

CASE 1

Words of Destruction

"Hey, Mr. Brooks. Did you see this?"

This call comes from Tommy across the cafeteria. Tommy is one of our students with a significant lack of an "inner locus of control." He seems to be eager to share a secret with me. I'm glad to be drawn into his confidence. I am aware that Tommy also has the attention of a large number of students sitting around the tables. As I move closer, the other students begin to disappear. Now I am on the alert.

"What's that Tommy?" I ask, noticing his wicked grin.

"Here, look on page 27, Mr. Brooks."

Tommy passes this year's school yearbook to me. It has just been distributed this morning to all our students. He is pointing to a page written by Jethro, our school council president. Tommy seems pretty amused at something that I am unable, as yet, to clue into.

"What am I supposed to see, Tommy?"

"There, Mr. Brooks." Tommy points to the page and circles the bolded letters in a number of paragraphs with his index finger.

"So?"

"There, Mr. Brooks," he reiterates, as if he is explaining calculus to a struggling student. "Put the bolded letters together Mr. B, and you get the message." He laughs. "Pretty good, huh?"

The message registers. Oh no! I quickly excuse myself. I know this needs my immediate attention.

When I return to the office, Mrs. Montcrest, one of our math teachers, is already waiting for me. Her face is red. She waves the yearbook in my face even before I can close the door.

Heads turn in the outer office. Are they already aware of the situation?

In my inner office, Mrs. Montcrest rages. She is practically spitting. I'm shocked at her outburst and her plentiful use of foul language. Her voice is shrill. "I want him expelled. I want him out of here."

"Now Hilda, let's sit down and discuss this."

"I don't want to sit down and discuss anything. I want this student expelled," she yells.

"Tell me exactly what happened," I say calmly. She hurls the offending yearbook onto my desk and demands that I take a look.

Unfortunately, the page hasn't changed since I looked at it five minutes earlier. There, in bold print spaced throughout the text, are the letters that so clearly spell out, "**F--- you, Mrs. Montcrest.**"

"Hilda, I just found out about the yearbook moments ago. I know you must be furious. Please remember that we need to keep cool heads and deal with this in a professional way."

"I don't want to cool down. I'm going to sue you, the kid, the editor and the school board."

Finally, I get Hilda to agree to meet with me in the morning, and I escort her to her car. Thank goodness it is the end of the school day. When I return to my office I close the door and implode.

We have 1,100 yearbooks out there in the community. I can just imagine some of the students savouring the joke and boasting about how they put one over on the school. That is not, however, my understanding of our general school population. Most of the students are helpful, smart and supportive. I have felt honoured to be a member of the administration at this school. I have enjoyed the camaraderie and trust of many students on many committees. Now we have a teacher who is angry and offended, personally and professionally. I understand that she has every right to be angry.

Later that evening, I'm still thinking about the incident and Hilda's reaction. Hilda is well within her rights to be angry. Her reaction, however, seems to be more than one of anger. I believe that it also comes dangerously close to being vengeful and even somewhat irrational. That really worries me.

Earlier today, in my office, there was no way to reason with her. Hilda even suggested that the school administrative team was supporting the student because his family is prominent in the community. It complicates matters that the student who wrote the offending material is well liked by the school staff. Jethro, our school council president, is a young man whose record has been spotless. He has been a real asset to our school, a leader liked by his peers and an outstanding contributor to our extracurricular activities.

After a sleepless night, I meet with Hilda and ask her to allow us some time to consider an appropriate course of action. Ironically, the f-word again escapes from Hilda's lips several times. I once again feel that something is not right.

I call the superintendent and share the details with him. He asks me to keep him posted as the investigation progresses. We discuss the option of trying to recall the yearbooks. The superintendent indicates that, in the interim, he will contact the district school board lawyers.

Later that day, the administrative team gathers in my office to discuss options. We continue to be astonished that one of our students would do this. We are also doubly surprised that Jethro is involved. How did this happen?

We call in the boy.

"Jethro, whatever possessed you to do this?" I show him the page in the yearbook. There is no doubt that he has done it. He doesn't try to deny it. He actually seems to radiate pride. This is not the Jethro I know.

"Since the beginning of the year, Mrs. Montcrest has been teaching us math. From our very first class, she told us we were all f---ing stupid."

I am shocked to hear him actually use the word in my office. He looks away. "Every time one of us went to the board to do a math question and got a wrong answer, she would swear at us." Jethro is now obviously upset. Just as obvious is the fact that he is telling the truth.

"I didn't mean for anyone to find out about this. I just wanted to get a silent shot at Mrs. Montcrest for what she has done to us over the term. My buddies are pretty sharp though. I only told Paul. He always got the wrong answers in her class. I guess he told some of the others."

I can feel his embarrassment. He has always been supportive of school events, staff, peers and projects. It's a difficult position for me because I am torn between loyalty to staff and respect for Jethro's prior contributions to life in our school community.

"Why couldn't you tell us?"

"All of the kids in the class talked about this. But we didn't think anything would be done. We didn't want to endanger our marks for graduation and university."

The three members of the administrative team exchange glances. Jethro's last comments are hurtful and disturbing. We pride ourselves on putting people first and being student focused. If what Jethro is saying actually happened, then we have let these students down.

I am hurt. I have always felt that my open-door policy, breakfast meetings with student leaders, interest in their achievements and support through both their successes and failures have established a culture of trust.

Reflection on school policy and procedures will come later. What are we to do with this student? He should be graduating soon. As school council president, he will likely be nominated for an award. He is liked and respected by teachers and peers. The graduation formal is also coming up, and I expect that he has purchased tickets. How will his parents react? Should I expel him for one transgression over his 13 years of exemplary behaviour?

There are also 1,100 yearbooks out there. Do we recall them? How do we recall them? I begin playing out various scenarios.

And what about the teacher? What about the behaviour Jethro described? And what about my uneasy feelings about the way Hilda behaved in my office?

We telephone our superintendent.

"Hello, Bill."

"Hi, David. I was just about to call you. How is it going with Hilda?"

"Not too good, Bill. We'd better meet tomorrow. I'll share the details with you then."

The meeting with Bill is the beginning of a series of long and protracted meetings. We talk to our lawyers. She talks to hers. Letters are exchanged. Some of the meetings are truly horrible. Usually there are at least four or five of us in a small room including administration, union representatives and recorders for both groups. The meetings take their toll. At one of them, I begin visibly shaking with nervous tension and anxiety. I know the others in the room can see this. I feel ashamed.

We eventually ask for a psychiatric assessment for Mrs. Montcrest. She refuses. She applies for stress leave for a term. She gets it.

I wonder how I will ever be able to rebuild the relationships and trust that I so value. How will the staff react? What will the students and the community have to say? What does all this mean for Hilda Montcrest and for Jethro? I just don't feel that I have the answers.

PROFESSIONAL INQUIRY

The Professional Inquiry section is intended to support reflection, dialogue and the development of new understanding and insights. Engagement in the following processes can occur individually or collaboratively with colleagues. These processes are designed to facilitate new or revised interpretations of the leadership experience described in the case Words of Destruction. This additional knowledge may guide the subsequent leadership actions, thinking and decisions of the reader.

Reading and Reflecting on the Case

1. Record the facts, issues/dilemmas, leadership style and ethical responsibilities of the educational leaders in this case, using the following framework:

Case Reflection			
Facts of the Case *What are the pertinent facts of this case?*	**Issues/Dilemmas** *What issues or dilemmas are apparent in this case?*	**Leadership Style** *What leadership qualities, knowledge, skills and practices are evident in this case?*	**Ethical Responsibilities** *What are the moral and ethical responsibilities of the educational leader in this case?*

Values

1. Use the framework below to identify how the ethical value of *Trust* is apparent (or not apparent) in the actions of the participants in this case:

Trust		
Case Participants	**Value of *Trust* Apparent in Actions**	**Value of *Trust* Not Apparent in Actions**
Teacher (Mrs. Montcrest)		
Student (Jethro)		
Administrative team		

2. Discuss how the *Integrity* of the school administrator is challenged in this case.

Ethical Responsibilities

1. Identify the ethical responsibilities that the teacher and the administrative team have toward learners, the school community and the public in this case. Use the following framework to record your thoughts:

Ethical Responsibilities			
Case Participants	Toward Learners	Toward the School Community	Toward the Public
Teacher			
Administrative team			

2. Evaluate how commitment to the common good is addressed in this case.

3. Generate examples of how a commitment to the common good could be illuminated in similar situations.

Ethical School Culture

1. Identify the impact of the actions of the teacher, the student and the school administrative team on the ethical culture of this school.

2. Identify strategies to foster the development of ethical awareness, knowledge and action in this school community. Use the following framework to elicit your strategies:

Strategies to Foster Ethical Professional Practice		
Ethical Awareness	Ethical Knowledge	Ethical Actions

Ethical Pedagogies and Identity

1. Discuss the ethics behind the pedagogies used by Mrs. Montcrest and the administrator.

2. Explore what these pedagogies might reveal about the ethical identity of the professionals involved.

Culture of Professionalism

1. Examine how the issues of power, influence and politics impact on this case.

2. Identify whose interests were served in this case.

Ethical Decision Making

Reflect on and inquire into your own ethical decision making by using the following framework to explicate your thinking about the dilemmas in this case.

A Framework for Ethical Decision Making					
Ethical Dilemma/ Issue *What ethical dilemma(s) or issue(s) were apparent in this case?*	**Judgment/ Decision** *How would you respond?*	**Principle/ Value Guiding Decision** *What principle or value is guiding your action(s)?*	**Rationale for Decision** *What are the reasons for your action(s)?*	**Implication of Decision** *What are the possible consequences of your decision(s) or action(s)?*	**Reflections on Ethical Dilemmas of Practice and Action** *What new insight or understanding have you gained from listening to your colleagues?*
Dilemma One					
Dilemma Two					
Dilemma Three					
Further Inquiry: Inquire further into your own practice by reviewing your responses to each component of the ethical decision making framework and reflecting on the following questions. *What observations can you make regarding your own actions, principles and reasons for decisions?* *What themes emerge regarding your decision making?* *Do these observations affirm the educator you are and want to be or invite you to consider changes in your thinking and practice?*					

(Smith 2003)

CASE COMMENTARY CRITIQUE

1. Read the commentary(ies) written about the case.

2. Record your reflections regarding the commentary(ies) using the framework below:

    a. Identify the key points, perspectives or issues in the commentary.

    b. Analyze the key points, perspectives or issues identified in the commentary.

    c. List the new insights you gained from the commentary.

Commentary Critique			
Case Commentary Writer	Identification *What key points, perspectives or issues are identified in the commentary?*	Analysis *What is your analysis of the perspectives identified in the commentary?*	Synthesis *What new insights have you gained from the commentary?*

CASE COMMENTARIES

CASE COMMENTARY 1

Case: Words of Destruction

Rita L. Irwin
Professor of Art Education and Curriculum Studies,
Associate Dean of Teacher Education, University of British Columbia

The cultivation of judgment is essential in the professionalization of educators for it helps us consider how to act ethically in relation to others on particular occasions, while taking into account community engagements, action-based inquiry and personal reflection. Moreover, we can begin to address ways in which our perception is distorted by forms of bias. Discerning educators and leaders are sensitive to the particulars of students' lives and stories, even if they open up inconvenient complications and competing demands on practice. All educators need to appreciate that teaching is a moral activity because it is guided by conceptions of what is good for humans, what is educationally valuable, and how individuals ought to treat one another. This means that teaching requires political awareness as it involves decisions that affect the distribution of power, resources and opportunities. Ultimately, if teaching is consumed with ethical action then it becomes a *praxis* activity and is concerned with webs of relationships. Yet to understand praxis, one must work with particular relationships, in particular contexts and situations.

The words of destruction in this scenario suggest a lack of judgment on the part of the teacher who repeatedly criticized her students during class assignments. What bias did she hold toward these students? Her apparent continuing lack of judgment in addressing the particulars of the situation after the yearbook event occurred raises issues around her ability to discern what is best for the student in question, herself and the school community.

The words of destruction hit the school administrative team hard for they felt much closer to the student body than the student body felt to them. Discerning educators are sensitive to inconvenient complications and competing demands on practice – in fact, may even look for them. Being discerning is being open to alternative points of view and many times that means recognizing that a difficult relationship may have more to it than what is on the surface. Ethically, what web of relationships is the student being provided by staff, teachers, peers and administrators?

The words of destruction directed by the teacher to the students were difficult but so too were the words directed toward the teacher. The cultivation of judgment, discernment, and political awareness must also be an essential part of the curriculum for high school graduates. The student may have less power and opportunity in this situation but he asserted what power and opportunity he had with his own words of destruction. How should he treat teachers and his peers (it is their yearbook too)?

For everyone concerned, the particulars were neglected for far too long. The teacher did not share her frustrations with anyone or seek professional help. The students did not seek help either. The administration did not scratch below the surface and recognize the teachers' or students' need for assistance. Discerning educators need to be attentive to the particulars of individuals' lives and stories. It is in these details that one can begin to cultivate judgments and engage in ethical action that is contextually appropriate.

CASE COMMENTARY 2

Case: Words of Destruction

Patrick M. Jenlink
Professor of Doctoral Studies, Department of Secondary Education and Educational Leadership, Stephen F. Austin State University

The author of Words of Destruction presents a multi-layered, problematic situation, emblematic of the often complex and dynamic tensions that define schools today. In this case, Mr. Brooks, the school principal, is confronted with what on the surface appears to be a misguided action on the part of a student. But the use of inappropriate language on the part of Jethro, a school council president and soon to be graduating senior, is actually a symptom of a much deeper set of problems that lie beneath the surface of the daily activities of the school.

Mr. Brooks finds himself, along with the administrative team, challenged on one level by not having been aware of students' lack of trust in the administration, and challenged on another level by the inappropriate behaviour and language used by Mrs. Montcrest, a math teacher under whom Jethro and many of his classmates have suffered verbal and emotional abuse. Adding to an already problematic situation is the distribution of 1,100 yearbooks, each carrying into the public evidence of the deep-seated problem that has festered in the school for a full term. Jethro's attempt to "get a silent shot at Mrs. Montcrest" and his use of "words of destruction" symbolize a school climate in which students feel unsafe and trust is an issue.

The use of the phrase, "F--- You Mrs. Montcrest," reflects the power that words have over others, particularly when used by a teacher to devalue and dehumanize students. When words are used to attack, to take away an individual's dignity and belittle someone in public, as did Mrs. Montcrest, such words cultivate anger, resentment and emotional damage. In this case, Jethro elected to turn Mrs. Montcrest's destructive words back on her, not realizing that ultimately he would not only be taking a "silent shot" but that his action would negatively affect him and others in the school. In this case, the words had a destructive valence for the school and the community. Words are easily placed in the public realm, but the words cannot be withdrawn once spoken or printed, and the destructive power of words is felt for months and years to come. The destructive force of words is often not explicit or selective, as demonstrated in this case. Students, teachers and administrators, and the community all share in the damage done by the "words of destruction."

In this case, school personnel seems to have failed in many dimensions of ethical responsibility and this, in turn, undermines trust relationships between students and teachers and administration. Mr. Brooks, along with the school administrative team, is confronted with questions of trust and ethical responsibility. As well, they must address questions related to why the yearbook sponsor was not attentive to ensuring the appropriateness of content in the yearbook. Mrs. Montcrest's unwillingness to submit to a psychological evaluation presents a deep ethical question. What surfaces in the latter part of the case is yet another dimension of an already complex ethical dilemma. The policy-based options available to Mrs. Montcrest seem to advantage the teacher as contrasted to the options available to Jethro. The teacher is able to take a leave of absence, whereas the student must remain. The ethical dilemmas that Mr. Brooks resolves ultimately translate into how the destructive force of words can be mediated so that the student, teacher, school and community are able to rebuild trust and move forward in creating a safe space for students to learn.

CASE COMMENTARY 3

Case: Words of Destruction

Peter McLaren
Professor of Education, Graduate School of Education
and Information Studies, University of California, Los Angeles

Dianna Moreno
Doctoral Student in Education, University of California, Los Angeles

Jean J. Ryoo
Doctoral Student in Urban Schooling, University of California,
Los Angeles

Many of us who teach believe that the purpose of school is to transform and empower students as civically responsible agents of positive change. Some of us take it even further: to challenge social relations of exploitation that inform neo-liberal capitalist society and to work toward a post-capitalist society. Unfortunately, most school structures organized in a hierarchical dynamic of administrators over teachers over students do not engage learners in questions of social justice, rendering them invisible and powerless in the process of schooling. Students are told to respect teachers before themselves, when both parties should be held in high esteem. Students are taught to be passive pawns, teachers are taught to be stern disciplinarians and administrators are taught to be distant supervisors. This hierarchical structure often breaks bonds of trust between students, teachers and administrators so that individuals may not know how to deal productively with disagreements among different groups. Within this power structure, students, teachers and administrators may become either disengaged or violent in an effort to deal with conflict.

In this particular case, Mr. Brooks shows a desire to respect both Mrs. Montcrest and her student, Jethro, but all three are trapped in a power dynamic that clearly has resulted in verbally violent acts between teacher and student. According to Jethro, Mrs. Montcrest abused her power in the classroom, not only distancing her students, but also verbally assaulting them when they made mistakes. Because of the silencing of his voice, Jethro did not feel safe enough to talk openly about the situation with either teacher or principal, and thus channelled his desire for change by returning the verbal abuse that he and his classmates received from Mrs. Montcrest.

Although Mr. Brooks clearly cares about Jethro as a strong student leader and although Mr. Brooks wants to support Mrs. Montcrest and prevent her pending lawsuit, he may be approaching this situation in a destructive way by being more reactive than preventive. First of all, Mr. Brooks wisely recognizes Mrs. Montcrest's reaction as potentially "vengeful" and "irrational," but he passively absorbs her abusive language without trying to address the deeper reasons why Mrs. Montcrest is upset. Secondly, he treats Jethro like a criminal by questioning him in front of three other adult administrators, rather than treating him with respect by speaking with him one-on-one to understand his actions. Again, opportunities to develop trust between administrator and teacher as well as administrator and student were lost.

One possible way to remedy the situation is to create a shift in the culture of how people view discipline and punishment in Jethro's school. Instead of making isolated efforts that are mere reactions to aggression or violence, Mr. Brooks could use a restorative justice program in the school that would provide a safe space for all parties to engage in changing traditional responses to serious offences. Although a restorative justice program cannot provide such change overnight, it would allow for long-term improvement through four steps: (1) an "encounter" that allows all stakeholders in an aggressive act (Mr. Brooks, Mrs. Montcrest and Jethro) to meet and discuss the problem as equals after individually reflecting about the situation; (2) "amends" in which offenders (Mr. Brooks, Mrs. Montcrest and Jethro) make efforts to repair any pain they have caused; (3) "reintegration" that restores all participants as engaging members of the school culture; and (4) "inclusion" that provides a chance for all parties to participate in the school's healing process after discussing the aggressive offence. Such a four-step mediation process would allow for students, teachers and administrators to engage in valuable dialogue that recognizes each party's agency and strength despite functioning within the confines of a potentially dehumanizing hierarchical institution.

Words of Destruction reflects the frustrating isolation that many of our best and most sensitive school leaders, like Mr. Brooks, face in traditionally hierarchical school systems. However, the greatest challenge critical educators and administrators face is to recognize the multiple forces and social relations affecting student and teacher behaviour in educational institutions, and to directly challenge such structures without suppressing student, teacher or other administrator voices. Both Jethro and Mrs. Montcrest clearly wanted to be heard, but their words yielded negative repercussions rather than providing an opportunity for listening and change. In such a situation, we must come together to provide safe spaces for mediation, while recognizing which aspects of schooling (hierarchical structures, curriculum and so on) dehumanize education communities so that we can rediscover our human agency and engage in positive, dialectical relationships between all fragmented parties.

REFLECTION ON THE COMMENTARIES

Consider the comments of McLaren, Moreno and Ryoo regarding the impact of hierarchical school structures, Jenlink's reference to the failure of school personnel to fulfill their ethical responsibilities and Irwin's identification of the importance of cultivating judgment for both the professionalism of educators and for student development. How do these commentaries enrich your own perspectives regarding leadership and ethical practice?

ADDITIONAL READING

Beckner, W. (2004). *Ethics for educational leaders.* Boston, MA: Pearson Education.

This professional development book emphasizes the practical application of ethical concepts to realistic educational leadership challenges. Case studies illustrate the importance of developing ethical education organizations and the capacity of leaders for ethical decision making.

Begley, P. T. (1999). Guiding values for future school leaders. *Orbit, 30*(1), 19–23.

The author considers the special function of values and their influence on administrative action. The findings from multiple studies conducted at the Ontario Institute for Studies in Education, University of Toronto, identify which values predominate in school leaders' problem-solving processes and influence their decision making actions.

Brooks, J. S., & Normore, A. H. (2005). An Aristotelian framework for the development of ethical leadership. *Values and Ethics in Educational Administration, 3*(2), 1–8.

The importance of including ethical study and reflection in education preparation programs is explored in this article. Character, emotion and logic plus the Aristotelian framework studied from perspectives of theory, practice and wisdom aid prospective teachers and administrators in understanding the value of ethical orientation in their leadership practice.

Duignan, P. (2006). *Educational leadership: Key challenges and ethical tensions.* New York, NY: Cambridge University Press.

Duignan explores the ethical challenges and tensions experienced by educational leaders and presents practical frames for assessing ethical knowledge and enhancing ethical decision making. He identifies leadership presence and authenticity as important dimensions of leadership formation.

Langlois, L. (2004). Responding ethically: Complex decision making by school district superintendents. *International Studies in Educational Administration, 32*(2), 78-93.

In this study, Langlois looks at the ethical decision making processes of school superintendents. Through an examination of their processes and frameworks, she outlines essential ethical dimensions and offers key insights.

Shapiro, J. P. (2006). Ethical decision making in turbulent times: Bridging theory with practice to prepare authentic educational leaders. *Values and Ethics in Educational Administration, 4*(2), 1–4.

This paper explores the disconnection in theoretical development in programs that prepare education administrators. The author advocates for reflection, understanding, deep dialogue and critique, combined with skills, analysis and synthesis. This balanced approach focuses on the integration of practice and theory.

CASE 2

An Emotional Friday Afternoon

"She has something to say about everything. She has no right to treat me this way. I am a professional and should not be second guessed about the decisions that I make."

It is nearly three o'clock on Friday afternoon. Amy has just entered my office, sobbing, and sits down on the first available chair. Amy is a registered nurse who was hired to be with Terry all day. Terry is a student who has severe physical and learning challenges. He is placed in our developmentally challenged class with five other students identified as exceptional. Terry is a non-verbal student who has to be fed through a tube. He is confined to a wheelchair and must never be left alone. He needs help with all life skills. Including his teacher, Terry has three full-time caregivers to support his needs.

Suddenly, Irene, Terry's teacher, storms into my office pushing Terry through the door in his wheelchair. "Amy doesn't know what she is doing and puts everyone at risk," she yells.

Terry is crying hysterically. I am shocked. "What is going on here?" I ask in disbelief.

The next moment, Jane, the education assistant in the developmentally challenged class, pushes open my office door. "Here is my written statement," she says. "I refuse to work under these conditions. I will be contacting my union. Something needs to be done to change things before I return to that classroom." Jane turns and marches out of my office.

I thought that Amy, Irene and Jane all worked well together. Obviously I was wrong. My first instinct as principal is to intervene and take immediate control of the situation. However, I suppress my initial instinct and say, "I need to find out why you are all in my office. Please, let's settle down and examine what exactly is happening. But before we begin our discussion, would one of you please comfort Terry and help him to calm down. Our immediate task here is to reassure this student."

Irene tucks a blanket around Terry and begins to roll his wheelchair back and forth beside her chair. Terry focuses his eyes on his teacher's face and quiets down.

I begin by asking Amy, "What happened today that caused you to be so upset? I know that you have been successful working with Terry for the past six months and that you have handled many issues well."

Amy gives me an icy glance and replies briskly, "Things have not been going well. I have been undermined in my work constantly since I arrived." Her facial expression conveys her pent-up rage. She goes on. "Irene is continually asking me to perform tasks that are not part of what she calls her job description. She asks me to push Terry's wheelchair down the hall. She doesn't seem to understand that I am a professional nurse. I am not an education assistant. The chores that she is asking me to perform are not part of my job description either. On top of that, I never get a break."

Irene jumps in angrily. "She has not been assigned to any job outside of her job description. She has been told by all of us, including her supervisor, that she can take a break. However, she must take her break in the class, where she can keep an eye on Terry and be available if he needs medical attention."

Amy snarls her response. "Everyone is entitled to have an uninterrupted lunch break. What makes me different? When I take a break I can just disconnect his feeding tube for the time that I'm away. I'm sure he'll be okay."

Irene interjects, "It's the doctor's decision to keep the feeding tube in place continuously for as long as he's at school. Amy has been told that she is not allowed to leave the room without Terry or to disconnect his feeding tube for any reason."

Amy raises her voice and interrupts Irene. "This is not fair. The education assistants who work with Terry are continuously second guessing me.

They are always asking, 'Is he okay? Is he in pain?' Even when I tell them he's fine, they continue to hound me with their questions. I think that Terry is just bored with the school and the program he gets here."

Irene is indignant. She walks up to Amy and stands almost nose-to-nose with her. "You have no right to judge our program. You are a nurse. You are not a teacher. If you don't want to push the wheelchair then don't do it."

Terry starts to cry again. The two women yell louder in order to be heard over his sobbing.

I speak slowly in a firm but authoritative manner. "Yelling doesn't help us resolve any issue. We need to calm down and listen to one other. Terry is upset again and we need to stop his crying."

Amy looks directly at me. "Terry cries all the time. That is part of his disability. We must learn to live with it." She then proceeds to list all of Terry's daily needs.

I try again to defuse the situation. I motion for Amy to sit down. I'm thinking of Terry and what may happen to him if I'm unable to get these pivotal people in his life to work together. I'm furiously turning over strategies in my head while hoping that my efforts at dispute resolution will be effective. I try to establish a positive tone that will encourage them to put aside their grievances and to move on to focus on Terry's best interests.

I begin again. "Let's try to talk this through so I can better understand the issues. Irene, why don't you give me your side of what has happened."

Irene sighs and wipes away a tear. She continues to rock Terry by pushing his wheel chair back and forth. "Amy has been leaving all of Terry's medication on the counter, even after she has administered it. We're afraid that the other students will get into it. She also leaves Terry's syringe full of stomach fluids on top of the microwave oven and then empties it in the kitchen sink where we prepare food for other students. This is unacceptable. I will not continue to work in such unsanitary conditions. She leaves bloodied napkins in the bathroom that our other developmentally challenged students use. This is also very dangerous and unsanitary. I've encouraged the education assistants to file a health and safety claim and to submit a work-refusal statement. We fear for our own safety and for the well-being of our students."

I turn to Amy for her input. Amy shakes her head vehemently. "What lies," she huffs. "You just want to have me fired."

After an hour of discussion, I realize that we are getting nowhere. It's time for Terry to go home. We agree to meet again on Monday morning.

After everyone leaves my office I telephone Simone, the district board supervisor of Special Education. She has worked closely with both Terry's teacher and his education assistant. Over the five years I've known Simone, I have always been impressed by her experience and expertise.

Simone sounds exhausted but asks, "What's the problem this time?" I provide her with a summary of the afternoon's events. She quickly responds, "We've had nothing but trouble since Amy arrived. There is definitely a lack of communication and understanding on all sides."

I wonder why this is the first time I'm hearing about this situation but decide not to raise that issue now. I start off by saying, "My first priority is the refusal-to-work statement submitted by the education assistant. Did you know that Jane has put in a work refusal?"

Simone quietly replies, "No, but it doesn't surprise me. She's always complaining about something."

I'm also concerned about how Amy behaved this afternoon. She seemed almost hysterical and threatened to stay home from work if we don't find an immediate resolution. Besides Amy and Jane, I have a frustrated and upset teacher on my hands. It's also very disturbing to me that Terry is caught in the crossfire of this dispute. We must do something quickly.

I tell Simone that I'm calling a Monday morning meeting with all parties to try to resolve the situation. I follow protocol and inform my superintendent of the day's events. He suggests that I call Terry's parents and tell them that the school needs to work out a staffing situation concerning the developmentally challenged classroom. The superintendent wants me to request that the parents keep Terry at home until we have worked out a solution.

I call all the individuals involved in the situation, including the education assistant's union representative, and invite them to the Monday morning meeting. The last call I make is to Terry's home. I know this will be the most difficult call. Terry's mother blows up. She screams into the telephone, "Your staff is the most incompetent group of people I have ever dealt with. This is absolutely unacceptable. I will not tolerate this kind of incompetence."

I inform my superintendent about the mother's response. He tells me not to worry. He will be at our school at eight on Monday morning to try to defuse the situation before our meeting starts.

Everything seems to be falling apart. I don't know what to think or where else to turn. I feel like crying and screaming at the same time. I realize that I must remain calm. There are already enough irrational people around me. This will be a very long weekend.

PROFESSIONAL INQUIRY

The Professional Inquiry section is intended to support reflection, dialogue and the development of new understanding and insights. Engagement in the following processes can occur individually or collaboratively with colleagues. These processes are designed to facilitate new or revised interpretations of the leadership experience described in the case An Emotional Friday Afternoon. This additional knowledge may guide the subsequent leadership actions, thinking and decisions of the reader.

Ethical Responsibility

1. Describe the ethical responsibilities, commitments and obligations the professionals in this case have toward Terry, the learner with exceptional needs.

2. Investigate the type of "harm" (Starratt, 2004) the professionals in this case are collectively responsible for preventing. Assess the extent to which this ethical responsibility is achieved.

Ethical Leadership

1. Discuss the ethical dimensions associated with the superintendent's recommendation to keep Terry at home until the school is able to deal effectively with the personnel issues.

2. Identify the ethical beliefs evidenced by the words and actions of the staff in this case.

3. Analyze the extent to which the following ethical beliefs are evidenced in the actions of the principal. Use the following rating scale and framework to assist in your analysis.

   L: Limited evidence of this belief

   M: Moderate evidence of this belief

   H: High evidence of this belief

Ethical Beliefs			
Guiding Belief	**Limited Evidence of This Belief**	**Moderate Evidence of This Belief**	**High Evidence of This Belief**
Devoted to the best interests of the learner			
Caring and just treatment of individuals			
Concerned for the dignity and rights of the individual			
Committed to fostering effective learning environments			
Transparent, fair and equitable responses			

4. Analyse the dimensions of ethical leadership demonstrated by the principal using the following rating scale and framework.

L: Limited evidence of this dimension

M: Moderate evidence of this dimension

H: High evidence of this dimension

Ethical Leadership			
Dimension of Practice	**Limited Evidence of This Dimension**	**Moderate Evidence of This Dimension**	**High Evidence of This Dimension**
Authenticity of leader			
Presence of leader			
Care and compassion of leader			
Social justice commitment of leader			
Decision making of leader			

Ethical Awareness and Knowledge

1. Analyze and discuss the level of ethical awareness and knowledge reflected in the decisions and actions of the case participants.

Ethical Awareness and Knowledge			
Case Participant	Limited Ethical Awareness and Knowledge	Moderate Ethical Awareness and Knowledge	High Ethical Awareness and Knowledge
Educational leader			
Classroom teacher (Irene)			
Registered nurse (Amy)			
Educational assistant (Jane)			
Supervisor of Special Education (Simone)			

2. Examine the ethical standards and principles that were violated in this case.

Ethical Pedagogy

1. Discuss the ethics associated with the curriculum and pedagogies referenced in this case.

2. Analyze the current learning environment that Terry is exposed to from moral and ethical perspectives.

Ethical Capacity Building

1. Create a plan to develop ethical capacity and foster an ethical school culture in this learning community using the following framework. In developing the plan, consider the following questions:

   a. What strategies would I employ to foster ethical awareness, a commitment to social justice, enhancement of ethical decision making and leadership of all members of the school community?

   b. What approaches would I employ to meaningfully integrate ethical awareness, social justice, decision making and leadership throughout the curriculum, pedagogy, school polices and practices?

Fostering Ethical Capacity and an Ethical School Culture Plan of Action				
School Components	Ethical Awareness	Social Justice	Ethical Decision Making	Ethical Leadership
Learners				
Faculty				
Curriculum				
Pedagogy				
School policies				
Parents				

Ethical Principles

1. Review the case using the following framework of ethical principles. Identify how each of the ethical principles, *Care, Respect, Trust* and *Integrity*, is reflected in the actions and decisions of the participants.

Ethical Principles				
Case Participants	*Care*	*Respect*	*Trust*	*Integrity*
Educational leader				
Teacher				
Nurse				
Educational assistant				
Supervisor of Special Education				
Superintendent				
Parent				

Culture of Professionalism

1. Critique how *power* and *influence* are demonstrated in this case.
2. Discuss the *privileging* of some voices, rights and perspectives in this case to the exclusion of others.
3. Identify the *rights* of Terry and his family in this situation.
4. Examine whose *interests* are served.

CASE COMMENTARY CRITIQUE

1. Read the commentary(ies) written about the case.

2. Record your reflections regarding the commentary(ies) using the framework below:

    a. Identify the key points, perspectives or issues in the commentary.

    b. Analyze the key points, perspectives or issues identified in the commentary.

    c. List the new insights you gained from the commentary.

Commentary Critique			
Case Commentary Writer	Identification *What key points, perspectives or issues are identified in the commentary?*	Analysis *What is your analysis of the perspectives identified in the commentary?*	Synthesis *What new insights have you gained from the commentary?*

CASE COMMENTARIES

CASE COMMENTARY 1

Case: An Emotional Friday Afternoon

Julia O'Sullivan
Professor and Dean, Faculty of Education,
University of Western Ontario

Leadership on Paper versus Leadership on Legs

It is hard to accept that this case description is true – that any student, never mind a medically fragile boy named Terry who cannot speak or walk independently, was subjected to this situation in one of our schools. It is understandable to react with a myriad of emotions (shock, dismay, anger, sadness and disappointment), easy to attribute blame to the people involved, and reassuring to believe we would have handled this in a much better way. But would we have? Although the particulars of the situation are unique, the underlying issue of the dehumanization of children with special needs is not – not to this student and not to this school (Orelove, Sobsey and Silberman, 2004).

Throughout this case description, Terry, his needs, rights and best interests are consistently relegated to last place. Staff are shouting about their needs and making demands right in front of him, even arguing about who should push his chair. Accusations about the safety of the classroom (for example, bloodied napkins left lying around) and Terry's personal safety (for example, disconnecting his feeding tube contrary to medical instructions) are flying through the air. Everyone seems to have forgotten that he is present, that he is a person entitled to respect and dignity, that schools are first and foremost for students, not for teachers, nurses or those in leadership positions.

When Terry responds with evident distress, even his tears are denied him, dismissed out of hand as "part of his disability. We must learn to live with it." This serves to reduce him to his condition. It also implies that staff are dealing with factors over which they have little or no control. Attributing Terry's distress to his disability absolves staff of responsibility for causing it in the first place (Terry is not in tears; his disability is), denies them any power to effect change and relieves them of any real obligation to try (Weiner, 2004). Consequently, attention is focused not on Terry but on factors perceived to be within the school's control. Superiors are informed, parents contacted, meetings scheduled and so on. This is leadership on paper.

Imagine that a different type of leadership had been present on that late Friday afternoon. Imagine that leadership walking over to Terry, holding his hand, stroking his hair and yes – pushing his wheelchair as together they left the room for a safer, calmer place. With those simple, silent and compassionate gestures a message would have been shouted to the entire school community. It would have said, "Terry is the most important person here. I see beyond his disability to the boy in distress. My immediate concern is for him, and for him alone all the rest can wait. For this, I am not only responsible but accountable." Imagine the impact for children with special needs. This is leadership on legs.

CASE COMMENTARY 2

Case: An Emotional Friday Afternoon

Felicity Haynes
Former Dean of Education, University of Western Australia

The four main characters all try to dominate and take control. Even Terry manages to "control" his caregivers by crying hysterically. Senge (1990) recommends that administrators move beyond top-down control and allow all workers to participate equally in decision making in a complex open system. The principal first decides to do this but then defers to authority by asking the superintendent to step in.

As superintendent, how would I debrief on Monday? Discussing problems will resolve differences only if each person is ready to listen impartially to others and present cogent arguments for their actions and beliefs. For Habermas (1995), it has to be a rational process. Each participant must decide whether what is being said is true, is right by conventional standards, and whether each participant has good reasons for their beliefs and values.

We can begin by establishing questions of fact. Is it true that the safety and well-being of students are at risk because of Amy's practices? Is the staff incompetent, and in what respects? Is it a general incompetence or does it relate solely to Terry's needs? What are Jane's complaints about work conditions based on? What might be the consequences of changing things to meet the staff's requests?

These are not just questions of fact, but evidence helps to establish truth. A rational decision requires judgments based on evidence, principled values and feelings, and therefore one has to justify one's beliefs. Is it unreasonable to ask Amy to wheel Terry down the corridor, or for her to have to stay in the classroom with Terry all day? Is Amy justified in feeling undermined?

However, is such rational communication possible with this emotional group? The principal implies that they are all irrational. Terry cannot reason because he lacks language but his crying could be a "reasonable" attempt to communicate frustration. Amy appeals to rights in her demand for both equal respect ("She has no right to treat me that way.") and a lunch break, but is inconsistent in not according Terry his right to respect and care. What counts as a good reason differs according to the level on a Kohlbergian (1981) scale of rational ethics. Amy operates at a preconventional level, showing little concern for others, while Jane operates only within the conventions of her union rules. Irene is on the cusp of moving toward autonomy.

In any ethical situation, one must consider not only the level of reasoning but the equal demands of consistency (reasons/mind), consequences (knowledge/brain) and care (concern for others/heart). Irene seems more concerned with consequences than reasons for acting, accusing Amy of putting everyone at risk by her actions. However, she is concerned with fairness and importantly shows concern for Terry. The superintendent must allow for open consideration of all three aspects to ensure that Terry's treatment and the needs of the school move beyond issues of personal power. What is needed is not a briefing that presents information from the top, but an open and democratic community of inquiry in which all participants are enabled to question, reason, connect, deliberate, challenge and develop problem-solving techniques in a just community that evolves beyond power and control.

References

Argyris, C., & Schön, D. (1978). *Organizational learning: A theory of action perspective.* Reading, MA: Addison-Wesley.

Habermas, J. (1992). *Between facts and norms: Contributions to a discourse theory of law and democracy.* Cambridge, MA: The MIT Press.

Haynes, F. (1998). *The ethical school: Consequences, consistency, care, ethics.* New York, NY: Routledge.

Lipman, M. (2003). *Thinking in education* (2nd ed.). New York, NY: Cambridge University Press.

CASE COMMENTARY 3

Case: An Emotional Friday Afternoon

Elizabeth Campbell
Professor and Associate Chair of Graduate Studies,
Department of Curriculum, Teaching and Learning,
Ontario Institute for Studies in Education, University of Toronto

An Unethical Friday Afternoon: A Case Renamed

When filtered through the lens of ethical decision making, problems that could otherwise be seen narrowly as involving managerial, political or strategic choices become clearer, although not necessarily easier to resolve. The situation presented in this case is shown to be a complex interpersonal conflict that challenges the principal's administrative skills at mediation, conflict management and micropolitical sensitivity. However, to interpret the case only at that level greatly underestimates its moral and ethical dimensions.

The principal – whose commitment to the best interests of the student is not questioned but rather seems sidelined by an impulse to navigate strategically through a crisis – states that she/he suppressed an initial instinct to intervene and take immediate control of the situation. Instead, the principal opts to "furiously [turn] over strategies in my head while hoping that my efforts at dispute resolution will be effective." Perhaps this is the problem. Rather than vocally expressing moral outrage at the unprofessional, uncaring, disrespectful and unethical conduct of the three people responsible for Terry's well-being in the classroom, the principal seems driven by an almost desperate search for a way to bring about a reconciliation among them, regardless of who is right or wrong. It should also go without saying that yelling and arguing in the principal's office in front of the student is, under no circumstances morally or professionally justified.

Immediate concern about the care and safety of Terry and the other students in the class, coupled with an assessment of the truth of the situation that is fair to the staff (they cannot all be accurate in their account of the situation), should trump any worries about Jane's petulant refusal to work and Amy's similarly threatening attempts to blackmail the principal. If the allegations regarding Amy's dangerous practices and her insensitive and incompetent behaviour prove to be true, then Terry and the school would likely be better off without her.

The principal and superintendent seem intent on "defusing the situation." This could be interpreted as reasonably pacifying everyone, including Terry's mother, none of whom are being at all reasonable. This is likely the most rational approach to problem solving if accompanied by the necessary quest for the truth about what is and is not happening in the classroom. However, by staying focused on the need to mediate conflict, they may overlook the moral aspects that make the conflict necessary.

It may not be a practical response, and I doubt it would make it into an education administrator's guide to facilitating win-win resolutions, however, before embarking on the rational approach, I would suggest that the principal demonstrate clear moral outrage and take to task Amy, Jane, and possibly to a lesser extent, Irene for their unethical behaviour. They collectively reflect an uncaring disregard for Terry and an attitude of disrespect for each other and for the principal in a professional sense. They put ahead of their professional duties their own petty concerns over job descriptions, workplace grievances, injured egos, hurt feelings, and a shallow interest in asserting their own professional status. If the principal were to start from a position of outrage rather than conciliatory reasoning, the other professionals may be shaken into appreciating the moral dimensions at stake in the situation. Or they may quit, as they threaten to do. In that case, Terry's mother will have to be more patient and recognize that the principal is striving to do not what is strategically expedient, but what is ethically right for her son.

CASE COMMENTARY 4

Case: An Emotional Friday Afternoon

Stefinee Pinnegar
Teacher Educator, David O. McKay School of Education,
Brigham Young University

Lynnette B. Erickson
Associate Professor of Teacher Education, David O. McKay
School of Education, Brigham Young University

Positioning theory provides a tool that allows us to sort out the competing plot lines that flow under this case. In positioning theory, "Not only what we do but also what we can do is restricted by the rights, duties and obligations we acquire, assume or which are imposed on us in the concrete social contexts of everyday life" (Harré and van Langenhove, 1999, p. 4). Our question for this case: "How is Terry being positioned in relation to the other actors?"

Traditionally, the superintendent has the most power in the social order of schools. His decision to attend the meeting to "debrief and defuse" the problem positions the principal as incapable. This results in Terry's being positioned as a political problem to be defused rather than a child whose education needs have priority.

The principal positions Simone as a knower. Simone positions the principal as obtuse for not realizing the disruptive interpersonal dynamics that have existed for some time. Simone also positions Jane as a complainer, perhaps because that is how Irene has positioned her. Simone ignores any responsibility for Terry's well-being, positioning him as tangential.

The principal consistently calls for a plot line where disagreements are resolved through calm and co-operation. The principal assumed that Irene, Amy and Jane were working together to create an optimal learning environment for Terry. The principal consistently positions Terry and his needs as the central focus of concern in the education plot line of the school. However, the principal's reflections in the role of leader position her/him as unaware and unconcerned about its moral order.

Amy, as a recent hire, is positioned as the outsider and the outlier. All the other characters have a much longer history together. Implicit in each player's positioning of themselves and others are assumptions about their duties, rights and responsibilities. As we listen to the charges and counter-charges, we find that Irene and Jane have common assumptions that are not shared by Amy. In fact, Amy positions Irene as a tyrant who insists that she assume any duties that are not part of Irene's conception of the teacher role. Jane appears to expect Amy to assume responsibilities that potentially belong to Jane. The questions about Terry's behaviour and the reports of her nursing practices position Amy as incompetent. Amy's anger about her break is an assertion that her rights are being denied. Perhaps the last nurse accepted Irene's positioning and took on duties and responsibilities that belonged to Irene and Jane, thus sacrificing her own rights as Terry's nurse. Irene and Jane are positioned as incompetent educators when Amy contends that Terry is bored.

As these three women position and reposition each other, Terry disappears as the focal point and is used as an evidentiary bargaining chip in their attempts to establish themselves as dominant. The principal in this case is the only actor who consistently positions Terry's well-being as the focal point. Thus, this analysis reveals the ethical tensions that emerge through the positioning of children in relationship to the duties, rights and responsibilities of the adults charged with their education.

CASE COMMENTARY 5

Case: An Emotional Friday Afternoon

Lyse Langlois
Associate Professor, Department of Labour Relations, Université Laval

At the core, this case involves three people: a nurse, a Special Education assistant and a teacher, who are struggling with different perceptions of acceptable and unacceptable ways of providing Terry with better accompaniment. It may appear difficult in such circumstances to get a thorough grasp of the actual problem, because emotions are getting the upper hand and taking over the principal's office, where the people involved end up. When that happens without warning, it would be a good idea for the principal not to let the boy remain in her office; he should not have to witness the heated discussion. The primary consideration is to protect him so that the relationship of trust he has with the educators working with him can be maintained. Given the high emotions that are prevailing, I suggest that the principal ask each person to make an appointment to meet with her individually after school the same day, so she can get each one's understanding of the situation.

For the principal, it is important to calm down those involved and assure them they will be listened to individually, and then as a group, when they have gained some distance from the incident that acted as a trigger. During the one-on-one meetings, the principal can get a better idea of what everyone has to say by asking each one to suggest solutions in line with Terry's well-being (getting back to the primary consideration), and thereby clarifying the situation. This will give her an overview that takes individual perceptions into account. In addition, the negative emotions can be vented, for the most part, in her office, without excessively inflaming relations among those involved. This is a tactic designed to maintain communication without airing such emotions somewhat indiscriminately in front of everyone.

Following the individual meetings, there should be a group meeting to come up with a solution that satisfies everyone. The principal should lay out a framework for the discussion: set a time limit to prevent the meeting from getting out of control, emphasize the primary consideration, have each person outline her/his perception of the tasks involved in her/his role of caring for Terry, do not interrupt, listen respectfully to what each person has to say so that everyone's dignity is protected. It is very important that the principal articulate the goal of such a meeting. For instance, based on the information gathered, it could be to *find common ground concerning recognized tasks that truly help Terry with his learning while maintaining his relationship of trust with his educators* (teacher, nurse and education assistant). The principal's leadership is crucial in highly emotional situations: it is easy to let off steam and let fly cutting remarks that will only destroy any possible discussion. Moreover, the trap that a leader could fall victim to is to be paralyzed by one's professional inaction as a result of being vulnerable solely to the ethic of care.

It is important to remind each person of the vital importance of maintaining a professional relationship with others, because this is the base on which the identity of educators is built.

CASE COMMENTARY 6

Case: An Emotional Friday Afternoon

Craig E. Johnson
Professor of Leadership Studies, George Fox University

This case vividly demonstrates the urgency of real-life conflicts and dilemmas. Like Amy bursting into the principal's office at three on a Friday afternoon, problems often surprise us at the most inopportune times. When they thrust their way into our classrooms and offices, they demand our immediate attention.

The principal gets off to a good start when confronted with this crisis. She suppresses the urge to take charge and begins to ask questions instead. Then she tries to defuse the tension and establish a more positive tone. She also notes that the primary objective is to care for the student and follows procedures by notifying the district Special Education supervisor and superintendent. However, leaving Terry in the room during the outburst is disrespectful. His needs are ignored as participants vent their frustrations.

The other actors in the drama seem to have forgotten both professional and general ethical standards. Amy, the nurse, Irene, the teacher, and Jane, the education assistant should have brought this issue to the attention of the principal sooner. Amy and Irene engage in confrontation instead of collaboration. Simone, the district Special Education supervisor, has critical things to say about the parties but offers little in the way of assistance. Terry's mother is understandably upset but engages in name-calling.

The goal of Monday's meeting should be to shift the conflict from affective to substantive. Affective conflicts centre on the personalities of those involved and generate destructive outcomes. Substantive conflicts focus on resolving issues and generating win-win solutions. The emotional tone of Friday's encounter shouldn't obscure the fact that the parties involved have legitimate concerns that need to be addressed. Amy deserves to be treated as a professional and should not be asked to carry out tasks beyond her job description. She ought to be able to take regular breaks outside the classroom. Irene, the education assistants, and the students ought to have clean and sanitary work and classroom spaces. The teacher and assistants also deserve respect as professionals. Terry's parents have a right to see that their son gets a quality education that meets his needs. Terry should be treated with respect.

While the superintendent will likely run Monday's session, the principal can do her part to focus attention on problem solving. Participants should be reminded that they have a shared mission: to help Terry. Assertions have been made and charges levelled that may or may not be true. More fact-finding is in order. For example: Is Amy always required to stay with Terry as claimed? What are the job requirements for each party? How does Amy handle medications and dispose of Terry's stomach fluids? Do the education assistants treat the nurse disrespectfully or are they expressing concern about Terry's condition? Once the facts are established, the parties involved can go about addressing their concerns. Procedures will need to be put in place to monitor compliance to agreements made during the session and to address additional issues that will undoubtedly arise in the future. If these steps are taken, future Friday afternoons will not be so emotional.

REFLECTION ON THE COMMENTARIES

Identify the statements in the commentaries that resonate strongly with you. Reflect on how these statements align with your ethical principles. O'Sullivan comments on the dehumanization of children with special needs; Campbell suggests that the educational leader demonstrates moral outrage; Pinnegar and Erickson identify "positioning theory" as a key factor present in the case; and Haynes understands the case from an orientation toward Kohlberg's rational ethics. What is your reaction to each of these approaches? What role does your own leadership philosophy play in your responses?

ADDITIONAL READING

Browne-Ferrigno, T. (2003). Becoming a principal: Role conception, initial socialization, role-identity transformation, purposeful engagement. *Educational Administration Quarterly, 39*(4), 468–503.

The author presents findings from a study conducted with educators in various roles who engaged in a principal leadership program. The goal of the study was to discover the attitudes and perceptions of administrators, related to the transformations they face as they assume leadership roles.

Normore, A. H. (2004b). Ethics and values in leadership preparation programs: Finding the North Star in the dust storm. *Values and Ethics in Educational Administration, 2*(2), 1–4.

Normore offers a theoretical perspective on ethics and values as components of professional preparation for school leaders. His multi-dimensional ethical framework includes three themes: integrating the study of ethics into leadership preparation programs, incorporating ethics into administrative decision making, and using ethical rules and the ethics of individuals in leadership positions.

Starratt, R. J. (1999). Moral dimensions of leadership. In P. T. Begley & P. E. Leonard (Eds.), *The values of educational administration* (pp. 22–35). London, UK: Falmer Press.

This article proposes that a restructuring of the school system, in reaction to a changing society, requires that moral leadership be maintained in schools. It presents three hypothetical situations concerning a school principal, which outline and explain the characteristics of three modes of leadership: transactional, transitional and transformational.

Starratt, R. J. (2004). *Ethical leadership*. San Francisco, CA: Jossey-Bass.

The author argues that educational leadership requires a moral commitment to high-quality learning for all students. That commitment is based on three principles: proactive responsibility; authenticity, both personal and professional; and a supporting presence for educators and educational environments.

Starratt, R. J. (2005). Responsible leadership. *The Educational Forum, 69*(2), 124–133.

Starratt defines five domains of responsibility central to education leadership: responsibility as human being, as a citizen and public servant, as an educator, as an education administrator, and as an educational leader. He provides an ethical vocabulary that can be used by practitioners in describing their leadership challenges.

Stengel, B., & Tom, A. R. (2006). *Moral matters: Five ways to develop the moral life of schools*. New York, NY: Teachers College Press.

This book identifies various methods of enhancing the moral life of schools. Case studies illustrate the moral dimension of teachers' work, the moral education of students and the moral structure of schools. The importance of working in and nurturing moral environments that enable teachers to collectively respond to the moral dilemmas encountered in practice are highlighted throughout this text.

Zubay, B., & Soltis, J. F. (2005). *Creating the ethical school: A book of case studies*. New York, NY: Teachers College Press.

The authors address some of the ethical issues that arise daily in an educator's professional practice. They present case studies and ethical standards for educators at all levels in a school environment. The book is a resource for educators and a guide for pre-service candidates who want to create caring and supportive learning communities.

CASE 3

Initiated

"What camp?" I ask hesitantly.

"It's the Grade 9 three-day orientation. It will be a great way for you to get to know the students," my principal declares. "Yeah, it'll be your initiation into the school," quips the other vice-principal, David.

"Sure." My stomach is already starting to knot.

I've only been in the vice-principal role for two weeks. Now I'm leaving with 300 Grade 9 students, 40 senior student counsellors, 20 teachers and an organizational plan that befits a small military operation. The entourage consists of 10 school buses travelling in convoy. I clutch the large-size bottle of headache tablets that David presented to me for the trip.

I've been told that these senior student counsellors are "the best of the best." They have been recommended by their teachers and have been selected from twice as many student applicants. The lead teacher, Paulette, has everything carefully planned. She seems to be in control of bus groups, cabin groups, activity groups, group rotations, meal plans, spirit builders, and even the set of rainy-day activities.

Day one is no problem. There are no injuries. The students seem to be having fun. We have only two minor discussions with a couple of students about acceptable behaviour. The principal visits the camp for a few hours and comments on how well plans are being followed. The sun is beaming. Everything is going well. The first day ends successfully. I am starting to feel that this isn't such a bad idea after all. Perhaps I won't even need those headache tablets.

I think to myself as I drift off to sleep, "These senior counsellors are amazing. They are thoughtful, spirited, responsible and engaging. They are really like an extended staff."

The second day it is raining and we have the chance to test out the rainy-day activities. Once again, even with the rain, things seem to be going well.

When evening arrives, we remind the student counsellors of their responsibilities. All students are to be in their cabins for the night. Anything unusual is to be reported to staff members. The clouds roll in again as darkness falls. As I'm preparing for my rounds at three in the morning, I hear voices off in distance. I make a quick call to Paulette on our special hand-held radios, and then I'm off to investigate.

I see a string of Grade 9 girls being marched down the road ahead and placed in a circle in the middle of a field. At the lead are the senior counsellors. Then I hear the heavy feet of Grade 9 boys running down the hill. I watch as the senior students chase them into the field. The counsellors are running commando style, wearing night-vision goggles. The light from my flashlight reveals that the Grade 9 students are covered with shaving cream, toilet tissue and toothpaste.

Approaching a senior counsellor, I naively ask, "What's going on?"

"Don't worry, sir. We promise no one will get hurt. They're all having fun. It's a tradition." The senior counsellors appear to be proud of their leadership in this event. I am shocked.

"Get back to your cabins, now. And I mean all of you." One look at my face and they know I'm serious. They turn toward the cabins. Several counsellors mutter sheepishly, "We're going."

In the meantime, Paulette has arrived and together we walk back toward the cabins. Torrential rain, thunder and lightening begin just as we reach the camp.

Paulette and I begin to check the cabins to ensure that all students have returned. While we're doing this, the electrical power fails. Luckily, we have flashlights. We continue to check the cabins, groping our way around the property. I'm sure that some students are lost in the woods. We desperately try to account for every single student and soon realize that not all of the students are in the cabins that they were originally assigned. This makes our task even more confusing.

After an hour, Paulette and I conclude that two Grade 9 boys are still missing. We frantically organize the other teachers to search the woods around the cabins. We scramble in the dark and the mud, repeatedly calling out the names of the two students.

Mercifully, we locate both students after about 10 minutes. (Every one of those minutes, however, felt like an hour.) They were hiding in the trees for shelter, afraid to return to their cabins in the storm.

I am relieved beyond words that all the students are accounted for. No one is hurt, though some are trembling, a few are crying and others are angry. I finally take a few minutes to rest and dry myself off. Now I feel my rage beginning to swell. I cannot believe that these senior students could be so irresponsible. They have broken all the rules. They were informed of the trip's expectations. We had meetings and discussions. They convinced us they were ready and responsible. No one mentioned the words "initiation activity" during any of these meetings. How did this happen?

In the morning I phone the school principal. The principal phones the superintendent and the school council chair. The Grade 9 students phone home. Our interviews with the Grade 9 students reveal that they were doused with shaving cream and toothpaste, decorated with markers, toilet tissue and nail polish, marched outside in the night and made to sing songs and read poems. One boy was taped to a tree.

Some of the Grade 9 students begin to develop colds. Some are upset that the counsellors seem angry with them. Others are in disbelief that the counsellors they trusted during the day turned on them at night. A number of Grade 9 students from a variety of ethno-cultural backgrounds claim they were singled out and treated worse than other students.

When interviewed, the counsellors reveal that they themselves were all initiated in Grade 9. They say that the initiation activity has gone on for at least the last 25 years. Several senior students tell stories about their parents, who were involved in initiation rites years ago. They insist that the Grade 9 students expect this initiation tradition of them.

Back at the school, the parents of the Grade 9 students are demanding a full investigation. They are demanding the resignation of the incompetent school administrators who allowed this to take place. One set of parents goes so far as to demand that charges be laid against those who endangered their children. They characterize the incident as nothing less than assault.

I can't believe the parents are taking things so far. I reluctantly consult with police officers to get their opinion on whether or not charges are warranted. Parents of the senior counsellors, on the other hand, are worried about potential consequences. They assert that their children meant no harm to the Grade 9s, and several remind us that they went through the same thing themselves. Fearful of repercussions, as their children are about to apply to university, parents encourage the school administration to take a calm, reasoned approach. But these parents also acknowledge that times have changed and that initiation activities should probably be banned.

Some teachers add to the confusion. I overheard one group commenting, "It's just a minor hazing. It's always been done. It's just for fun. No one gets hurt. Remember, those senior kids are the best."

I am just one month into my vice-principal role. What have I got myself into? I feel like I am the one being initiated, although the principal is very supportive throughout the ordeal, and challenges our administrative team to come up with a creative solution.

This is the first time the issue of initiation has been tackled at this school. There is no written school district policy. Nor has any reference to initiation been included in the school code of conduct. The parents in the community represent diverse cultural backgrounds. They are generally well versed in the law and in issues related to safe schools. A number of them serve on the school council and have made important financial contributions to the school. The superintendent tries to appear sympathetic to all parties and to all sides of the issue.

We interview all of the students again. We communicate directly with every family involved. The school administration team then meets and begins looking for creative solutions.

We know we must address the issues. We decide on an approach that we hope will bring about community dialogue and change. We recognize that this is a turning point in the life of the school community. We know that, somehow, we must present the facts, demonstrate concern for the dangerous and explosive nature of events, and find a resolution that will put an end to this tradition.

Finally, we agree on a set of strategies.

PROFESSIONAL INQUIRY

The Professional Inquiry section is intended to support reflection, dialogue and the development of new understanding and insights. Engagement in the following processes can occur individually or collaboratively with colleagues. These processes are designed to facilitate new or revised interpretations of the leadership experience described in the case Initiated. This additional knowledge may guide the subsequent leadership actions, thinking and decisions of the reader.

Vision

1. Examine the vice-principal's vision of education in this case.

2. Critique this vision from the perspective of your own educational philosophy.

3. Identify processes that might facilitate a collective and shared vision for this school.

Ethical Practice

1. Identify the ethical responsibilities the educators (principal, teachers, vice-principal and superintendent) have toward the learners in this case.

2. What ethical principles or norms should a school possess?

3. Examine the ethical principles or norms that are not honoured in this case.

4. Develop a plan to foster a more ethical school culture in this learning community.

5. Discuss how the best interests of students, teachers and the community could be served in this case.

School Culture

1. Explore issues that are related to the culture of this school (power, privilege, tradition, silence, etc.).

2. Identify the components of the school culture that need to be addressed in order to assure both students and parents that a safe, trusting and just learning community will be provided to learners in this school.

Leadership Practice

1. Develop a leadership entry plan for the vice-principal new to this secondary school.

2. Describe the multiple forms of leadership exhibited in this case.

3. Design a plan for developing ethical leadership for the students and the teachers in this school.

School Policy

1. Discuss how school and board policy can be used to support ethical professional practice.

Public Trust

1. Explore the strategies the administrative team and faculty might employ to maintain trusting relationships with parents and deal responsibly and ethically with the situation.

2. Discuss how a lack of commitment and action to preventing harm for all students impacts on the public's view of a professionally responsible and trustworthy teaching profession.

Reflective Practice

1. Reflect on the role of the principal and supervisory officer in this case. Identify areas of professional growth for both of these educational leaders.

2. Reflect on the dilemmas in this case and write a commentary in response to the inherent issues.

3. Explain what you have learned about educational leadership from this case.

CASE COMMENTARY CRITIQUE

1. Read the commentary(ies) written about the case.

2. Record your reflections regarding the commentary(ies) using the framework below:

   a. Identify the key points, perspectives or issues in the commentary.

   b. Analyze the key points, perspectives or issues identified in the commentary.

   c. List the new insights you gained from the commentary.

Commentary Critique			
Case Commentary Writer	Identification *What key points, perspectives or issues are identified in the commentary?*	Analysis *What is your analysis of the perspectives identified in the commentary?*	Synthesis *What new insights have you gained from the commentary?*

CASE COMMENTARIES

CASE COMMENTARY 1

Case: Initiated

Jean Clandinin
Professor and Director, Centre for Research for Teacher Education and Development, University of Alberta

When I encounter a dilemma, I am asked to think of a way to live with, or through, a situation where I feel competing or conflicting demands. There are no sure answers or tidy solutions. I felt the dilemmas for everyone involved in Initiated, that is, for the vice-principal who narrates the case, the senior counsellors, the Grade 9 students, the principal, the other teachers, including Paulette, and the parents of all students. While I appreciated that, for some, the events might be seen as a problem in search of a solution that assigned blame, or a question of missing policy that could be answered by filling the policy gap, the administrative team understood the events as creating a dilemma for how they might restory the landscape of their school.

Initially, I thought about the lives that bumped against each other, each person's plot lines visible in ways not apparent before the bump. For example, the vice-principal, new to his position and trying to figure out what stories to live by, follows Paulette's lead and together they follow the plot lines of the stories they heard about previous trips, trips in which secret stories not visible to school administrators were lived. The Grade 9 students, too, at least as far as we are told in the piece, follow the plot lines of becoming Grade 10 students. The senior counsellors appear to have a different story, a secret story, perhaps an open secret for some parents and for teachers. The parents, those who did not know the secret story, lived the plot line of parents who trust the story of school, a familiar plot line parents expect to live out.

When these stories bump against each other on that stormy night, everyone awakens to how the stories conflict and do not follow a coherent plot line within the safe story of school. When stories bump together, we awaken in ways that make us attend to the storied landscape in new ways: we find ourselves in what seems to be an unfamiliar landscape and we struggle to find our place in that altered landscape. When stories bump, the bumps occlude the flow, the coherent unfolding of lives in a familiar and perhaps comfortable landscape, and create moments where, with hard work, careful attending to each other, and respectful listening, restoried stories of school can be composed. Events such as these create the rupture, the occlusion that allows something different to be composed, an opportunity for hearing the stories of the others and allowing familiar storied landscapes to be restoried.

Is it possible, I wonder, to create spaces where people can come together in genuine dialogue to tell their stories and be attended to in order to restory the landscape of school and allow new stories of school to flourish? I am not sure that strategies that work toward "presenting the facts" will create spaces for everyone's story to be told, heard, valued and inquired into, and in that way, allow the restorying that is necessary in the landscape.

As the administrative team looks for strategies to move forward, to hear the stories of the community that might lead to the change they are seeking, they need to allow for the possibility of composing a restoried story of school that picks up on what happened before and allows each person to be a part of, and locate her/himself in the new story. Restorying cannot be imposed. One story cannot merely replace the other; but we need to work to create spaces for dialogue where all participants' stories are told.

CASE COMMENTARY 2

Case: Initiated

Steven Jay Gross
Associate Professor of Educational Leadership, Temple University

Initiated depicts a dilemma that is at once volatile and complex. Because the situation quickly becomes divisive and because the new vice-principal is getting little help from others in the administration, he is left with a disturbing and potentially dangerous dilemma. One useful way for the vice-principal to respond is to consider both turbulence theory (Gross, 2006; Shapiro and Gross, 2008) and the multiple ethical paradigms (Shapiro and Gross, 2008; Shapiro and Stefkovich, 2005).

Turbulence theory will help the vice-principal in two ways. First, using the scale of air turbulence that pilots are trained in, he can determine the current level of volatility. While the scale runs from light turbulence, where there is little disturbance, to extreme, where the aircraft is about to break up, the current problem seems to be at level three: severe turbulence. In schools, severe turbulence can be caused by a clash of values in a given community and can lead to large-scale demonstrations. Both seem to fit this case.

Next, he should consider the dynamics of turbulence that have made things so potentially explosive. This means thinking of three interrelated forces: *positionality* – the way a situation can seem different from various vantage points; *cascading* – the tendency of one turbulent issue to build on and propel the next; and *stability* – where fault lines may exist in an organization. He should examine the case through the eyes of ninth graders, seniors, parents and teachers at the school to appreciate the difference position makes. Applying cascading might mean mapping the events and seeing how one leads to another and accelerates the speed and intensity of the situation. Understanding stability is critical to this case since there seems to be a divided school and community when it comes to this issue.

Once turbulence has been considered, it would help to use the multiple ethical paradigms. Of these ethics (justice, care, critique, and the profession), the ethics of care and the profession seem most relevant. In the ethic of care, we worry about the welfare of the ninth graders. But we should also wonder what can be done for the senior counsellors, who have betrayed their trust by turning on the younger students. The guiding question of the ethic of the profession is, "What is in the best interests of students?" Obviously, protecting younger students from aggressive older students is crucial. But the vice-principal should also ponder the welfare of the seniors. What resolution would help them learn and help to break the cycle of victimization?

Considering turbulence theory and multiple ethical paradigms is meant to lead to a deeper reflection for the vice-principal. One outcome may be a form of restorative justice where the ninth graders and seniors can enter into a thoughtful dialogue about hazing, followed by a co-operative effort to establish new policies and continued communication. The turbulence level may rise a bit as seniors meet with younger students but should decline as sensitive dialogue deepens.

COMMENTARY 3

Case: Initiated

Kay Johnston
Professor of Educational Studies and Women's Studies,
Colgate University

I had several ideas after I read this case, but the one that I most want to focus on is how the case illuminates the moral dilemmas embedded in the building of school communities.

At first I thought that perhaps the expectations for the senior counsellors had not been well articulated. The vice-principal states that the students "were informed of the trip's expectations," but I wondered if the senior students had been informed of the expectations that the adults had for *them* and why they had them. There is a difference between expectations for a trip and expectations for a person or a group of people, and I wondered if these senior counsellors had discussed both kinds of expectations with the adults in charge. The seniors clearly had expectations for the trip and those expectations were to carry out "the tradition" of hazing the Grade 9 students. The fact that these seniors were proud of their leadership in this tradition is an indication that they had not yet thought about the difference between conformity and leadership. The second issue is that the parents also seem not to have a focus on community. How would the vice-principal and other administrators take responsibility for introducing that issue into the conversation with the parents? Let's take each idea separately.

Young people need to understand that doing something because "everyone does it" or "it has always been done this way" is not a good reason for behaviour. They need to be helped to understand the importance of judging things as right or wrong rather than just going along. How would educators facilitate this kind of learning? I would suggest that they need to lead discussions about responsibility in relationships. These discussions can't be a one-off event in preparation for a trip; instead, the administrators must develop a culture of responsibility in the school. The adults in charge must develop a working theory about what responsibility means for their students, in their actions both in school and outside of school. The students need to learn to critique conformity and this learning takes time. It is work to develop a culture of care in a school, however, I think that seeing themselves responsible to the ninth-grade students, rather than to some tradition, would prevent this hazing from happening.

The students also need to be taught to understand reciprocity to the adults who gave them responsibility. Again, this is the kind of learning that must be done in the ongoing work of developing a school culture rather than in a meeting or two before an event.

The second issue also deals with community and reminds me of the John Dewey quote, "What the best and wisest parent wants for his own child, that must the community want for all of its children" (1990, p. 7). In this case, parents of the ninth graders are "demanding a full investigation" and parents of the senior counsellors "are worried about potential consequences" for their children. As I think about this, I wonder if there is a way for all the parents to be concerned for all the children. Is there a way that the administrators at the school could arrange for a conversation in which all the parents discuss the moral implications of this experience for both the seniors and the ninth graders? I imagine this conversation to be a space where, as Dewey suggests, all parents are concerned about the consequences for all students.

My reflection on this case makes me question how those involved – parents, administrators, teachers and students – can work to make this an experience that builds community and develops the moral thinking that is needed in order to take responsibility for treating others with care and respect. It is the kind of work that takes time and effort but it is the kind of work that needs to be done in schools.

CASE COMMENTARY 4

Case: Initiated

Stéphane Thibodeau
Professor, Department of Education, Université du Québec
à Trois-Rivières

This case study highlights the importance of leadership, especially in the problem-solving process. It also raises a number of fascinating points.

First, the case study concerns a vice-principal's initiation into his position. In this process, it would appear essential to introduce steps that encourage the integration of new school administrators, ensuring, for instance, that the incumbent administrative team provides them with adequate accompaniment and support. This would certainly foster the development of strong and effective leadership among young principals.

Next, the principal calls on the entire administrative team to resolve the problem facing the school, a model that may be referred to as shared leadership (Marks and Printy, 2003), leadership as a partnership (Moxley, 2000), co-operative leadership (Bronckart and Gather-Thurler, 2000), distributed leadership (Elmore, 2000), a community of leaders (Barth, 1990) or empowerment (Peel and Walker, 1994). Whatever the term used, this sharing of powers and responsibilities among various actors who join forces for a common goal can certainly further the development of the teaching profession and school effectiveness (Brunet and Boudreault, 2001).

In addition, to resolve the problem, the principal challenges his team to generate an innovative solution, which is in line with the concept of *intellectual stimulation* that is part of Bass's theory of transformational leadership (1985, 1998). The intellectual stimulation provided by a leader involves a set of behaviours that motivate or intellectually stimulate the members of her/his team. A leader who provides others with intellectual stimulation challenges their perceptions, reformulates problems and takes an innovative approach to difficult situations. To solve problems, the leader asks her/his team members for fresh ideas and creative solutions – because they are part of the problem-solving process. In short, the leader encourages the others to try new methods of doing things and does not criticize their ideas, even if they differ from her/his own. Such a leader can help the team become more creative and original.

Lastly, the administrative team makes no attempt to cover up the incident and seems prepared to assume its responsibilities. The transparency and accountability of the school team are two qualities required by government authorities as well as by the community and parents. By acting in this manner, the leaders can benefit from the effects of *charisma* within their school. Charisma is a trait that makes a leader exemplary; that is, it indicates an influential person who is held up as an ideal by members of her/his team (Bass, 1985, 1998). Such a leader appears to command admiration, respect and trust, and the others identify with and wish to emulate her/him.

In conclusion, leadership in education is one of the most researched concepts in the field of school administration (Brunet, 2003; Langlois, 2004). Since its necessity in a school environment has been proven beyond question, extensive development in this area would appear to be crucial for anyone hoping to become a school administrator.

REFLECTION ON THE COMMENTARIES

The commentators suggest a variety of frameworks for responding to the leadership dilemmas experienced by the vice-principal in this case. Consider Clandinin's concept of stories bumping together, Gross's discussions of the dynamics of turbulence, Johnston's references to John Dewey and Thibodeau's highlighting of transformational leadership. Identify the new understanding you have gained regarding educational leadership and ethical practice from reading these commentaries.

ADDITIONAL READING

Barkley, S., Bottoms, G., Feagin, C. H., & Clark, S. (2001). *Leadership matters: Building leadership capacity*. Atlanta, GA: Southern Regional Education Board.

This guide offers strategies for building leadership capacity. It addresses the following four questions: What do leaders do to create curriculum and instruction that push all students to higher levels of proficiency? How do school leaders demonstrate that nearly all students can master challenging curricula? How do leaders generate the efforts of many to focus on the success of every student? How can leaders put these ideas into practice?

Fullan, M. (2001). *Leading in a culture of change*. San Francisco, CA: Jossey-Bass.

This book identifies five competencies as important for educational leaders. The author proposes that educational leaders need to develop the skills necessary to encourage and empower education partners during times of change.

Hargreaves, A., & Fink, D. (2006). *Sustainable leadership*. San Francisco, CA: Jossey-Bass.

The authors set out a framework of seven principles for sustaining leadership. Explanations concern the depth, length, breadth, justice, diversity, resourcefulness and conservation of leadership, along with action principles for achieving sustainability in practice.

Ogawa, R. T. (2005). Leadership as social construct: The expression of human agency within organizational constraint. In F. W. English (Ed.), *The Sage handbook of educational leadership: Advances in theory, research, and practice* (pp. 89–108). Thousand Oaks, CA: Sage Publications.

Ogawa begins with the need to control one's own destiny and how that has shaped his conceptualization of leadership. He examines existing theories on the difficulty of defining leadership and the link between leadership and organization success. He focuses on shifts in theory and research on educational leadership.

Theoharis, G. (2006). *Woven in deeply: Identity, calling, and urban social justice.* Paper presented at the annual meeting of the American Education Research Association, San Francisco, CA.

The author investigates the experience of seven urban public school principals who maintain a strong commitment to their vision of social justice and equity. They empower their staff and facilitate school-wide, shared decision making.

Section II

Leaders as Facilitators of Community

LEADERS AS FACILITATORS OF COMMUNITY

Educational leaders who nurture relationships of trust, openness and mutual respect will be able to cultivate a shared commitment to community in the school environment. Facilitating a school ethos based on community helps to build interdependence toward the collective project of optimizing student learning. Fostering collaborative communities of practice based on reflection, inquiry and shared leadership is an essential requirement of effective educational leaders. As facilitators of learning communities who are deeply committed to enhancing student learning, school leaders need to be highly knowledgeable in the areas of curriculum, pedagogy, assessment and evaluation, ethics and professional learning, as well as deeply committed to enhancing student learning. Developing the collective capacity and leadership of all staff members to enable them to effectively support the success of all students is an important area of focus for the school leader. Involving all members of the community in the mutual pursuit of student learning requires the school leader to foster the development of a shared vision. The leader needs to be invitational, open, service-oriented and unwaveringly committed to teaching and learning. The ethical orientation and values that guide the actions, discussions and decisions of educational leaders need to be made visible and articulated. These elements play a critical role in shaping and influencing the ethical nature of the school community. The effective educational leader ensures that the voices, perspectives, leadership and experiences of all members are authentically included so they can meaningfully contribute to the common vision created for the school.

CASES FROM PROFESSIONAL PRACTICE

The three cases in this section invite contemplation regarding the importance of ethically responsible practice in the development and sustenance of effective learning communities. The essential role of the educational leader's vision, skills, professional knowledge and instructional leadership is illuminated in these illustrative cases. Essential to the implementation of effective learning communities is the creation of a culture of professionalism where shared leadership and joint responsibility become the norm. In this professional climate, teachers are empowered as pedagogical leaders and their sense of professional efficacy is supported, thus enabling them to collectively enhance student learning. In this open professional environment, educators collectively commit to be responsible for achievements toward a common purpose.

> ### Cases
>
> *Striptease on Day Three*
> *A School Divided*
> *Growing Pains*

CASE COMMENTARIES

The case commentaries in this section are written by educational scholars and practitioners. The commentary writers highlight a multiplicity of concepts associated with educational leadership. These concepts include: reflection, authenticity, core values, leadership responsibilities, organizational culture, student learning, ethical dilemmas, the ethics of justice, care, critique and the profession, presence, trust, moral leadership, teacher leadership, shared professional growth, disengaged teachers, and the role of dialogue in school communities.

Commentaries

Striptease on Day Three

Pauline Leonard
Brenda Beatty
Andy Hargreaves and Pauline Hargreaves
Theresa Shanahan
Ulrika Bergmark

A School Divided

Joan Poliner Shapiro
Patrick Duignan
Lorraine Savoie-Zajc
Ben Levin

Growing Pains

John M. Novak
Ann Lieberman
Jeanne Doucet
Ellie Drago-Severson

CASE 4

Striptease on Day Three

Margaret Stanfield, better known as Maggie to her friends and colleagues, sits on the stage in the school gym and resolutely eyes the audience. Today is her third day as principal in a school dubbed "the flagship." The school is not quite four years old and is equipped with the latest and the best of everything. The front entrance to the building is beautifully landscaped. The furniture gracing the main foyer and administrative offices is cherrywood. The classrooms are furnished with laptops.

Maggie's predecessor retired unexpectedly on the last day of December. The quick turnaround did not give Maggie the opportunity to visit the school before her first day on site in January. Her request to the superintendent to visit the school before the former principal left was denied.

However, as an experienced secondary school administrator, she feels quite comfortable. Ironically, she was invited to be a part of the design team for this school building and was directly involved in the selection of its first staff. She remembers that the community at this end of town took a special interest in the proposed school from the moment the announcement was made about construction. Prospective parents attended public meetings and even held fundraising events to help supplement the district school board's allocated start-up funds.

On this, Maggie's third day at the school, John, the vice-principal calls an assembly of the student body to formally introduce the new principal. The student athletic council has taken this opportunity to showcase the school's athletic teams. One team after the next comes forward. The student audience claps and cheers for each one.

The last team to come on stage is the boy's basketball team. As the team is introduced, music begins to blare. The boys strut across the front of the stage. Each one is gyrating to the music in a provocative way. Maggie soon realizes that the spectacle is a mock striptease. The student body is yelling and screaming.

Maggie can see John, the vice-principal, from the corner of her eye. He deliberately avoids looking in her direction. The cheering reaches a crescendo in anticipation of the finale. Maggie stands up.

Suddenly, someone turns off the music. The boys stop. Their momentum is lost and they scatter off stage. John runs to the nearest microphone and directs the teachers to return with their students to their classrooms. The group departs in silence.

"What is going on here?" Maggie demands of John behind the closed doors of her office. She has been an administrator for 15 years and never has she experienced such lewd and inappropriate behaviour in a school setting. She asks John, "Is it because there is no established protocol for school assemblies? Is it poor leadership on the part of a group of teachers in the athletic department? Is this an isolated incident of unacceptable behaviour?"

This incident is just one more thing to add to Maggie's list. The list that began on her first morning in the school has continued to grow over the last two days.

On Maggie's first morning, she greeted the office support staff warmly. Their response was, at best, lukewarm. In some ways she anticipated this. The talk around the system is that she's been sent to "clean up" the school.

That same morning, Maggie continues through the reception area and enters her office for the first time. Trying to orient herself to her new surroundings, she begins to search for the usual documents. She looks for staff lists, schedules, student timetables, budget statements, and the district-board-issued principal's handbook. She opens and closes drawers. She finds nothing. Perhaps her predecessor used a computer to store this essential information. Maggie calls in Janet, the school office manager and asks, "Could you please log me in to the principal's laptop?"

"Oh, I'm sorry," Janet replies. "Were you not advised that the principal's computer isn't working? I sent in a repair requisition a couple of weeks before Christmas but no one showed up. I could contact them again."

"Thank you, Janet. In the interim, are there hard copies of both a staff list and the school timetables?"

Janet scurries off to make copies.

Maggie also decides on her first day to take a tour of the school. She plans to do a walkabout and at the same time give herself an opportunity to calm down. She invites John, the vice-principal, to join her.

Fortunately, a number of the staff members know her. As she walks the halls and peers into classrooms, Maggie relaxes a bit. Teachers are actively engaging students. She is always encouraged when she observes students learning.

As Maggie and John move from one floor to the next, Maggie wonders why John seems nervous and why the students snicker as he approaches. She knows that he's been a teacher and vice-principal at the school for some time. She'll make a point of discussing this with him later. She doesn't want to put him on the spot right now. She knows how to wait for the right time.

Her final stop is at the custodian's office. She congratulates the custodian on how well maintained and clean the school looks. He is clearly grateful that she's noticed.

As Maggie and John return to the main office, the lunch bell sounds. Students flood out of the classrooms and into the cafeteria. Maggie notes that teachers move out of the way of students instead of students moving out of the way of teachers. The consistency of this behaviour bothers her.

From a distance, Maggie sees that the lunchroom supervisors are already in place. She compliments John on this. "I'm glad to see that the lunchroom supervisors are here to receive the students as they come in. You must have prepared a schedule and a list of expectations for the supervisors. Thanks." Maggie hopes this will help put John a little more at ease.

"With 450 students at lunch, supervision is very important," he replies proudly.

Maggie can barely hear his words for the noise and the confusion in the area.

She remembers that, during the design meetings several years ago, the cafeteria was regulated to house only 300 students at a time. The fact that it might be too small was a topic of discussion during the preliminary planning. Maggie asks, "John, do you know if fire regulations have been addressed regarding the cafeteria? There are so many students crammed into this space."

"We know that it should only have 300 students but there are 450 students who need to eat here," John replies.

Back in her office, Maggie contemplates where to start. Her superintendent has already pointed out that the school is now in its fourth year and should have reached a projected enrolment of 850 students. The present 450 is a far cry from the target. Maggie wonders if the expectation is that she will bring that goal to fruition as soon as possible.

Tom, one of the English teachers, interrupts Maggie's thoughts. He is knocking on her open door. She invites him in. He hesitates. She invites him again, thinking that perhaps he hasn't heard her. Tom enters and remains standing.

"What can I do for you, Tom?"

"First, I would like to welcome you to our school. I missed you earlier. Do you have a moment to talk to me or would you like me to make an appointment?"

"I have time now," Maggie replies.

"I'd like to close the door," whispers Tom.

"I don't usually close my door." Maggie focuses on his eyes. She smiles and gestures for him to sit down.

"This is important," says Tom.

"Please sit down, Tom."

"No thank you. I prefer to stand. Being in this office makes me nervous."

Tom says that he is the English teacher for the two graduating classes. He explains to Maggie that these students are viewed as the school pioneers. They were the first students in the first year that the school began.

Right from the beginning they were treated differently. Tom explains that because the school was partially under construction in its opening year, promises were made to these students and their parents, many of whom are prominent individuals in the community and active on the school council. They were promised many things, from special timetables to bussing from any location in town.

Tom complained to the previous principal a number of times about minor problems with this elite group of students. Now he is experiencing major difficulties keeping them on task and making them work. Their grades are dropping. He explains that at mid-semester some students were given passing grades by teachers in spite of the fact that they had not met the curriculum expectations. January finals are around the corner and Tom wants Maggie's advice. He feels that maintaining a positive image of the school is very important. However, he is also wondering what would happen if not all the students of the first graduating class received diplomas? Will teachers be expected to adjust marks to accommodate the first graduates?

Maggie tries to comprehend exactly what has been going on for the last four years. It is just her second day and she has already encountered a broad range of problems. Now this.

She looks directly at Tom. "Thank you for coming to see me well in advance of the exams and the report cards. You realize that it is only my second day here. However, it has always been my understanding that a student earns her/his mark. I believe it is the student's choice to work or not. Could we focus on how to help as many of your students as possible to be successful? We also need to remember though, that no matter what we do, it still may be that not everyone will pass. Why don't we meet again tomorrow during your planning period? In the meantime, I'm going to ask the English department head to join us for the meeting. I'm sure the three of us will come up with some helpful strategies."

As Tom leaves the office, Maggie wonders, "Is the image of this school so important that a teacher would consider adjusting marks?"

Later that day, Janet reminds Maggie that a meeting of the subject department leaders to review curriculum and budget needs is traditionally held on the first Tuesday of every month. Maggie's second day at the school is also the first Tuesday of the month. Janet volunteers to type the standard agenda. "Thanks for the heads up," says Maggie.

The meeting is short. Maggie soon discovers that these curriculum leaders are accustomed to accepting office directives and following instructions without question. Discussion is halting and limited. Clearly, these staff members see their role as delivering an office-generated message rather than assuming a real leadership function.

Maggie's day began with the assembly fiasco. Throughout the day, her list of concerns continued to lengthen. It is five o'clock on day three. Maggie is sitting alone in her cherrywood office.

PROFESSIONAL INQUIRY

The Professional Inquiry section is intended to support reflection, dialogue and the development of new understanding and insights. Engagement in the following processes can occur individually or collaboratively with colleagues. These processes are designed to facilitate new or revised interpretations of the leadership experience described in the case Striptease on Day Three. This additional knowledge may guide the subsequent leadership actions, thinking and decisions of the reader.

Vision

1. Describe the vision of teaching and learning that the principal is trying to foster in this school community.

2. Identify the leadership vision that is communicated in the actions and words of the principal.

Leadership Practice

1. Pinpoint the values that are modelled in the actions and decisions of the school principal.

2. Describe and analyze the principal's leadership style in this case.

Professional Efficacy

1. Analyze the professional efficacy of the teachers and vice-principal in this case.

2. Outline the steps you would take, as an educational leader, to further develop the professional efficacy of the teachers in this school.

Shared Leadership

1. Identify the strategies an educational leader could employ to foster a sense of responsible and effective shared leadership in this school.

2. Using the following framework, explore the various forms of leadership depicted by the learners, teachers, school personnel and vice-principal in this case.

Case participants	Forms of Leadership
Learners	
Teachers	
School personnel	
Vice-principal	

Ethical Practice

1. Identify the ethical issues inherent in the assessment processes used in this school.

2. Using the following framework, ascertain what ethical responsibilities and obligations the superintendent, school board personnel, teachers and vice-principal have in supporting the effective transition of a new principal to this school.

Supporting the Transition of a New Principal	
Case Participants	**Ethical Responsibilities and Obligations**
Superintendent	
School office personnel	
Teachers	
Vice-principal	

Collaborative Community of Inquiry

1. Examine the effectiveness of this professional learning community.

2. Discuss the ethical implications of providing special privileges to an identified "elite group of students."

3. Develop a plan, using the following framework, for fostering a collaborative community of inquiry based on the principles of collaboration, transparency, respect, trust, social justice and equity.

Fostering a Professional Learning Community Action Plan		
Foundational Principles: Collaboration, Transparency, Respect, Trust, Social Justice, Equity		
Student Learning	Teacher Development	Relationships with Parents

CASE COMMENTARY CRITIQUE

1. Read the commentary(ies) written about the case.

2. Record your reflections regarding the commentary(ies) using the framework below:

   a. Identify the key points, perspectives or issues in the commentary.

   b. Analyze the key points, perspectives or issues identified in the commentary.

   c. List the new insights you gained from the commentary.

Commentary Critique			
Case Commentary Writer	**Identification** _What key points, perspectives or issues are identified in the commentary?_	**Analysis** _What is your analysis of the perspectives identified in the commentary?_	**Synthesis** _What new insights have you gained from the commentary?_

CASE COMMENTARIES

CASE COMMENTARY 1

Case: Striptease on Day Three

Pauline Leonard
Associate Professor and Department Chair of Curriculum, Instruction and Leadership, College of Education, Louisiana Tech University

Despite the apparent ease with which she observes her comfortable surroundings as the newly appointed principal of a celebrated secondary school, the principal in the opening scene in this case portrays an alert leader poised for action. Early on, it becomes clear that her seemingly enviable position is one that has placed her in a challenging environment where she is beginning to uncover a multi-layered, complex school culture in need of change. As the case unfolds, we catch promising glimpses of principal Margaret Stanfield's *reflective timing* (Coombs, 2003) and *authenticity* (Begley, 2004; Starratt, 2004) as a leader in her endeavour to understand the challenges and needs of this flagship school.

Reflective timing refers to when reflection takes place: *before* (reflection-for-action), *during* (reflection-in-action), or *after* (reflection-on-action) the event or action being reflected upon occurs (Coombs, 2003, p. 3). In this case, there's ample evidence of principal Stanfield's reflection-on-action processes as she contemplates the events leading up to her acceptance of the principalship position. Additionally, she carefully and methodically gathers information before taking any irreversible action, a testament to her ability to reflect-for-action. However, it is her reflection-*in*-action agility that is arguably her most important resource as she charts these unfamiliar waters. For example, consider her response to the mock striptease performed at the assembly. Principal Stanfield's decision to stand up at a crucial moment during the performance quietly marked her disapproval. Was this merely a reflexive reaction on her part? Or was it a result of her *reflecting-in-the-moment* on what was happening while using her intrinsic moral compass as a gauge to determine action? Clearly, her action did not go unnoticed, sending an extremely important message about her expectations for student (and teacher) behaviour in the school.

Conscious engagement in reflective practices is the hallmark of an authentic leader (Begley, 2004). Simply put, an authentic person is real, not fake (Starratt, 2004). In our brief visit with principal Stanfield, we see someone who appears to be genuinely concerned about the academic direction of the school and her role in facilitating change for school improvement. She gives the impression that, despite the ambiguous and uncharted course she is travelling, this educator is crystal clear about who she is and what she stands for. Undoubtedly, her 15 years as a school administrator have helped her arrive at this juncture in her professional career. However, in addition to confronting her core values as an educational leader, she appears to be clarifying her leadership responsibilities "as, to, and for" (Starratt, 2004, p. 63) in this school. This is evident as she negotiates the multiple arenas of valuation (Begley, 2004) to uncover the shared and contested values of students, teachers, staff, parents and the community at large.

Attending to these valuational processes will also help principal Stanfield better understand the organizational culture of her school, an important prerequisite to organizational change. According to Deal and Peterson (1999), the heart of leadership is the ability to read school culture and, if necessary, shape it for a new direction. Principal Stanfield's astute reflective timing and her authenticity as a leader should assist her immensely in reading the organization's culture. In fact, it is these leadership characteristics that will guide her incremental and long-term decision making for culture change as she navigates – mid-stream – the evidently troubled waters of this flagship school.

CASE COMMENTARY 2

Case: Striptease on Day Three

Brenda Beatty
Designer and Director of the Monash Master in School Leadership and the Human Leadership: Developing People programs, created for the Victoria State School Department of Education

To introduce my reflection, I shall begin by stating some inferences and therefore assumptions I have made based on my reading of this case story. Maggie prefers to operate with an "open door policy" and sees herself as a consultative, collaborative, relational leader. She is aware of the emotion factor as it affects others and their responses to her and each other. She knows that her priority is to put safety first. Maggie practises the wisdom of separating the problem from the person. She recognizes the need to lead change in this school so that all members of her staff can become members of a proactive, cohesive, collaborative *learning* community.

As I see it, Maggie has her hands full to become attuned to the existing culture and begin to lead change in this school. The school has been riding high on its initial reputation as a "flagship" school, and some cracks are beginning to show. But things could be worse. Resources are not an issue, except perhaps the use of them, as in the cafeteria overcrowding situation. The parents are interested in being involved but it is unclear what their present role is relative to the decision making process. (Maggie may want to consider engaging them beyond a traditional bake-sale function by clearly defining her own values and her intentions about involving them in other ways, including having them in the school during regular hours.) Indeed, the flagship status may even be working against the people in this school at the moment. The need to seem to be excelling can create performativity pressures (Ball, 2000) that have been known to encourage contrivance and even the misrepresentation of performance data. And while resources can seem like a boon, resource-lean systems have been positively correlated with better performance patterns (Musella and Leithwood, 1991). In his model of aesthetic leadership, Duke (1986) suggests that "leadership, in fact, helps bring meaning to the relationships between individuals and greater entities – communities, organizations, nations" (p. 13) and advocates that we measure leadership in terms of what meets the eye of the beholder – direction, engagement, fit and originality – as four properties that matter the most.

Establishing a clear direction needs to be front and centre in Maggie's entry plan. But first, active engagement in her own reflective emotional meaning making could help her avoid falling into the trap of lurching for control against her better judgment and even her own preferred leadership style. Maggie's instincts for managing her own emotions are sound, given her decision to have a walkabout to calm down, but she may need more than emotional control. Indeed, too much emotional control can create numbness and disconnection in a leader, making it harder to stay present to others (Beatty, 2005). If she has a support system of trusted peers in whom she can confide about what she is feeling and thinking, this would be ideal. If she doesn't have such a support system, she needs to create one. Even connecting regularly with one trusted mentor/colleague outside of her school would be a place to start. If her regional school board doesn't provide a mentoring scheme, this might be something that it should consider developing.

Maggie needs to emulate the collaborative processes she values and will need to quickly establish a different working model for communication, one that is likely more invitational and responsive than that of her predecessor. At the same time, she will need to be noticeably assertive. The way Maggie's entry plan asserts her role as principal with all others in her community will be defining. The word will get around quickly, based on her earliest dealings with its members. As she asserts what she stands for, she needs to demonstrate strategically that her commitment to these things is substantial, both in principle and in practice.

In her new school, there are clearly some issues that need attention – the safety factor in the overcrowded cafeteria first and foremost. There are also apparent issues associated with what seems to be a lack of mutual respect between adults and children. There is a tradition of passive followership by the curricular heads that needs to change. Signs of some underlying patterns of distrust suggest the need to work on developing a shared sense of mutual trustworthiness – in honest *communication*, commitment to the implicit *contract* through honouring obligations, and trust in *competency* (Reina and Reina, 1999) – to ensure that the values and best interests of the whole school community are served. These, and trust in respectful relationship, can form a new foundation for working together if the associated expectations are addressed explicitly and become normative in the culture.

After four years of launching this new flagship, it is a good time to take stock – re-examine the vision and mission of the school and each person's daily contributions to the whole school's sense of moment, its progress to date, its causes for celebration and opportunities for improvement. A full-day retreat, carefully structured to allow for small group discussions and collection and consideration of findings, with clear plans for follow-up in subsequent action plans, could provide the opportunity to do just that. When these new consultative and collaborative ways of operating through shared leadership have begun to take hold, the qualities in real relationship can begin to provide a secure base for addressing emerging issues and establishing new directions.

Maggie's openness in meeting with Tom is a sign that she prefers to *work with* rather than *hold her authority over* others. Maggie is likely quite aware that it is important to lead with teacher emotions in mind (Leithwood and Beatty, 2008). Her teachers' sense of safety, opportunity for growth and belief that they are respected, cared about and professionally supported (Beatty, 2007) will need to be protected and fostered so that the usefulness of individual and school-wide changes can emerge and be embraced in a culture of connectedness. This base of support can become the foundation from which teachers will be able to engage in peer learning, coaching and mentoring schemes, to examine their own practices and to grow professionally. From a position of security, as they become engaged in data-based dialogues – with each other and their curricular and administrative leaders – teachers will be able to weather the emotional challenges of venturing into this new territory. Some professional development in focusing on data and interpreting it together wouldn't go astray. Given Maggie's overt support and openness to her own learning, her staff will be able to work through the threats to their sense of self-efficacy as they acquire the new skills that can support them in addressing problems and developing solutions together.

Meanwhile, back at the office, in addition to getting access to existing records and sorting the overcrowding in the cafeteria (likely through a restructured timetable to allow for a split lunch), her relationships with John, her curricular heads and the office staff could provide a worthwhile direction for some of Maggie's earliest energies.

Importantly, there is always apprehension when a new leader takes the helm. This apprehension is not all bad. But it is palpable. There are ghosts of the outgoing regime that are permeating the perceptions of leaders and leadership itself. Old anxieties die hard. Maggie can sense John's discomfort and the English teacher has openly stated his. In combination with Maggie's own need to get things into shipshape and her rising desire to assert control, there are many obstacles to her achieving the non-anxious presence she really needs. Again, her own peer support system will help her strengthen her ability to reach out to others on staff to encourage them to join her in acknowledging their real fears and worries and envision better things to come.

By addressing together the school's progress to date and opportunities for improvement, Maggie and her staff can establish confidence in mutually respectful and openly communicative relationships. From this new relational dynamic, they can refocus their shared purposes and create opportunities for new learning. They will soon be ready to do some root cause analyses on the matters of the moment. As they address the root causes, they will be well advised to start building from their strengths. A SWOT (Strengths, Weaknesses, Opportunities and Threats) analysis is a good vehicle for this kind of thinking. Still, there will be a range of concerns that will see people moving through stages. Making explicit the expectation that people will feel emotionally intense about change, and giving people the opportunity to use emotional meaning making in collaborative reflection with colleagues, is smart leadership. One framework for looking at some fairly predictable stages with one's staff is the CBAM (Concerns Based Adoption Model). Another is an emotional epistemologies framework that helps people recognize emotional silence and its damaging properties, flag the emotional feeling rules that are and are not serving the organization well, and then move into transitional and ultimately resilient emotional relativity as they learn to let respectful, dignified acknowledgment of actual feelings enter their professional discourse (Beatty and Brew, 2004).

Finally, but not necessarily lastly, the matter of student voice needs to figure in this flagship school's strategies. Students need to discover the rewards of sharing in the responsibility for keeping their school tone respectful and responsive. This is most likely to occur if they are invited into the communication and decision making process. Students need to be consulted and informed, perhaps to begin with, using a simple online survey that they can take using their laptops. Student conduct, morale and academic engagement are closely linked. Often a tone, such as that reflected in the striptease incident and the general pattern of teacher-student interaction in the halls, is a reflection of less than meaningful student-teacher relationships in terms of respect and mutual trust. A survey to determine students' sense of connectedness with school – trust in leaders, trust in teachers, sense of belonging with peers, confidence in the school's learning opportunities, and their own expectations of success – can create a baseline and help to determine where some of the issues may lie (for example, Beatty and Brew, 2005). The shared consideration of results of such surveys can help to foster data-focused dialogues in staff meetings, in professional development, and most importantly in classrooms, where real culture change makes itself felt. By contributing to the data-gathering process and being involved in follow-up discussions of the need for change and plans of action, students can begin to take ownership of the results by contributing to the discovery as well as the implementation of solutions. This kind of engagement can help shift the culture from the status quo. However, discussions of survey results and action planning with students are important parts of the cycle for improvement that are regularly forgotten. Together, Maggie and her colleagues could make the decision to do things differently.

The professional ethics of the individual school personnel at all levels need to emanate from a solid base of shared values and relational connectedness. By demonstrating her commitment to teachers' organizational, personal and professional learning needs, Maggie can begin to foster an ethic of bold self-critique among collaborating educators. But this will not happen until people feel safe enough to admit that they still have something to learn. Maggie needs to demonstrate her own interest in learning and her own sense of entitlement to being a work in progress, rather than a fait accompli, if she expects others to embrace this ethic. This will put her stamp of originality on her own leadership, as Maggie's authentic self will be present to others. She will also save the depleting energy drain of pretending to be perfect. Declaring one's entitlement to being incomplete and needing to learn can be a daunting, counterintuitive endeavour for a leader, one that takes real courage, as it defies the glib managerialist pseudo-perfectionism of outmoded yet lingeringly popular leadership styles. Staying connected to one's inner meaning-making processes, including the emotional dimension, ensures connectedness to one's ethical self (Margolis, 1998). By modelling this with her staff, Maggie can ensure that not only is she a good fit for this school, but so is everyone else, as their actual points of progress are honoured and integrated into the spirit of learning together. Symbolic affirmations, threaded through humane and accountable relationships of respect, trust and genuine interest in real inquiry, can make human leadership a natural fit and everyone's business.

As Maggie no doubt knows, the relationships among teachers and other staff in the school are the most influential school-wide factor associated with all methods of leader influence (Musella and Leithwood, 1991). Furthermore, levels of trust among adults in schools are associated with student performance patterns (Bryk and Schneider, 2002). To get to the matters of student attitudes, conduct, morale and engagement will involve new conversations with teachers, parents and students. A position of genuine interest and inquiry will be required of Maggie if she is to avoid putting the whole school on the defensive and alienating everyone through their fear that she does not recognize, respect or value what they have already created together. These early days will be exciting and challenging, as Maggie and her colleagues define their new pathways for pursuing their potential together.

CASE COMMENTARY 3

Striptease on Day Three

Andy Hargreaves
Thomas More Brennan Chair in Education, Boston College, USA

Pauline Hargreaves
Assistant Head, The Learning Project Elementary School, Boston

The naked truth of leadership

This case raises central issues of care, respect and responsibility. Though lurid and licentious in representation, it is an all too common instance of an innovative school that has revealed in and exploited its marginal status within the system, flagrantly flouted professional and ethical standards while actively cultivating envy among peers, and not only failed to plan for the succession of a charismatic founder, but actively baulked those who would try to tarnish the special innovative identity that set it apart in its Golden Age. The mysteriously sudden departure of the incumbent principal, his/her refusal to cooperate with advanced entry planning, signs of passive and even petulant resistance from some inherited staff, as well as indicators of drift in academic standards and basic behaviour among students all point to a leadership and improvement challenge of significant proportions.

The striptease is the very visible tip of a large and dangerous iceberg. It's important to pay attention to it; clearly, yet briefly indicate that it is inappropriate and unacceptable, and then move on. Perseverating on it will provide a rallying point for dissenters and distract attention from the more serious, underlying issues.

The first thing to know is what not to do. The tempting extremes of leadership in taking over from a charismatic predecessor of an innovative institution are to accept and endorse the past on the one hand without challenging those aspects that are ineffective, harmful or limited; or to dismiss and deny the past on the other, treating everything to which teachers and students have committed many years of their life as having no relevance or value. The nature and challenge of leadership lies, as always, in understanding and mastering the ambiguity that stands between and beyond these positions.

First, in the wake of the previous principal's defiance and amid signs of at best tepid support from the vice-principal, Maggie must establish her presence and authority. She must walk the halls, enter classrooms, be confident in meetings and show she is interested in and unafraid of all. Without authority, there can be no effective action. Picking a winnable issue with unarguable implications for students and their wellbeing is an early priority. The cafeteria is the key issue here. It is a question of law and safety. An immediate solution must be decided in a single meeting to limit lunches to 300 with emergency accommodation for the rest – overflow space, second sittings etc. Implementation must be instant.

Second, a more lasting solution to the cafeteria crisis can be developed collaboratively with the vice principal, bolstering his leadership and partnership and what is already now seen as a high profile issue, and also with staff and students. Cafeteria provisions are high profile issues for students, and involving them will give legitimate avenues for student voice that might then incorporate their input on behavioural issues etc. A crisis can be turned into an opportunity to demonstrate and develop both care and respect.

Third, the principal should take a longer period to engage in inquiry regarding standards in English classes, for example. This should be in a spirit of shared professional inquiry leading to subsequent jointly developed action, not of administrative snooping.

Fourth, the school has lost its way and needs to reconnect with and redefine its founding and preceding vision. Staff development work reconnecting teachers to their core values and passions through bringing and talking about inspiring photographs or meaningful possessions can unlock these discussions. Addressing whether these values are still active, how they have come to be lost and how they can be revived and developed can all follow on from this. Parents and students, at some point, need to be engaged in this process too.

Fifth, relationships have to be rebuilt. Working with Tom to be very visible as a team around the school and relentlessly appreciative of all who work and learn there demonstrates this through the leader's own behaviour...the first task of leadership. Then rebuilding relationships among others through engaging staff meetings of high expectation and great enjoyment, a retreat after one semester to re-vision the school, a joint inquiry into standards and how to raise them even further, and a celebration of positive innovative successes that remain in line with the school's long-standing character can all drive the community forward.

And last – do not perpetrate the predecessor's error and follow one iconoclastic leader with another, but act early on distributing leadership widely and wisely so as to create the culture and conditions for one's own succession in years to come.

CASE COMMENTARY 4

Striptease on Day Three

Theresa Shanahan
Assistant Professor, Faculties of Education and Graduate Program in Education, York University

This is a case about leadership in a time of transition. When I read this case I was struck by the importance of a systematic entry plan to orient an incoming principal: orientation to the school, to the staff, to the students, parents and local community. Regardless of how experienced a person may be in administration, the need for informed transition cannot be over emphasized.

A successful transition in school leadership can be accomplished if the incoming principal is given an opportunity to meet and talk with the departing principal and the superintendent responsible for the transition, ideally in advance of her tenure at the new school. It would be helpful for the new principal to know from the superintendent why she was chosen and what the school board's expectations and long-term plans are for this community. A meeting with the departing principal allows a new principal to review staff and personnel issues, budget and banking procedures, school learning plans and unique school initiatives, to identify established relationships between the school and the community, identify facility and resource issues and understand the culture and traditions within the school community.

At an early stage in the principal's leadership (if possible before the school year has started) it is also helpful to meet with the administrative team and review the student-teacher handbook to gain familiarity with all policies and procedures at the school (in this case school assembly protocols were an issue) and identify gaps and alignment with school board and ministry policies. In this process the principal should avoid comparisons or judgments of previous leadership. Ultimately, a principal will be answerable for any shortcomings in the school's policies even if they were inherited from a previous administration. So she must be proactive and positive. It is also important at this stage to review the status of the school learning plan, staff schedules and emergency/crisis and safety procedures. At this administrative meeting, the assignments and duties of the administrative team (including the office manager and the vice-principal) may be established. The agenda for the first-day staff meeting and the agenda for the first department-heads meeting may also be created at this time under the principal's leadership. In this case, a standard agenda was created by the office manager without consultation with the principal or staff, which is inappropriate. These important first meetings are an opportunity for a new principal to establish rapport and to communicate her leadership style to her staff.

On her own, the new principal needs to review the curriculum, course offerings, grade allocations and class sizes to ensure they conform to the collective agreement and ministry mandates, and to ensure that they meet the needs of all the students. As well, teaching assignments must be reviewed for fairness and equity, and to ensure that teachers are properly qualified for the courses they have been assigned to teach. A new principal will also need to review and analyze student academic achievement data, identify at-risk students, arrange meetings with key staff, and determine if strategies or initiatives have been put in place to address the needs of the students.

With information gathered at this point, a new principal can arrange informally to meet, at different times, the school teaching staff, support staff, department heads, program and committee leaders, parent council, student council, and custodial, secretarial and cafeteria staff in a manner that is organized and suits her particular leadership style. Spending this time will allow her to understand how the school's constituents view the school. These meetings not only serve as her informal introduction to the school community but also give her an opportunity to establish relationships, gather information about roles and jobs, listen to issues and concerns, show her interest and support for her staff, establish lines of communication and, importantly, to clearly articulate for students and staff her expectations for conduct and the consequences for inappropriate behaviour. For example, in this case Maggie needs to communicate clearly that the students' behaviour at the assembly was inappropriate, and she needs to clearly articulate consequences. This goes to an educator's statutory duty to maintain order and discipline in the school. Maggie also needs to establish clearly that passing students who have not met the curriculum expectations is unethical and could constitute professional misconduct and will not be tolerated. Teachers should not adjust marks to accommodate the first graduating class in order to maintain the positive image of the school. (As an aside, Tom's revelation could be interpreted as "adverse reporting" on his colleagues, which could trigger reporting protocols involving teacher-union representation at the school. This unfortunate situation could lead to conflict among staff members, which would further undermine staff morale. It might have been avoided had Maggie had the opportunity to arrange timely meetings, as described above, as part of her entry plan.)

These early meetings and tasks inform a new principal about the school's history and characteristics (in this case a young "flagship" school). Priority issues that need to be addressed immediately in the school community may be identified and responses developed. A deficiency list regarding equipment and facilities may be created and systematically acted upon. For example, in this case we see: equipment is not functioning; students in the first graduating class may not receive their diplomas; a lunch room is over capacity, which is a safety and supervision issue; disrespectful student conduct; and low staff morale. All of these issues need to be prioritized (with student safety first) and addressed.

At this point, the new principal can turn her mind to her "formal" introduction to the school community. In this case, Maggie is introduced to the school by way of a school assembly led by the student athletic council. In such an unpredictable environment, much depends on the respectful relationship between the students, teachers and administration, which this case reveals was clearly lacking. Further, the objective of the assembly as an introduction of the new principal was obscured by the showcasing of the athletic teams. Maggie might have circumvented this by asking for the assembly to be delayed until later in the year when she had time to implement her entry plan. In the meantime, a letter of introduction to staff, parents and various community leaders, with follow-up meetings around general issues, could have averted the striptease welcome Maggie received at the school assembly.

Time spent at the early stages of transition is invaluable. Ultimately, these early tasks and meetings will inform a new principal's plan of action. Some issues that emerge will need to be addressed immediately. Others will take time, patience and concerted strategies. In general, a new principal need not rush to make grand or sweeping changes (except for priority issues such as safety, as evident in this case). She may wait until she has gained familiarity with the new school and had a chance to build relationships and trust – two essential ingredients to successful leadership.

CASE COMMENTARY 5

Case: Striptease on Day Three

Ulrika Bergmark
PhD Student, Department of Education, Luleå University
of Technology, Sweden

When I read the dilemma Striptease on Day Three, I imagined the school as a fancy-looking car randomly driving around with no driver in it. This fancy car is just a couple of years old and has all the new technology you can imagine, however riding in this car is not very smooth. The exterior of the car projects a positive image; however, what does this image really mean if the real truth about the functioning of the car is hidden from the reality of many?

The school in this dilemma appears to have a bright and attractive facade on the outside, but it faces a lot of challenges inside. At this point, it feels like the students are in power and control many of the activities in the school. Where are the responsible adults? One question that arises is – do the students and the adults (principal, vice-principal, curriculum leaders and teachers) really talk to and meet with each other? Maybe the mock striptease is a symptom of underlying problems embedded in the culture of this school. Issues that come to mind for me include: power relations, genuine communication and responsibility for each other. What can be improved in order to create a positive community in this school?

As Maggie, the new principal, wanders around in the school, she sees insufficient knowledge in how to organize a school from an administrative point of view and she feels that the responses of staff are not that friendly and warm. This suggests that the leadership in the school can be strengthened in both administrative and relational aspects. How can the administration of the school be done in a more rigorous and organized way? How can principals and teachers create teams striving for shared goals? How can staff and students create together a collective feeling of being a community of "we" as opposed to divisive groups of "we" and "them?"

In a dilemma such as this, there is a risk that the thinking of the members of this school community is fixated on the problems, issues and strategies for improvement. This form of thinking leads to an excessive focus on problem solving. What would happen if we turned things around and considered the possible positive factors and growth possibilities in this dilemma instead? One of them is Maggie herself. She demonstrates ethical leadership qualities such as care, patience, respect, ethical awareness, a deep commitment to student learning and a desire to collaboratively create an equitable and fair learning community. The following quotations illuminate these dispositions:

She *greeted* the office staff *warmly*.

She does not want to put him on the spot right now. She knows how to *wait for the right time*.

Maggie *notes* that teachers move out of the way of students instead of students moving out the way of teachers.

The *inconsistency* of this behaviour *bothers her*.

Maggie's leadership style, values, awareness and commitments hold much hope for fostering positive interpersonal relationships and authentic dialogue among staff and students in this school. Another possible positive factor and growth possibility in the school can be seen in this reflective comment made by Maggie:

Teachers are actively *engaging* students.

The teachers' ability to engage students in their learning seems to be something that *works well* in this school. How can the school rebuild its community by *amplifying what really works*?

It is clear that Maggie's knowledge of teaching and learning and her belief in building on the school's central purpose of optimizing student learning as a catalyst for creating true community are leadership strengths.

A principal plays a central role in inspiring, arousing enthusiasm and modelling ethical action for school staff. The congruent and consistent actions of a principal can help to propel staff toward further ethical awareness and development. Creating an ethical school is the collective responsibility of members of a school community. Maggie, in this case, cannot enhance the ethical decisions and practices in this school alone. Principal, vice-principal, teachers and students have a shared responsibility for improving their school. All must participate in ensuring that practices, policies and decisions serve all students in the most fair and equitable manner.

If we contemplate the school as an expensive car, it is important that the outside aligns with all persons in this car engaged in the shared journey toward creating a school that is safe, ethical and learner centred. Maggie certainly has the leadership potential to steer this car on the road to becoming a more ethical school community

REFLECTION ON THE COMMENTARIES

The educational leadership strengths of this school principal are identified and discussed in the commentaries. Review these identified strengths and prioritize them using your own values and ethical principles as the lens for your decision making.

ADDITIONAL READING

Arriaza, G., & Krovetz. M. (2006). *Collaborative teacher leadership: How teachers can foster equitable schools*. Thousand Oaks, CA: Sage Publications.

> This book reveals how collaboration, the use of data, a focus on equity, and job-embedded professional development have been incorporated into real-world settings so that teachers can lead and manage change successfully.

Forster, K. (1998). *Promoting the ethical school: Professional ethics for school administrators*. Discussion paper presented at the symposium on The Ethics of the Teaching Profession, Sydney, Australia.

> The author presents a profile of an ethical school culture, discusses ethical awareness and staff responsibilities, and explores the difference between a prescriptive code of conduct and an aspirational code of ethics. She explains how to create an ethical community and addresses the importance of ethical training programs.

Hargreaves, A., & Fink, D. (2006). *Sustainable leadership*. San Francisco, CA: Jossey-Bass.

> The book sets out a framework of seven principles for sustaining leadership. Explanations concern the depth, length, breadth, justice, diversity, resourcefulness and conservation of leadership, along with action principles for achieving sustainability in practice.

Leithwood, K., & Beatty, B. (2008). *Leading with teacher emotions in mind*. Thousand Oaks, CA: Corwin Press.

> The authors examine teachers' emotional well-being in five key areas. They suggest that mental wellness has an effect on teachers' daily practice and that educational leaders are responsible for school environments that enhance teachers' well-being.

CASE 5

A School Divided

I should have tried to learn more about the school before I walked in as the new vice-principal. Perhaps some prior knowledge about the school staff would have better prepared me to deal with the situation.

The school currently has 24 teaching staff. There was a large turnover in teachers in June. Most of the remaining staff members have been at the school for 10 years or more. This experienced group is a complacent lot. Their motto seems to be, "This is the way it has always been done around here." They are set in their ways and confident in their skills.

The new teachers who joined the staff in September seem open to my frequent suggestions for school activities and initiatives. They volunteer for committees or coaching duties. They enjoy interacting with the students and their parents.

The parent community has not generally been supportive in the past. Some have even chosen to communicate their dissatisfaction to the local newspapers. Some parents seem to search for every opportunity to confront teachers. I am told that last year one group of parents even staked out the school parking lot to watch for teacher behaviour that they considered unacceptable. This situation was compounded by the fact that several community members, who were not qualified teachers, had been brought into the school as short-term supply teachers when certified teachers were not available. These teacher replacements shared information with other community members about teacher absences and confidential school matters.

Following these incidents, the experienced staff members made every effort to avoid interaction with parents and the community. This attitude was obvious at the open house barbeque in late September. The new staff mingled and ate hot dogs with the parents in the gymnasium. The experienced group barricaded themselves in the staff room.

I often notice that the new teachers chat with parents before and after school and make regular use of the office phone to maintain contact about student progress. They seem less intimidated, more friendly and receptive. These teachers also greet students with smiles and nods in the hall. The experienced teachers continue to avoid parents whenever possible and limit their interaction with students to the classroom setting.

The experienced group also avoids the school administrative team. A morning greeting is not part of their regular early-day routine. In October, I started to play a game. I gave these teachers a hearty morning greeting and observed how many responded in kind. My game scores were consistently low.

Even the staff-room lunch table is divided. The experienced teachers sit at one end and the rest of the staff at the other. I find myself consistently sitting at the end with the new staff. I refuse to occupy the transition zone in the middle of the table. My position at one end of the room affords me clear vision of the other. I see Mildred, one of the long-term teachers, rolling her eyes when the lunch conversation turns to the wedding plans of one of the new female teachers. She barely stifles a laugh at the inaudible but obviously derisive comments made by Monique, who is sitting next to her.

During the same lunch period, the new teachers begin discussing an upcoming student activity that will require staff involvement. Monique, who overhears, interjects loudly, "My contribution will be my absence." She guffaws scornfully. Her lack of professionalism stuns me.

The next day I decide to make the move to the transition zone at the lunch table. My goal is to participate in conversations at both ends of the table. An icy silence is my only response when I try to initiate conversation with the experienced group.

Later that day I ask myself, "Can I continue to live with this situation?" I'm not sure yet of my answer. The long-term teachers are at least basically competent in their teaching practice. I have seen Monique sparkle as she actively engages her class in discussions and activities. Mildred's testing scores are consistently the highest in the school.

The principal's plan for building community and raising school spirit is slowly beginning to happen. I have observed some progress since September.

The reality is that the teachers stationed in this school for 10 years or more expect to be here long after the current administrative team leaves. However, during my tenure as vice-principal, I am determined to ensure that the classes are places of learning. Maybe if we build on a common goal around student success, the teachers will work together more. Maybe we can establish at least a civil relationship with the community. Maybe, in time, the staff as a whole might develop a spirit of camaraderie.

One teacher in particular seems to be the centre of a sphere of influence. Norman has taught at the school for more than 10 years. He is a charismatic fellow when he wants to be. During his years at the school, he has occupied the same classroom and taught the same grade. His students are arranged in neat rows that all face the front of the classroom. He uses outdated textbooks that he insists are central to his program. Norman is always easy to locate at the front of the class, ensconced in a comfortable chair.

Norman has not engaged in any form of professional development since he was hired. He refuses to even consider activities or professional development opportunities offered through the school or district school board that require a time commitment outside of the regular school day.

Brian is Norman's long-time colleague across the hall. He, too, refuses to have anything to do with the development of a professional learning plan, personal growth or even new curriculum expectations. Last week, he openly complained about possibly having to participate in an early-release professional development session that involved staying until 4:00 p.m.

I ask myself, "Am I totally unrealistic in expecting a teacher to be open to activities designed to enhance professional learning and benefit our students? Am I naive to think that teachers should be willing to stay an extra 30 minutes after the normal 3:30 p.m. dismissal time and participate in a program to upgrade their professional knowledge and skills?" What should be my response when both Norman and Brian ask me, "Do we really have to attend?"

With a little nudging from both the principal and myself, Norman ends up joining the early release session. This was a first. In good weather, Norman is usually off to his golf game as soon as his contractual duties are fulfilled. His departure is timed almost down to the second. He leaves the school exactly 15 minutes after the dismissal bell rings.

In the spring, the entire staff is asked to contribute to a school performance that is part of our school education-week activities. Norman, as usual, asks, "Can we be forced to do this?" The night of the performance I'm not surprised at the lack of inspiration reflected in the part of the program prepared by Norman, Brian and their long-term colleagues. Their attitude is really beginning to grate on me. I feel discouraged. Nothing is changing.

Where do I go from here? Will Norman cruise along, continuing to undermine new initiatives? Will the attitude of one group continue to be a major influence in the school? Will more staff members be drawn into this web of negativity? What impact does this atmosphere have on our students and our relationship with the community? Can I make any difference in a school divided?

PROFESSIONAL INQUIRY

The Professional Inquiry section is intended to support reflection, dialogue and the development of new understanding and insights. Engagement in the following processes can occur individually or collaboratively with colleagues. These processes are designed to facilitate new or revised interpretations of the leadership experience described in the case A School Divided. This additional knowledge may guide the subsequent leadership actions, thinking and decisions of the reader.

Vision

1. Describe how the school leadership team's practices convey a vision for this school.

2. Critique the implications of this vision for the school.

3. Analyze the vice-principal's ability to translate the school's vision into agreed-upon objectives and operational plans in this learning community.

Leadership Practice

1. Analyze the leadership style of the vice-principal in this case.

2. Identify the beliefs that appear to guide the practices of this educational leader.

3. Why does she/he seem to encounter resistance?

Leadership Authenticity and Presence

1. Critique the authenticity of the vice-principal in this case.

2. Analyze the vice-principal's ability to be fully present to the faculty in this school.

Instructional Leadership

1. Explore how this school might benefit from explicit demonstrations of instructional leadership by the school vice-principal.

2. What strategies might be used to raise awareness of issues in this school?

Culture of Professionalism

1. Describe and critique how teacher professionalism is enacted in this case.

2. Explore how professional inquiry processes might enhance professionalism in this school community.

Collaborative Community of Inquiry

1. Assess the vice-principal's knowledge and application of different models of effective partnership.

2. Identify the actions you would take as an educational leader to foster a collaborative community of inquiry in this school.

CASE COMMENTARY CRITIQUE

1. Read the commentary(ies) written about the case.

2. Record your reflections regarding the commentary(ies) using the framework below:

   a. Identify the key points, perspectives or issues in the commentary.

   b. Analyze the key points, perspectives or issues identified in the commentary.

   c. List the new insights you gained from the commentary.

Commentary Critique			
Case Commentary Writer	**Identification** *What key points, perspectives or issues are identified in the commentary?*	**Analysis** *What is your analysis of the perspectives identified in the commentary?*	**Synthesis** *What new insights have you gained from the commentary?*

CASE COMMENTARIES

CASE COMMENTARY 1

Case: A School Divided

Joan Poliner Shapiro

Professor of Educational Administration, Department of Educational Leadership and Policy Studies, College of Education, Temple University

In A School Divided, the vice-principal faces an ethical dilemma that feels very authentic. The tension between the new and experienced faculty is palpable. In light of this problem, it might be useful to utilize two ethical frameworks – turbulence theory (Gross, 2006; Shapiro and Gross, 2008) and the multiple ethical paradigms (Shapiro and Stefkovich, 2001, 2005; Shapiro and Gross, 2008).

For example, using turbulence theory, which focuses on the pilots' scale of light, moderate, severe and extreme turbulence, the vice-principal would need to assess the current level of unrest in the school. As described, the problem does seem to border on severe turbulence, and there is a need to bring the level down so that rational decisions can be made. One way to do this is to meet with individual experienced staff members, rather than approaching them as a group, to find out why they are angry and to determine, with their advice, ways to change the culture. In this particular case, singling out Mildred and Monique might be appropriate as each of them is a competent teacher. If the vice-principal can show respect for these teachers by listening to their concerns, trust can begin to develop and there is a chance that some of the anger might dissipate within the experienced teachers'. group.

Turning to the multiple ethical paradigm of the ethics of justice, critique, care and the profession, here is a chance to begin to resolve the dilemma in a rational manner once the turbulence level is managed. For example, calling on the ethic of justice, the vice-principal could ask: Are there any laws, rules, procedures or contracts that would help her/him in regards to the need for faculty development? Are there any legal impediments that might prohibit the faculty from spending extra time in working together? If the vice-principal turns to the ethic of critique, further questions could be raised: Are the laws, rules, procedures or contracts appropriate in this case? Who made them? When were they made? Above all, should they be followed?

Moving to the ethic of care, ignoring the rules and procedures, the vice-principal might ask: Who will be helped by the two opposing groups working together? Who will be hurt? How can I make certain that professional activities build on teachers' expertise and do not make some of them feel disrespected, ignored or even silenced? And finally, turning to the ethic of the profession, the vice-principal should consider: First and foremost, what is in the best interests of the students? Then determine: What is in the best interests of all the teachers? What is in the best interests of the local community? And what approach resonates most with the personal and professional ethical beliefs of the vice-principal and the principal?

Working through these questions should help the vice-principal and the principal determine what would be the best ways to break down the barriers between the experienced and new teachers, enabling movement toward a shared culture.

CASE COMMENTARY 2

Case: A School Divided

Patrick Duignan
Emeritus Professor and President, Australian Council
for Educational Leaders

To paraphrase Abraham Lincoln (1859), a school divided against itself cannot stand. I find this case deeply concerning, even disturbing. The new vice-principal admits that she/he should have tried to learn more about the school before taking up the position, but even this admission may be missing the point because the vice-principal does not seem to appreciate that she/he is dealing with deep organizational, cultural and sub-cultural subtleties and tensions, including the different norms for professional behaviour and interaction across and between the groups. The facts as the vice-principal describes them seem to be symptoms of deeper issues.

Getting to know the people – as individuals and in their groups – is more important than merely attributing generalized characteristics to the groups. The vice-principal too easily attributes stereotypical characteristics to each of the groups of teachers – new, old or experienced. Generalizing about the experienced group as a "complacent lot" isn't helpful as a leader. Approaching the problem from an either/or, black-and-white perspective and blaming one group for the malaise is unlikely to resolve the issues, even though it would appear that there is considerable professional disengagement by the "experienced group."

As far as the vice-principal is concerned, simply occupying the transition zone in the middle of the staff-room table does not signify a well-thought-out leadership strategy. Better to hold personal and professional dialogue with key individuals to find out the root causes of their frustrations as well as seeking their suggestions for ways forward. Blaming one side or the other or singling out Monique and Norman as negative and bad influences is not on its own likely to lead to improved positive outcomes.

It appears that the principal lacks leadership presence and initiative and the reference to "the principal's plan for building community and raising school spirit" is vague. If, as suggested, this plan is "slowly beginning to happen," then there is genuine reason for concern at the rate of progress, given the very negative state of affairs at the end of the case. I believe that Starratt (2004) would score the principal's leadership low on the ethics of authenticity, responsibility and presence.

There is a serious lack of trust from parents and between the two groups of teachers. There is little evidence of a systematic approach by the leadership team to build a professional culture of learning with a definite moral purpose based on the need to maximize learning opportunities and outcomes for all students. There is also little evidence to indicate that learners and their learning are central to the school's moral purpose and culture. There is an urgent need to create such moral purpose and to create conditions within which all teachers are encouraged and supported to take much greater responsibility for the quality of their own teaching and learning in order to better engage with students and parents, and thereby raise everybody to higher levels of professional responsibility, motivation and morality. Open and responsible professional conversations, dialogue and engagement are urgently needed.

CASE COMMENTARY 3

Case: A School Divided

Lorraine Savoie-Zajc
Director, Département des sciences de l'éducation,
Université du Québec en Outaouais

Overall Response

Another title for the this case study could be Uneasy Intergenerational Relationships within a School. The case study clearly reveals an unresolved conflict between experienced teachers and parents, a situation which the young, newly hired teachers prefer to ignore. The new teachers don't want to fan the flames of old disputes; they have no desire to become involved in a matter that has nothing to do with them, hence the experienced teachers' resentment of the new teachers. But who can blame the new teachers for not wanting to get embroiled in an unfortunate history with the parents that can only undermine a desirable co-operation between home and school? In such a situation, what steps can a principal take to build community? The writer of the case study makes two experienced teachers' lack of interest in professional learning the focal point; this is how she/he describes Brian and Norman's challenging behaviour. Such disinterest is the writer's starting point for expressing her/his discouragement with the prevailing work environment.

Existing Strengths

It is important, however, to note the strengths on which the principal can rely in rebuilding a more harmonious working environment. Among the experienced teachers, these strengths include Monique's ability to engage her students and the excellent academic results of Mildred's students. These are indications of the two teachers' professional competence that should be highlighted, cited as examples, valued. The young teachers have strengths as well, especially their willing involvement in school activities. This also deserves to be encouraged and strengthened by the principal. The principal must send a clear message to the young teachers concerning her/his appreciation of this attitude and her/his wish for it to continue.

Taking on an Education Project

The writer's pondering about the importance of acquiring a common goal, which I would refer to as an education project consisting of a number of teaching and learning projects, is a key mode of action. I agree with the writer that in order to establish what she/he calls a civil relationship with the community and staff camaraderie, it is a good idea to encourage the emergence and implementation of unifying and meaningful teaching and learning projects targeting student success. Such objectives are the heart of a teacher's professional ethics, a galvanizing force few teachers can resist. Likewise for the parents who have differences with the school: They cannot remain unresponsive to the school's efforts to enhance student success. This is a step in the right direction. And teaching and learning projects targeting student success could be the way to make Norman and Brian realize the relevance of professional learning, if they subscribe to a common goal like this and are asked to plan their own teaching and learning projects which they find worthwhile and which stimulate their professional commitment and enthusiasm and encourage them to identify professional-development needs.

Research on change clearly indicates that it is individuals who decide whether or not to review their practices and make any necessary changes. However, external surroundings may be helpful and may offer support. The school's administrative team plays a key role! Its members must encourage teachers to reflect on their professional practice while performing the same exercise themselves; they must support individuals' efforts to adjust their teaching and learning strategies and must promote an atmosphere that welcomes open reflection and is designed to strengthen and stimulate rather than to punish.

The Emergence of Differentiated Leadership

A principal's leadership is not automatically conferred; it is built up with experience over time. Fullan (1997) and Sergiovanni (1992, 1995) refer to the concept of moral leadership: The important thing for principals grappling with complex problems confronting their schools is to sort them in order of priority so that the action they take is meaningful and the team does not become exhausted. Being a leader also means having the ability to develop approaches that are adapted to different people, because each individual possesses talents and strengths. By fostering each person's reflective practice and encouraging her/him to develop a teaching and learning project targeting student success, the principal will be able to identify each teacher's driving force: What motivates Norman, Brian, Monique, Mildred, the young teachers? What is the extent of their professional learning? The answers to these questions should help the principal develop approaches for offering support, taking action and providing intervention that is adapted to each individual, resulting in leadership that is not only moral but also differentiated in its concern to take the unique needs of each member of the team into consideration.

CASE COMMENTARY 4

Case: A School Divided

Ben Levin
Professor and Canada Research Chair, Department of Theory
and Policy Studies, Ontario Institute for Studies in Education,
University of Toronto

The first thing to say about this scenario is that it is quite common.
Many secondary schools have divided staffs or significant minorities of
teachers who are disengaged from the administration, if not from students
and teaching. In an organization of 60 to 100 professionals with a range
of disciplines, backgrounds and experiences, some significant divisions
among people are almost inevitable.

Following from this position, it is advisable not to panic or to assume
that these problems can be remedied or done away with in any short time
frame. It is equally important not to develop, as the writer of this case is
close to doing, a frame that places some of one's colleagues as the enemy,
because no progress can be made from such an oppositional point of view,
just as one cannot engage students if one regards them as the opposition.
People behave as they do for a reason. One has to understand the reason
to be able to move in a better direction. For many high school teachers,
alienation results not from sheer orneriness but from perceived poor treatment by previous administrators or from feelings of ineffectiveness in the
classroom.

I have four suggestions to make for managing in this situation.

First, it is the responsibility of school administrators and leaders to
find ways to re-engage individual staff members. There are many possibilities for doing so, ranging from different assignments to in-depth conversation, but all of them involve a real effort to understand the sources of
frustration and to find ways of moving people in new directions. Another
positive side of this approach is that re-engaged teachers are happier in
their work as well as more productive; nobody really wants to count the
years until retirement if they can see a better option.

Second, students and parents can be key to a teacher's approach to
her/his work. In this school, it seems that at least some parents are also
oppositional in their approach (we are not told about students). Teachers
overwhelmingly want to do well by and for their students; actuating this
impulse through students and helping people discover new ways to be

effective in their teaching is potentially a valuable strategy, especially if, as in this case, some of the disaffected staff members are in fact still quite competent or better classroom teachers.

Third, start by working with those who are potentially easiest to move in a positive direction as a way of reducing the influence of the most problematic staff. This can be done, in addition to earlier suggestions, by the way staff meetings are organized or department work is structured, or through school learning communities. If the overall number of disengaged teachers decreases, those who remain will be less important and perhaps less inclined to carry on in the same way.

Finally, it may be necessary to move a small number of people to other schools. As long as such action is seen as building a stronger staff team, not as punishing dissent, it will generally be accepted – even applauded – by most staff. Even a small number of changes in key people can make a big difference, but other avenues mentioned should be attempted before people are moved.

REFLECTION ON THE COMMENTARIES

The commentators make several suggestions regarding leadership and ethical practice. Identify the recommendations that resonate strongly with your own leadership philosophy. Consider how these recommendations reflect your own espoused and lived values about educators, leadership, community and shared vision.

ADDITIONAL READING

Camburn, E. M., Spillane, J. P., & Sebastian, J. (2006). *Measuring principal practice: Results from two promising measurement strategies.* Paper presented at the annual meeting of the American Education Research Association, San Francisco, CA.

The central topic in this study is the need for more precise measurement of the day-to-day practice of school principals. The authors present data from two separate models, EDL (End of Day Log) and ESM (Experience Sampling Method) to estimate a principal's engagement in a core set of six leadership functions: building operations, finances, student affairs, personnel issues, instructional leadership, and professional growth.

Fullan, M. (2005). Professional learning communities writ large. In R. Dufour, R. DuFour, & R. Eaker (Eds.), *On common ground* (pp. 209–223). Bloomington, IN: National Education Service.

This brief article focuses on building school learning communities. The author describes a tri-level model based on his education research. He describes each of the three levels in detail: the school/community level, the LEA or district level, and the state or national policy level. He presents implications for his model approach and concludes with a description for widespread, longitudinal success.

McCay, L., Flora, J., Hamilton, A., & Riley, J. F. (2001). Reforming schools through teacher leadership: A program for classroom teachers as agents of change. *Educational Horizons, 79*(3), 135–142.

This article reviews a teacher leadership program that focuses on current and future leadership roles in the classroom. The authors provide a thorough overview of the program that includes curriculum as well as assessment and evaluation analysis. They provide a theoretical framework regarding school leadership, give three differing perspectives on school transformation, and discuss the opportunity for student feedback.

Retelle, E. (2007). *The preparation and promotion of vice-principals to the principalship.* Paper presented at the annual meeting of the Canadian Society for the Study of Education, Saskatoon, SK.

The author investigates the leadership development and promotion of elementary vice-principals in two school districts in western Canada. She looks at how vice-principals prepare themselves for their roles as principles and explores the micropolitics of interview procedures and promotion.

Wilmore, E., & Thomas, C. (2001). The new century: Is it too late for transformational leadership? *Educational Horizons, 79*(3), 115–123.

This article reviews educational leadership trends. In particular, the authors describe transformational leadership, including the skills, knowledge and attributes that define a transformational leader. They conclude by discussing the multiple roles and responsibilities of a successful principal leader.

CASE 6

Growing Pains

"I don't buy it. Nothing you can say will convince me. We are overwhelmed. We need to slow down." Larry looks around at the other teachers at the meeting. Heads nod.

The staff meeting grinds to a halt. As principal, I realize that there are really only two options. I can intervene in the heated discussion or keep silent. I quickly process the pros and cons of each option.

Larry is a well-respected staff member with over 30 years of experience at our secondary school. He always has the best interests of our 800 students as his priority. He is also a school basketball coach who inspires tremendous loyalty in his team players. Larry usually gives any new idea a chance, but he needs to be sure that there is validity in the change. I have worked with Larry for almost 13 years and have found it very helpful to listen carefully to his input. Today, however, I am surprised by his tone and his comments.

I look over at Jessica. She catches my eye and nods her head slightly. "Larry," she says, "I understand your concerns. My hope is that the literacy strategies that we have been working on during the last two staff meetings will help to improve student performance."

Larry remains silent. The stony expression on his face reveals that he is not convinced by Jessica's calm and reassuring words.

Jessica is an aspiring principal. She needs to learn to face challenges like the ones in today's staff meeting. As she brings the staff meeting to a close on this blustery day, I reflect on how much she has grown. Almost 12 years ago I taught Jessica Grade 11 English in this very school. But in many ways, she hasn't changed. Her cheerful and positive nature still shines through. She has a bright smile, confident manner, insight and intelligence. She is a very active staff member who loves teaching science and English. She also coaches our track-and-field team and sits on the staff social committee.

Prior to the summer break last June, Jessica dropped by the office to tell me that she had decided to pursue her dream of becoming a principal. I was pleased, and proud of her decision to enrol in the required course for her leadership development.

In July, Jessica asked me if there was a school project that she could work on for the required practicum component of her leadership course. I immediately replied, "This is such great timing, Jessica. I've been grappling with how to promote more staff involvement in our school growth plan. Do you remember in May when our planning team identified the need for more professional development?"

"Yes, I remember. The staff planning team targeted literacy and thinking skills as hot topics. Our team suggested that we introduce professional development activities to promote these skills as part of our monthly staff meetings."

"That's right. That's why I'm so pleased about your request to do your practicum with our staff. I've been trying to move the staff forward. Here is your opportunity to take a leadership role in the actual implementation of the professional development activities."

I knew that I had not been very successful in getting staff to take the initiative on our professional development plans. I rationalized that staff members were very busy with their courses, their extracurricular activities and their personal lives. However, if teachers were aware that other staff members were actively involved in promoting professional development as a part of our school growth plan, more might be willing to take on leadership roles. "Jessica, I can't tell you how happy I am about your offer," I said.

Jessica smiled. "I'm willing to help out wherever you see the need."

Now, Jessica has just finished the third of her professional development sessions with the staff. I remember Larry's comments as I gather up my papers and prepare to leave the school for the day.

Jessica stops me in the hall. "Do have a few minutes, Michelle?"

"Sure," I answer. "Let's go back to my office."

As we walk together, I tell Jessica I feel that the meeting went well for the most part. For her practicum project, Jessica has taken on the responsibility of modelling strategies for promoting cross-curricular thinking and literacy skills. The professional development part of today's meeting focused on related teaching strategies.

During the first staff meeting, she surveyed the staff members to determine what strategies they felt should be included in the in-service sessions. Then she designed an interactive format to encourage professional dialogue and the sharing of successful teaching strategies. Jessica put a lot of thought into making these sessions meaningful. I felt that her efforts were well received by staff, and Jessica told me that she had received encouraging feedback from her colleagues.

This is why Larry's statement in today's meeting confused me. I make a mental note to talk with him in the morning.

Jessica begins hesitantly. "Michelle, first of all I want to thank you for your belief in me. I'm so pleased that you trusted me to take on such an important role in our staff's professional development. I have learned so much. For the most part, I believe that the staff has found the sessions meaningful."

"Jessica, you handled the challenge from Larry very well."

"Thanks, Michelle. But Larry hasn't been my only challenge. I wanted to let you know that two other staff members approached me today before the meeting. They felt that they should not have to put in time just so that I can satisfy the requirements of the leadership course and eventually become a principal." I see the embarrassment and disappointment in her eyes.

I'm stunned. I thought I had clearly communicated that the in-service at the staff meetings was part of the plan put in place by the staff's professional development committee. Jessica's practicum is just a way of achieving the goal that the staff has agreed on.

"Jessica," I begin, "Obviously I have not effectively explained your role to the staff." I want her to know that she has my support. Perhaps I can alleviate any misunderstandings that the staff members are harbouring.

"I don't know, Michelle. I think you were clear in your introductory comments. There's something more going on, but I don't know what it is. Lately, I've noticed a change in the way some staff are treating me. I really can't put my finger on it but I can feel it."

"Okay Jessica. Let me talk to a few staff members to see what I can find out. Let me also reassure you that you have done an excellent job of leading the staff meetings. However, I do want to inquire into these staff concerns before we continue with your practicum. Hold off on doing any further planning for the next few days."

As I drive home, I wonder what is going on. Why are some teachers reacting so negatively? How can I continue my support for Jessica? We seemed to be following the professional development plan so well. What happened?

PROFESSIONAL INQUIRY

The Professional Inquiry section is intended to support reflection, dialogue and the development of new understanding and insights. Engagement in the following processes can occur individually or collaboratively with colleagues. These processes are designed to facilitate new or revised interpretations of the leadership experience described in the case Growing Pains. This additional knowledge may guide the subsequent leadership actions, thinking and decisions of the reader.

Instructional Leadership

1. Explore the experienced teacher's perspective regarding the staff being "overwhelmed" and his suggestion that the school "slow down" with curriculum-change initiatives.

2. Discuss effective methods for promoting a sense of shared ownership and commitment toward school-level curriculum change.

3. Analyze the principal's knowledge and understanding regarding the impact of change on individual teacher practice and the school organization.

Collaborative Community of Inquiry

1. Critique the barriers to professional learning in this school community.

2. Explore the school principal's assumptions regarding professional learning.

3. Analyze the principal's role as a facilitator of a collaborative community of inquiry.

4. Develop a plan for building and sustaining a collaborative community of inquiry in this school context. What must be considered and why?

5. Why has Jessica not been supported in her attempts to foster community within the school?

Leadership Capacity

1. Identify issues that educational leaders need to be cognizant of and responsive toward when fostering leadership capacity.

2. Discuss the principal's ability to empower and sustain individuals and teams in this scenario.

3. Critique the principal's capacity to be fully present to the teachers in this school.

Democratic Practices

1. Explore the differences and implications between institutionally driven professional learning and practitioner-driven professional learning.

2. Identify what democratic and authentic professional learning might look like in a school community.

3. Explore the ways in which the experiences and perspectives of teachers can be heard and respected within institutionally driven initiatives.

4. Identify and discuss the practices that would be in the best interests of learners and the teachers in this case.

Reflective Practice

1. Reflect on the leadership issues and dilemmas in this case. Identify the insights you gained regarding leaders as facilitators of community.

2. Role play the faculty meeting outlined in this case. Assign each participant a character from the case. Invite participants to re-enact the case based on the perspective of each character involved in the situation.

CASE COMMENTARY CRITIQUE

1. Read the commentary(ies) written about the case.

2. Record your reflections on the commentary(ies) using the framework below:

   a. Identify the key points, perspectives or issues in the commentary.

   b. Analyze the key points, perspectives or issues identified in the commentary.

   c. List the new insights you gained from the commentary.

Commentary Critique			
Case Commentary Writer	**Identification** *What key points, perspectives or issues are identified in the commentary?*	**Analysis** *What is your analysis of the perspectives identified in the commentary?*	**Synthesis** *What new insights have you gained from the commentary?*

CASE COMMENTARIES

CASE COMMENTARY 1

Case: Growing Pains

John M. Novak
Professor of Education, Department of Graduate Studies,
Brock University

The best-laid plans of mice and principals can sometimes go awry. Those darn ornery humans have a tendency to mess up the perfectly logical plan set up by the wise and benevolent leader in charge. At first glance, this is what seems to have occurred in the case of Growing Pains. What's wrong with the picture?

We have an established principal (Michelle), who thinks she has orchestrated a win-win situation whereby she can meet some school instructional objectives and provide an opportunity for an aspiring principal (Jessica) to obtain credentializing requirements. The joys of masterminding such a confluence of events are the subtle peak experiences that make administration worth doing. So how could the veteran teacher (Larry) rain on this administrative parade?

Oscar Wilde noted that those who go below the surface do so at their own peril. It could be added that in handling ethical leadership concerns, those who stay on the surface do so at the demise of educational experiences. Since peril can often be the source of growth, going below the surface would seem the way to begin to examine these growing pains. But how do you go below the surface to get at what might be the underlying factors contributing to the tensions in this situation?

If, as John Dewey said (Fesmire, 2003), imagination is the chief instrument of the good, then we need to focus our imaginative attention on why someone as solid and conscientious as Larry might have interrupted the meeting in such a hostile manner. After all, on the surface, all the principal was doing was intentionally inviting Michelle's professional growth and meeting the school's growth plan.

After all, however, this was not all that was occurring. Other things might also be happening. For example, the principal noted that Jessica had been her student nearly a dozen years before. Might the faculty have felt that some sense of favouritism was being bestowed on Jessica? Are there gender overtones to this perception? In addition, the principal noted that Jessica talked about her "dream of becoming a principal." Might some of the faculty have felt a sense of resentment with Jessica about wanting to leave the classroom for administrative glory?

Teachers, especially experienced teachers, can be suspicious of those who seek to be in positions of power over them. Is Jessica aware of this? Also, the principal seemed delighted in having constructed an efficient arrangement that fit her requirement for staff development and aided a faculty member's professional requirements. Might some of the faculty have felt they were being done-to as opposed to being done-with in this process? Might the faculty feel that they were not treated as valuable, able and responsible participants in their shared professional growth? Finally, can being intentionally inviting to one faculty member be perceived as unintentionally disinviting to others? How can a principal be perceived as fair in distributing professional and personal invitations?

This is just the beginning of the restorative learning process. Ultimately, the principal needs to provide a setting so that a constructive conversation can occur about what has happened and what should happen next. Done well, such a conversation will provide a principled and caring way to proceed. Done well, everyone involved will have participated and grown through the initial pain. Such ethical leadership is a self-correcting process that is not easy, but it is worth the effort.

CASE COMMENTARY 2

Case: Growing Pains

Ann Lieberman
Professor, Teachers College, Columbia University

This is a very familiar situation that clearly describes the way many teachers internalize their school culture. We are all teachers, even though some of us teach different subjects or grades, and even though some of us have been teaching for 30 years and others are in their second year. Teachers internalize a sense that their school is an egalitarian culture and that no matter who we are, nor how experienced, we are all somewhat the same. So when someone attempts to be something different or do something else in their school, that person is often suspect.

In the last decade or so, small schools have created a new definition of schools that focuses on a more collaborative culture. From the beginning, teachers take on different roles and everyone accepts leadership from a number of people. Also, the current discussion (and sometimes reality) about "distributive leadership," that is, literally, different people taking on different responsibilities, changes the egalitarian ethic and introduces a different way of thinking about who leads and for what purposes.

Linda Friedrich and I just completed a study of 31 teacher leaders in the National Writing Project in the US. (Teachers go to a summer institute for five weeks during the summer. During the institute, teachers teach each other their best teaching strategies and they all participate in writing groups where they produce some piece of work. In addition, they read research together, share books and listen to their colleagues who are already "teacher consultants." Teacher consultants or TCs are teachers who take on responsibilities for professional development in their own or other districts after they have taken the summer institute.) Our study sheds a bit more light on this very topic. We had teachers write vignettes – six- to 10-page short cases – of a set of events that showed their experiences in learning to lead. Two of these vignettes were very much like the preceding case. One vignette was titled *Kicked Out of the Club* which, in journal-like fashion, told the story of a much-admired English teacher who became a department chair in a fractious department. Through her tireless work she changed the department, helping to make it co-operative, productive and smooth running. Because of this, her principal then asked Yarda to become the vice-principal. She decided to go for it. But soon Yarda watched teachers stop talking to her, ignore her, and even tell her that she wasn't a teacher anymore. How could she understand their plight? When she went home and told her husband, he said "Honey, you have been kicked out of the club!" She was a first year VP when she wrote this vignette.

Also in my group was another woman who had been a teacher who became a VP in her own school in the Bronx, NY. She had experienced this role for five years, so she served as an interesting contrast to Yarda. Ronni's vignette describes her approach to the vice-principalship honed over the years. She can now describe her life with great clarity and is more comfortable in the role. As she says:

> It seems I always have three voices in my head as I plan the weekly English meeting. One is the voice of the assistant principal, one [is the voice of a] teacher, and the other is my Writing Project voice. The three have sometimes worked together as collaborators. But it is the struggle, the tension, the questions the voices raise independently, the conversations they have among each other that excite me, stress me, and move the work forward ... My experiences with the Writing Project have taught me about working alongside

teachers, facilitating, mentoring, celebrating, learning from mistakes, questioning, raising issues, sharing practice ... treating teachers as professionals. It is the culture of the Writing Project that I bring to my weekly English team meetings.

These two vignettes illustrate well the negative impact of the egalitarian culture. In Yarda, we see it in full flower. In Ronni, we see a teacher who has learned from her experience that she must work through the natural tensions of her beliefs and values and the new knowledge that comes with her new role. Because she has a strong set of values and experiences about how she is going to lead, she embraces the struggle and *learns* that this is going to be a part of the role. (Needless to say, Ronni and Yarda made friends and immediately shared their stories, their learning and their support for each other).

About 10 of the teacher leaders lead in their own schools and this too can add to the discussion. They all described the risks involved in leading in their own school.

As one said:

It is one thing to give advice to teachers you don't know. But it is far different to teach someone in your own school who you will see the next day and the day after.

Despite this challenge, all of them talked about the way they had learned to make changes in their school and figured out how to deal with the uncertainties and risks that came with leading in their own school. There were examples of *linking change to a widespread challenge in the school.* One teacher who knew that teachers were having a hard time admitting that they didn't know how to teach writing was asked by her superintendent to teach them what she knew. With the help of the principal, she called a meeting where everyone was to bring a piece of student work. All were coded and together they built rubrics about writing. She didn't allow teachers to compare and make it personal, but rather insisted that they build rubrics together. Others *created collaborative forums to learn together and make their practice more public.* Still others, learning from the writing project, *celebrated good work* by creating anthologies of student work from all grades. Eventually, peers began to ask for help, but it took time and patience. Lastly, we learned that teachers seemed to be more accepting of their peers when they had *ancillary roles* such as mentor, literacy coach, teacher on special assignment ... These roles were seen as somehow more legitimate for a teacher leader as they appeared less formal and somehow not part of the "administration."

I think we are learning from research and experience that outside networks give teachers opportunities to learn to lead, which helps them when they return to their own schools. And we are learning that when teachers work together, making their teaching public, they are more likely to accept the leadership of their own peers. But we also know that changing from isolated cultures where roles are tightly drawn to more collaborative cultures where people are more open to peer leadership takes time, effort and patience.

CASE COMMENTARY 3

Case: Growing Pains

Jeanne Doucet
Professor, Faculty of Education, University of Ottawa

The Growing Pains case touches on a number of important issues related to the various roles that a school principal must play. This case prompts me to ask several questions about principal-staff relations, inter-staff relations, mentoring and the place of practice teaching, communication strategies, the dynamics of attitudes, and learning communities.

I feel that the principal was right not to react immediately. The first thing was to identify the real problem. However, this question should have been asked when she realized that she, too, was having difficulty winning the teachers over to the school's growth plan and securing their commitment to it. The first question in such a situation is: "What is the culture of this school, that is, what attitudes, values and beliefs orient the teachers' behaviours and could therefore influence their commitment to the growth plan?" When we have a good understanding of a group's culture, we can better comprehend its environment, values, needs and concerns and thus choose better intervention strategies to effect in-depth changes. A more precise question is therefore: "What attitudes, beliefs and behaviours stand in the way of the staff's commitment to the professional learning community meetings and the growth plan?" According to Fullan (2002), the effectiveness of an organization is directly linked to the degree of commitment of those within it and to the ideas and intrinsic motivation held by the vast majority of that organization's members; school principals must therefore ask themselves such questions, find answers and establish a plan to change attitudes, beliefs and behaviours.

The group/school dynamic would also seem to be an issue. The way in which Jessica's role is perceived appears problematic. Did this assignment produce negative reactions? Explaining Jessica's role again and showing that she has the principal's support will not automatically resolve the problem. Indeed, the issue seems to run deeper than that because some teachers treat Jessica differently. Why do they do this? Did the principal and teachers have the same perception of Jessica or were things done in a way that was consistent with the staff's development as a group? Is this where the problem lies or does it lie with Jessica herself? How did Jessica handle the portfolio? Did she let other staff members have their say? Was she too directive in her approach? Did she show professional respect for the other staff? Did she let each have her/his say in the project or did the situation become even more difficult simply because the teachers were not involved? Did they truly perceive this practicum by another teacher as something negative? The principal could have sounded things out even before giving this assignment to Jessica as part of her practicum. Could it be that another teacher felt she had ownership of this portfolio and that the problem arose because it had been given to Jessica?

If the principal was not able to win the support of her staff, why did she give the portfolio to a teacher who was fulfilling her practicum requirement without becoming personally involved to at least some extent? Dialogue is needed to develop ethical leadership in a school and to support people to use their leadership skills. Leadership seems to have been in short supply before this incident. Was it realistic to give the responsibility to someone else without providing some mentoring? Could the problem have been more easily identified and resolved, with no further action required, if people had worked together? This type of collaboration would have constituted a valuable mentoring experience, motivating both individuals to progress as leaders. Mentoring, with follow-up, would have enabled each person to bring her/his perspective to the situation – and to find more effective solutions. Such an experience would have been enriching for everyone.

According to Fullan (2002), every individual in a leadership position finds that interpersonal relationships are an extremely important component of any culture of change. Has the problem surfaced because the teachers are overstretched or feel powerless to cope with the anticipated changes? If so, how could the principal have supported the teachers in their career development? How can the teachers be shown that the requirements to meet the new expectations and implement the school's growth plan are known and understood? Working with Jessica, they could have found support mechanisms for the staff. The principal could have set aside a few occasional teaching days for Jessica to assist the teachers, or she could have allowed Jessica to organize multi-class activities so the teachers could have some extra work time. During the mentoring period, the principal and Jessica could have discussed the various activities or resources needed to support the teachers, thereby facilitating the new approaches to the growth plan. Once the teachers become involved, it is extremely important to highlight the efforts of the team/school. Sincere expressions of appreciation for their work result in greater teacher involvement.

Mentoring, with follow-up, would have enabled Jessica to learn a great deal about the importance of interpersonal relationships; it would have helped her to accurately define the problem and understand the group culture; and mentoring would have shown her how important it is to provide meaningful resources and express appreciation. I need to ask myself how I, as a leader, can become involved in activities that will nourish and sustain my teaching community so that the members of this community can play a role in their own professional progress.

CASE COMMENTARY 4

Case: Growing Pains

Ellie Drago-Severson
Associate Professor of Educational Leadership, Columbia University Teachers College

Growth *is* difficult – and worthwhile. This timely, powerful case illuminates critical issues that crop up when leading to build capacity, share leadership, support adult growth, and create learning communities in 21st-century schools. I will focus on two intertwined dilemmas that the principal, Michelle, named as she reflected on the situation that had evolved in her high school: why had some teachers reacted so negatively, and how could she continue to support Jessica?

These quandaries, from my perspective, are inherent in the *process* of cultivating a learning community. In this process, open, direct and honest communication is the norm and spaces for dialogue are given priority. Below, I share one way in which Michelle could address her concerns. It is designed to support and challenge the teachers as well as Jessica by opening up a space for dialogue. It will also strengthen the learning community by surfacing underlying or unspoken concerns.

As discussed in the case, Michelle and Jessica have taken important steps toward building a learning community. And yet, as Jessica noted privately to Michelle, "Something else is going on" among the faculty. And as Michelle thought to herself during the faculty meeting, "I can intervene in the heated discussion or keep silent." What might be the result if the community explored – openly – what was happening and why?

As a first step, what might happen if Jessica, rather than Michelle, met privately with the two faculty members who had voiced their dissatisfaction? She could ask them to discuss their concerns before opening the discussion to the larger community. This conversation would create an opportunity to promote honest communication and build trust.

Second, what might happen if Michelle were then to open the next faculty meeting in the following manner?

> I know we all care about working together to build a true learning community. For us to have this, we need to be able to communicate openly and honestly. We need to cultivate a new soil for this.
>
> I've given a lot of thought to what happened during our last faculty meeting and I think it would be helpful to us as a community and to our shared mission if we created a space where we can talk openly about how we are feeling. Before doing that, though, I want to share why I invited Jessica to assume this leadership role. And I think it might be helpful for Jessica to share why she wanted to assume this role and how she is feeling about her work.

After Michelle and Jessica shared their hopes and feelings about the work and invited others to respond, Michelle might say something like this:

> Before engaging in an open, honest learning conversation about what is happening, which I hope will bring us together, I want to acknowledge Larry's concerns – he and his colleagues are "overwhelmed" and feel the "need to slow down" – voiced in response to Jessica's proposal. Larry, I know you expressed these concerns because you care deeply about your work and your colleagues. I know that you've all been working hard, and I also realize that we all have extraordinary demands placed on us. And I know we share the hope of making our school even better.

Michelle could then invite faculty to journal privately in response to questions such as the following: How do you feel about the professional development initiatives? What do you think is going well? What could be improved? What kinds of support would help you to implement our new plan? What role, if any, would you like to assume in this initiative? After writing privately, faculty could gather in groups of three or four and discuss what they had written, and afterward each group could share their responses with the large group and together all could decide on next steps.

While these kinds of conversations will certainly be risky or challenging for some – especially initially – they are essential steps toward building learning communities. Modelling open communication and prioritizing the need for spaces where adults come together in genuine dialogue to share their thoughts and feelings can build trust. Yes, it takes courage and time. Yes, there will be "growing pains" associated with it. And yes, it can help us grow.

REFLECTION ON THE COMMENTARIES

The commentaries suggest that significant issues beneath the surface of this case need to be understood and addressed. As facilitators of community, educational leaders need to consider school culture, teacher autonomy, professional knowledge, experience, and the implicit messages regarding teacher professionalism that can be conveyed by the leader's actions and decisions. Identify the perspectives and approaches that you would employ as an educational leader to the visible and invisible issues apparent in this case.

ADDITIONAL READING

Adalbjarnardottir, S., & Runarsdottir, E. M. (2006). A leader's experiences of intercultural education in an elementary school: Changes and challenges. *Theory into Practice, 45*(2), 177–186.

The article explores a principal's pedagogical vision, his motivation for his work and how he relates it to incidents in his life history. He also explains how he promotes students' intercultural competence within the context of an elementary school.

Armstrong, D. (2004). Constructing moral pathways in the transition from teaching to administration. *Values and Ethics in Educational Administration, 3*(1), 1–8.

Armstrong looks at the challenges, tensions and dilemmas of eight new administrators in their journey of constructing ethical pathways as they move from teaching to administration. He describes the iterative cognitive, emotional and social development encountered by recently appointed vice-principals.

Bezzina, C. (2006). The road less traveled: Professional communities in secondary schools. *Theory into Practice, 45*(2), 159–167.

The article considers the benefits of professional learning communities while acknowledging the personal, psychological and professional difficulties faced by principals and teachers in their attempts to establish such communities in their schools. Issues include self-management, leadership, collegial relationships, the development of collective capacity, and a focus on teaching and learning.

Browne-Ferrigno, T., & Muth, R. (2004). Leadership mentoring in clinical practice: Role socialization, professional development, and capacity building. *Educational Administration Quarterly, 40*(4), 468–494.

The studies discussed in this article were conducted at the University of Colorado at Denver. They include an exploratory study with aspiring principals in training and a cross-cohort investigation that compares the field experiences of students in preparation for principalship. The authors give their perspectives on best approaches to the development of future principals.

Noddings, N. (2002). *Educating moral people: A caring alternative to character education.* New York, NY: Teachers College Press.

This book explores the ethic of care and provides practical implications for care theory in education and daily life. The differences between character education and care ethics are outlined.

Pearce, C. L., & Conger, J. A. (2003). *Shared leadership: Reframing the hows and whys of leadership.* Thousand Oaks, CA: Sage Publications.

The authors present a view of leadership that is communal and shared. This leadership model distributes leadership among members of an organization. A team concept is discussed where leadership is determined not by positions of authority but rather by an individual's capacity to influence peers and by the needs of the team.

Shoho, A. R., & Barnett, B. G. (2006). *The challenges of new principals: Implications for preparation, induction, and professional support.* Paper presented at the annual meeting of the American Education Research Association, San Francisco, CA.

The authors investigate the efficacy of a professional induction program for beginning principals by determining their initial preparation experiences and their continuing professional development needs. Interviews were conducted with 62 new elementary and secondary principals. The findings suggest that leadership preparation programs need improvement in the areas of course content and instructional strategies.

SECTION III

Leaders as Reflective Practitioners

LEADERS AS REFLECTIVE PRACTITIONERS

Educational leaders who engage in reflective practice support their own professional learning and significantly contribute to the ongoing enhancement of professional practice within the school community. Leaders who are reflective practitioners serve as role models for other educators. Modelling the importance and impact of professional inquiry within a learning community is a leadership responsibility. Professional inquiry enables educators to explore practice through reflection, exploration and critique. Leaders are more effective in fostering professional learning communities when they authentically engage in processes associated with reflective practice. Reflecting on and inquiring into the ethical dimensions inherent in professional practice can enhance visionary leadership, strategic leadership, authentic leadership, instructional leadership, organizational leadership, educative leadership and community leadership. Many of the issues related to school leadership benefit from and can be further informed by reflection. School leaders who model reflective practice listen to others, inquire into their own practices, and engage in authentic dialogue as a means to improve practice.

CASES FROM PROFESSIONAL PRACTICE

The three cases in this section of the book illustrate the ethical tensions, challenges and dilemmas that are often associated with school staffing assignments, instruction, curriculum change, staff relationships and working with parents. These dimensions of professional practice can have a profound impact on the culture of a school and subsequently require strong leadership. The school leaders in the three cases in this section engage in varying degrees of reflective practice. The impact of engaging in meta-cognitive processes to reflect on one's practice, thinking and values is illuminated by two of the school principals in the cases. Another case depicts a school principal who does not appear to question her/his own thinking and actions. As a result, this principal's concern with rising test scores seems to be a factor influencing her/his thinking, decisions and actions. Reflecting on the assumptions, beliefs and values that guide professional practices can help leaders to see possible inequities, injustices and omissions in their judgments.

> ### *Cases*
>
> *A Staffing Hotspot*
> *Life Changes*
> *The Principal in the Middle*

CASE COMMENTARIES

The commentaries that accompany the three cases in this section are written by educational scholars in the fields of initial teacher education, self-study, ethics, leadership, case methodology and narrative. The commentary writers highlight issues of empathy, communication, equity, transparent decision making, individual rights, legal and contractual obligations, jurisdiction of staff advisory committees, organizational dysfunction, curriculum implementation, consultative management, power, pitfalls of participative management and the best interests of students.

Commentaries

A Staffing Hotspot
John Loughran
Margaret Olson
Paul Axelrod
Jean Plante

Life Changes
Alice Collins
Pat Rogers and Lara Doan
Katherine Merseth

The Principal in the Middle
A.G. Rud
Julie Mueller
Denise E. Armstrong

137

CASE 7

A Staffing Hotspot

Britannia Drive Secondary School is a large, well-established school in the suburbs of an urban centre. Many of its highly skilled teachers have been teaching at this school for their entire careers. Their vision and values have shaped and maintained the school's culture for more than 20 years.

I've enjoyed my years as a teacher and now as one of the vice-principals at Britannia Drive. Lately, however, there has seemed to be more unrest among staff members than ever before.

The principal, Joan Turgeon, must consider many variables in order to effectively run this large secondary school of 1,800 students. She must ensure that qualified and competent teachers deliver the curriculum. She must also encourage staff members to engage in professional growth opportunities. She tries to be sensitive to teacher interests and workload.

Historically, the school administrative team has always worked on staffing issues with a teacher advisory committee. The teachers on this committee expect Joan and the rest of the administrative team to consult with them regarding staffing assignments. Based on preliminary input from the teachers, Joan drafted a school timetable to be reviewed by the advisory staffing committee. There are many changes in the timetable this year as a result of the new secondary school curriculum. Several of these changes will mean new teaching assignments for staff members.

Change can be more difficult for some teachers than others. Jim, one of my teaching colleagues, is already concerned about the possibility that his assignment might be different next year. Jim cherishes the old curriculum. He has found that his lesson plans are based on tried and true methods that really work for him. His colleagues, however, have commented that what is really behind Jim's resistance to change is that whatever is less work appeals to him most.

Jim appears unconcerned that, for the last three years his colleagues have assumed the work of designing and implementing new courses and updating evaluation strategies while he himself has clung to the old curriculum. He doesn't seem to notice that several of the teachers aren't as friendly with him as they once were, and that fewer and fewer students are selecting his courses.

Recently, Jim took a stress-related medical leave. The administrative team was told that he was to return to work at the beginning of the second semester. His doctor indicated in writing that he should not teach in his former subject area, as doing so would pose a health risk for him.

Joan asks me to meet with Jim to gather more information about the conditions that appear to be associated with his return to work. We wonder what really lies at the root of his stress. Is it purely related to his former computer studies teaching assignment?

The next day, Jim arrives at the meeting accompanied by Bart, the school federation representative. The principal, Joan, and I are also present. Jim looks angry even before we start. Shortly, he exclaims, "You need to know that I am not able to teach any computer courses."

Joan calmly replies, "Jim, you realize that there are quite a large number of computer courses and that you are the most qualified teacher on this staff to teach them."

Jim responds, "I guess you'll just have to give those courses to Debbie. She is younger and has less seniority. If she wants to stay in this school, she'll just have to do it."

The principal and I are shocked at Jim's retort. I ask him, "How is it that you think you can personally tailor the staffing process and your teaching assignment?" Jim impatiently reminds us that he has just come back from a medical leave. He demands, "Can't you be more sensitive to my situation?" At this point Jim and Bart both leave the meeting.

The next day, Joan receives an e-mail from the local federation president questioning the staffing process at Britannia Drive Secondary School. "How could an administration be so indifferent and insensitive to the needs of a disabled teacher?" The federation's perspective appears to be that staff should understand and support Jim. The federation e-mail also indicates that this perspective has been shared with the district school board superintendent.

The principal is shocked. Joan feels that she has always been approachable and open to compromise. She feels that she has tried hard to work closely with all staff members and encouraged them to participate in team decision making and leadership building. She has always worked well with the teacher advisory committee on staffing issues. She asks, "Am I really insensitive and uncaring toward my staff?"

Joan asks me, "Isn't change a challenge at the best of times for most teachers? Isn't it a normal part of being a teacher? Why hasn't Jim been able to adapt to any changes over the last few years?" How could the superintendent know as well as the administrative team and advisory committee what might have initiated and motivated staffing decisions at Britannia?

Toward the end of the day, the office telephone rings. It is the superintendent and the district school board lawyer. Joan calls me into her office and puts on the speakerphone. The superintendent and lawyer recommend that Joan provide Jim with three teaching-assignment choices at Britannia Drive. He describes each of the three options.

The principal knows she is obliged to honour the collective agreement and recognize past practices within the school community. She also understands that the superintendent and lawyer are well informed about legal issues related to staffing matters. Joan indicates to the superintendent that she will bring his three suggestions forward to the staff advisory committee.

The committee members have a number of questions and concerns about the three options. Cecil begins with, "Why are we being asked to choose a timetable from three scenarios for Jim? Why is he being given undue consideration?"

Cathy reminds the entire staff that they all have to assume their share of responsibilities regarding the implementation of the new curriculum.

She moans, "Every curriculum area is struggling with new courses – without exception."

Cecil, even more agitated than Cathy, chimes in, "Why are we being asked to consider exceptions then? Isn't everyone on staff meant to share the workload related to the implementation of the new curriculum?"

Sarah questions, "Where did these scenarios come from?"

Trudy asks, "How would a superintendent know what is best for our situation?"

At the conclusion of the meeting, the advisory committee rejects all three scenarios.

By the end of the week, the decision is made by the district school board superintendent to "accommodate" Jim. The Britannia Drive Secondary School business-studies-department staff members are all called to a meeting with the superintendent, the federation president and the school administrative team. Jim also attends. His department colleagues are surprised at his participation since he seldom attends their meetings or engages in department dialogue around staffing.

The superintendent informs the group about the decision to assign Jim to teach the business ethics courses in the department. He asks the teachers, "What do you think of this decision?"

Elizabeth is very upset. "I have the curriculum expertise to teach the senior business ethics course." She looks directly at Jim. "You have not taught it. You haven't been interested in taking on new courses in the last few years. Why would you want to do this now?"

The group is confused and angry. Jim sits smugly, making no comment.

Mona turns to Jim directly and says, "You have the computer expertise. Why aren't you teaching in the area that you are qualified to teach?"

Jim does not respond. The superintendent makes a few closing comments and the meeting is over.

The principal and I realize that the real staffing issues are only just beginning.

PROFESSIONAL INQUIRY

The Professional Inquiry section is intended to support reflection, dialogue and the development of new understanding and insights. Engagement in the following processes can occur individually or collaboratively with colleagues. These processes are designed to facilitate new or revised interpretations of the leadership experience described in the case A Staffing Hotspot. This additional knowledge may guide the subsequent leadership actions, thinking and decisions of the reader.

Ethical Leadership

1. Explore the ethical dimensions associated with the principal's decision making processes.

2. Identify the values that appear to be guiding the decisions and responses of the principal, superintendent, teachers, Jim and the federation representative.

3. Consider how these values influence the ethical actions and stance of these educational partners.

4. Define the ethical responsibility of the educational leader in this case.

5. Analyze the ethical leadership capacity of the educational leader using the following inquiry process and framework.

Analyzing Ethical Leadership

Inquiry Process
- Identify from the case a response to an ethical dilemma by an educational leader.
- Analyze the response(s) from the perspectives of justice, care and critique (Starratt, 2004; Langlois, 2008).
- Map your own response to the identified ethical dilemma using the second section of the framework.
- Discuss your analysis with colleagues.

The Educational Leader in the Case

Response to an Ethical Dilemma	Ethic of Justice	Ethic of Care	Ethic of Critique
How did the educational leader respond to the ethical dilemma?	How did the educational leader's response reflect fairness, equity and respect for policy and the common good?	How did the educational leader's response reflect care and compassion toward others?	How were power, influence and transparency reflected in the response of the educational leader?

My Educational Leadership

Response to the Ethical Dilemma	Ethic of Justice	Ethic of Care	Ethic of Critique
What would my response or professional judgment be to this ethical dilemma?	How would my commitment to fairness, equity, policy and the common good be reflected in my decision making?	How would my commitment to care and compassion toward others be reflected in my decision making?	How would power, influence and transparency be reflected in my response and judgment?

Leadership in a Collaborative Community of Inquiry

1. Identify the messages that are conveyed in this case scenario about:

   a. the culture of this school

   b. teacher professionalism

   c. responsibility toward students

   d. responsibility among staff

   e. responsibility of an individual teacher.

2. Generate strategies that the administrative team might use to foster a culture of professionalism and inquiry in this school community.

3. Use the framework below to begin to develop your action plan for enhancing this school community's ability to act in the best interests of learners.

Fostering a Collaborative Community of Inquiry				
Action Plan				
School Mission and Vision *What do we collectively believe?* *What do we want our school to look like in three years?*	**Commitment to Students and Student Learning** *How will we collectively demonstrate our commitment to students and student learning?*	**Professional Knowledge and Practice** *What are our collective plans for fostering our professional knowledge and practice on an ongoing basis?*	**Teacher Professionalism** *How will we interact with our colleagues?* *How will we support shared leadership with students and teachers?*	**Relationships with Parents** *How will we interact with parents?*

CASE COMMENTARY CRITIQUE

1. Read the commentary(ies) written about the case.

2. Record your reflections regarding the commentary(ies) using the framework below:

   a. Identify the key points, perspectives or issues in the commentary.

   b. Analyze the key points, perspectives or issues identified in the commentary.

   c. List the new insights you gained from the commentary.

Commentary Critique			
Case Commentary Writer	Identification *What key points, perspectives or issues are identified in the commentary?*	Analysis *What is your analysis of the perspectives identified in the commentary?*	Synthesis *What new insights have you gained from the commentary?*

CASE COMMENTARIES

CASE COMMENTARY 1

Case: A Staffing Hotspot

John Loughran
Foundation Chair in Curriculum and Pedagogy, Faculty of Education, Monash University

A Staffing Hotspot is a very interesting and well-constructed case. It builds a sense of tension and frustration, dropping the reader into the situation in a most realistic way as it works toward the dilemma that the principal and vice-principal are left with as a result of the way in which the situation unfolds.

The way that the issue of change ebbs and flows in this case is interesting as it invites the reader to consider what change might mean and how it impacts teachers differently. In this case, the elements of change that might be challenging for Jim are not canvassed in particular detail, rather the reader is left to think about what some of the underlying issues and concerns might be. In so doing, the case encourages the reader to think about Jim's situation in light of one's own experiences, thus bringing to the surface many of the emotional issues that inevitably impact the way one responds to challenging or confronting situations.

The case makes clear how a failure to establish a genuine answer to the question at the heart of the issue leads to ongoing confusion, tension and frustration. For those who will have to deal with Jim's apparent inability to cope with his teaching allocation, the lack of reason or explanation for his recalcitrant attitude makes the sense of frustration all the more intense; "Why is he being given undue consideration?" As a consequence of this failure to establish the *real reason* underpinning the problem, the tension escalates.

Because the lack of explanation and reason for the situation is allowed to continue, resolution becomes all the more difficult and, increasingly, less likely. Adding to this is the lack of empathy. Jim expects understanding and acceptance of his position: "Can't you be more sensitive to my situation?" but at the same time appears to ignore the needs and concerns of his peers. Inevitably then, confrontation arises: "You have never been interested in taking on new courses ... Why would you want to do this now?" and the sense of frustration and lack of reason is compounded.

Despite the apparent fair and open approach of the principal toward Jim's inability to accept his teaching allocation, all those who are drawn into the situation or impacted by its consequences pay a cost. The group is confused and angry. Mona turns to Jim directly and says, "You have the computer expertise. Why aren't you teaching in the area that you are qualified to teach?" Jim does not respond. The need for a solution is palpable but when one is imposed by the superintendent, it is far from acceptable as the underlying cause for the difficulty is never made clear. Although Jim and the superintendent may have found some sense of resolution, it is perhaps only a temporary measure because "the real staffing issues are only just beginning."

As this case makes clear, when the reasons for actions are not open to discussion and critique, confusion, tension and frustration reign supreme. Sadly, in such situations, conflict arises and trust becomes the first victim.

CASE COMMENTARY 2

Case: A Staffing Hotspot

Margaret Olson
Associate Professor, BEd Program, St. Francis Xavier University

This case reminds me of Clandinin and Connelly's (1995) metaphorical "professional knowledge landscape," which they describe as "composed of a wide variety of components and influenced by a wide variety of people, places, and things," leading them to "see it as both an intellectual and a moral landscape" (p. 5). Clandinin and Connelly describe how teachers inhabit two essentially different epistemological places in this landscape: *out-of-classroom places* permeated by an abstract rhetoric of conclusions funnelled through the conduit into schools in the form of policies; and *in-classroom places* where teachers live their narrative understandings through stories of practice. Moral dilemmas emerge as teachers and administrators shift back and forth between these epistemologically different places.

The author of this case sets out three policy abstractions she believes Joan, as principal, is required to facilitate: (1) ensure that qualified and competent teachers deliver the curriculum, (2) encourage staff members to engage in professional growth opportunities, and (3) be sensitive to teacher interests and workload. While this appears to be a straightforward list of administrative responsibilities, when seen through the professional-knowledge-landscape metaphor, the narrative entailments of several competing and conflicting plot lines soon become apparent. I outline a few below.

Joan needs to ensure that qualified and competent teachers deliver the curriculum and to provide professional growth opportunities for them. Teachers in the school appear to value this, having created a collective story focused on continual improvement through designing new courses and updating evaluation strategies. This story of professional competence through professional development permeates the out-of-classroom landscape. Jim's in-classroom story of competent teaching through using tried and true methods that really work conflict with this dominant out-of-classroom story of other teachers in the school. As principal, Joan needs to be sensitive to the implications of these competing stories of professional competence in in-classroom and out-of-classroom places within the school.

The need for Joan to change the timetable and teaching assignments due to new curriculum being funnelled down the conduit onto the school landscape threatens teachers' professional pride in their in-classroom competence. Joan would need to facilitate a delicate balance between individual teachers' in-classroom competence, workload, and interests with what is funnelled into the school as a new version of what students need to know.

Added to the complexity of these dilemmas – tensions surrounding perceptions of good teaching emanating from within the school and tensions surrounding the imposition of external curriculum mandates that challenge all the teachers' perceptions of good teaching – are external personnel mandates concerning Jim's teaching assignment funnelled into the school by his doctor, then the teachers' federation, and finally the school board superintendent. While the recommendations for Jim's teaching assignment might appear to those positioned outside the school to affect only Jim and his in-classroom place, it is vividly apparent from the moral indignation expressed by other teachers that any decision about Jim's teaching assignment, especially in light of tensions created by the imposed curriculum changes, is perceived as inextricably intertwined with all teachers' interests, workload, and teaching competence as well as what the advisory committee perceives to be its role in having input into yearly teaching assignments.

As principal, Joan's decisions involve a delicate balance between competing and conflicting stories from in-classroom, out-of-classroom, in-school and out-of-school places on the landscape. Many more competing stories and ethical dilemmas could be teased out using the professional knowledge landscape metaphor. As the author of this case points out, "The real staffing issues are only just beginning."

CASE COMMENTARY 3

Case: A Staffing Hotspot

Paul Axelrod
Professor, Faculty of Education, York University

Two important questions arise from this scenario: what led to the current confrontation within the school, and how can a positive and effective working environment be restored?

In most organizations, including schools, there are individual employees who may be very competent in their jobs but who make enormous demands on management and on their fellow workers. Such individuals may be quite self-serving and uncompromising, and resistant to collaboration and collegial working relations. But as long as they remain on the job, their rights must be respected – particularly in a unionized work setting.

In consultation with the superintendent and school board legal advisers, Joan Turgeon, the principal, should carefully review the circumstances that precipitated both the conflict and the outcome through which Jim is perceived to have secured a preferred teaching assignment. In the original proposal to change Jim's classes, were all administrative rules and protocols followed? Did the principal ensure that Jim's legal rights were protected? Were the terms of the collective agreement ignored or violated? Did the school originally fail to meet its obligations to provide accommodation for a teacher returning from medical leave? Answers to these questions should be thoroughly pursued so that the principal can avoid similar situations in the future.

The use of a "teacher advisory committee" to draw up a draft school timetable is double-edged. On the one hand, it speaks well of the principal's attempts to foster collaboration and consultation within the school. When the process works, it gives staff a degree of ownership with respect to important school policies. On the other hand, in the absence of a co-operative spirit, or in the face of recalcitrant individuals, the system can founder. It would appear, too, notwithstanding its "advisory" mandate, that the staff committee acted as if it had *actual* decision making power with respect to teaching assignments. This is problematic. Teaching assignments should remain the prerogative, in practice as well as theory, of the principal who, in turn, is required to meet all legal and contractual obligations. Personal agendas and conflicts of interest could easily erupt in situations where teachers strongly influence, let alone effectively determine, the working arrangements of fellow teachers. If the principal intends to maintain the teacher advisory committee, then she must set new ground rules which ensure that her authority to make class assignments is understood and upheld.

The principal should encourage continuing dialogue about curriculum direction in the school, but in ways that avoid public discussion of personal situations and individual teaching assignments. These should be treated as personnel matters outside of the committee's jurisdiction. Principal Turgeon will have a lot to do, and this will include managing and, ideally, containing Jim's demands. She should meet with him as required and encourage him to be more of a team player. If, historically, she has been as respectful of teachers as the scenario implies, and if she has a fuller and clearer understanding of administrative protocols, then she and the staff should be able to put the current episode behind them. Time, patience and clarity are her allies.

CASE COMMENTARY 4

Case: A Staffing Hotspot

Jean Plante
Director, Department of Educational Fundamentals and Practices, Faculty of Education, Laval University

A problem that develops into a crisis is indicative of profound organizational dysfunction. Is the situation with Jim the real problem facing Britannia Drive Secondary School? Why is Jim experiencing stress? Why is this situation surfacing now? In this circumstance, the superintendent and the principal are clearly in disagreement; is this a latent situation that has reached crisis proportions? These are some of the questions prompted by a reading of this staffing-related case study.

The implementation of a new curriculum means major change within an education system; the new way of doing things creates upheaval for all of the actors within both boards and schools. A school, of course, is a professional bureaucracy with unique characteristics. It is a Weberian bureaucracy, that is, roles and duties are standardized and organizational life runs according to impersonal rules and standards. Furthermore, legality is often intensified (the superintendent is accompanied by the lawyer). Lastly, school systems are part of the machinery of government and are highly centralized politically. For instance, collective agreements are negotiated by the central authority (the province). But the school is also a professional organization in that the teachers and other professionals within it enjoy a certain freedom of action on the basis of their competencies, which are recognized by the central authority, in some cases through a professional body. The act of teaching, like all professional acts, is decentralized.

This being the case, how is the education system regulated? Each state establishes legislation and policies that regulate its education system as a whole, defining spheres of competence, authority structures and funding sources. In this particular case, funding sources are not at issue, but questions may be asked concerning the spheres of competence attributed to the principal of Britannia Drive Secondary School; similarly, the legitimacy of the teacher advisory committee on staffing does not appear to be accepted by the superintendent and some of the teachers, such as Jim. Britannia Drive Secondary School apparently operates according to the principles of consultative management, but the superintendent involves the board's legal counsel in her communications with the principal of the school, and Jim attends the meeting accompanied by the union representative. Is this not a serious conflict in which power relationships hold sway and attempt to redefine interpersonal and organizational relations?

In my opinion, in fact, this is not merely about a curriculum change but a renegotiation of the fields of jurisdiction of the superintendent, the principal, the advisory committee on staffing and even the teachers' interpersonal relations. For instance, the statement is made that Jim is governed by the least-effort principle, but also that he is a good computer studies teacher. Likewise, the principal and her vice-principal are shocked by the superintendent's response, yet within the school, the only apparent power relationship is the one consisting of the advisory committee allied with the principal against Jim.

This case also illustrates the pitfalls of participative management. The case study states that "The administrative team has always worked on the staffing issues with a teacher advisory committee." The rest of the paragraph sets out the rules under which the committee operates with the principal. Since not all the teachers serve on the committee, those who are not members of the committee cannot be expected to behave like so many sheep. Some, like Jim, rebel, but he is not the only one. Apparently, "Change can be more difficult for some teachers than others." Should the principal not have taken a different approach to staffing this year because the implementation of a new curriculum brought many changes with it? Didn't participative management require the principal to make sure that all the teachers could express their expectations?

Although everything appears to be functioning normally within this district school board, an analysis quickly reveals that it is having tremendous difficulty coping with the change. Was the change planned or was it simply assumed that it would take place without any need for actual effort? The example of Jim reveals firstly that he believes lesson plans should be based on tried and true methods, and secondly that he is prepared to teach business ethics. Yet his expertise apparently lies in computer studies. How can he agree to teach business ethics? How can the school and board administrations justify their proposal?

In short, staffing disputes at Britannia Drive Secondary School are not the problem; they are the expression of a much greater, board-wide maladjustment. The superintendent uses legal leadership to put forward a proposal for conflict resolution in one of her schools; the principal and her vice-principal believe that the school's organizational structure has not changed even though the curriculum, a key factor in the education system, has been changed; the teachers on the advisory committee do not feel the need to rely on their colleagues when implementing a new curriculum. In my opinion, Britannia Drive Secondary School is experiencing inter-personal and organizational conflicts that will most likely result in a restructuring of the power and leadership of all members of the district school board.

REFLECTION ON THE COMMENTARIES

The commentaries illuminate the issues and implications associated with educational change. Olson's statement that the new curriculum "threatens teachers' professional pride in their classroom competence" invites reflection on the ways in which educational change can disempower, disenfranchise and contribute to the disillusionment of teachers.

ADDITIONAL READING

Blouin, P. (2006). A profile of elementary and secondary school principals in Canada: First results from the 2004–2005 survey of principals. *Education Matters: Insights on Education, Learning and Training in Canada, 3*(2).

The author provides an analysis of the characteristics of school principals in Canada based on a survey of principals conducted by Statistics Canada during the 2004–05 school year. The survey asked principals about their perception of problems that occur in schools, actual and ideal levels of responsibility, job satisfaction, and aspects of school climate that obstruct the proper functioning of their schools.

Kouzes, J. M., & Posner, B. Z. (2001). *Leadership practices inventory (LPI): The facilitator's guide* (2nd ed.). San Francisco, CA: Jossey-Bass.

This facilitator's guide is part of a package that provides a variety of ways to enhance leadership abilities and roles. The authors identify five essential leadership skills: challenging the process, inspiring a shared vision, enabling others to act, modelling the way, and encouraging the heart.

Starratt, R. J. (2004). *Ethical leadership*. San Francisco, CA: Jossey-Bass.

The author argues that educational leadership requires a moral commitment to high-quality learning for all students. That commitment is based on three key principles: proactive responsibility; authenticity, both personal and professional; and a supporting presence for educators and educational environments.

Strike, K. A., & Soltis, J. F. (2004). *The ethics of teaching* (4th ed.). New York, NY: Teachers College Press.

This book offers authentic cases of the day-to-day ethical dilemmas faced by educators. It covers topics such as: punishment and due process, intellectual freedom, equal treatment of students, multiculturalism, religious differences, democracy, teacher burnout, professional conduct, parental rights, child abuse and neglect, and sexual harassment.

Zubay, B., & Soltis, J. F. (2005). *Creating the ethical school: A book of case studies*. New York, NY: Teachers College Press.

The authors address some of the ethical issues that arise daily in an educator's professional practice. They present case studies and ethical standards for educators at all levels in a school environment. The book is a resource for educators and a guide for pre-service candidates who want to create caring and supportive learning communities.

CASE 8

Life Changes

I thought that I had a perfect opportunity to make a significant impact on the success of our primary division. The solution, I believed, was to just move this one staff member to a situation where I was certain she would be better suited. Then all would be well with the world! The students would learn. Test scores would rise. The parents would be happy.

Some teachers establish their identity and their sense of self-worth through their classroom assignment. Susan was an energetic, enthusiastic, boisterous teacher with a heart of gold. She took great pride in delivering an enhanced arts program to the Grade 2 students. All year, they prepared for special recitals, plays and community presentations using dance, visual art and music.

Susan was highly committed to this enhanced arts program. She even appeared for a scheduled evening practice session with her students and their parents on a day that she had been absent due to illness. Susan enlisted parents and other volunteers to assist with preparing stage props, makeup, scenery, costumes and recital-room decorations. She worked hard to ensure that every event was a polished performance with all the extras.

Susan, however, missed at least 18 to 20 days of school every year due to her recurring illness. Parents were becoming increasingly concerned about the number of days that occasional teachers were assigned to her classroom. They were also becoming worried that Susan's emphasis on the arts program was having an adverse effect on the implementation of her mathematics and language curriculum expectations.

I began to wonder about moving Susan to another teaching assignment. During her performance appraisal, I took the opportunity to discuss her health and the impact that her recurring absences might be having on her students. Susan recognized that her frequent absences made it difficult for the students to develop consistent classroom routines. She looked like she felt guilty.

Susan voluntarily enrolled in a wellness program called Migraine Prevention and Management offered by the district school board. During the remainder of the school year, she tried to engage in professional dialogue, goal setting and collaborative planning with her Grade 2 colleagues.

Later during the year, I took the opportunity to explore with Susan a move to a teaching assignment in the junior division. I carefully suggested that she consider teaching music on a rotary basis for the junior classes. At the time, she seemed very open to my suggestion for a professional change sometime in the future.

For organizational reasons, however, Susan's relocation to a new teaching assignment did not materialize in September. Susan was still teaching Grade 2. She seemed unhappy and was just barely meeting her professional responsibilities. She made no sustained efforts to add rigour to her daily lessons. She didn't make any significant steps toward delivering a program that was more strategically consistent with the primary division initiatives.

My anxiety grew. I realized that our testing scores would probably remain low for the second year in a row. As well, Susan's headaches were occurring more frequently. She attributed this to the challenges of managing the new expectations for her classroom curriculum.

Susan complained, "I don't know why, but more and more students are misbehaving. They're not working independently. They're falling on the floor. They're talking when they should be working. They just are not paying attention to my lessons."

Parents began to complain about Susan's lack of patience. Jenny's mom described a scenario in which Susan had actually yelled and berated the whole class. In May, many parents requested that their children not be placed in Susan's class the following September. Something had to change.

I optimistically approached Susan. "I have a wonderful opportunity for you. This assignment draws on all of your teaching strengths."

I asked her to take on a new role. "I'd like you to begin September with a half-time Grade 5 and a half-time rotary music schedule for the classes in the primary division."

Susan's cheeks turned red. Her eyes widened. Her body stiffened. "Don't make me make this change. I don't want to do it. Other teachers have less experience in the primary area. They should be the ones to change!"

I knew immediately that there was a contract grievance in the making. I felt that Susan would complain that I had ignored her seniority in the division and moved her to the new assignment as a public declaration that her performance was inadequate in the Grade 2 placement.

When I discussed the issue with my superintendent, she indicated that I was fully within my mandate to make this staffing decision. She also suggested that a round-table discussion might help address some of Susan's concerns about the change. I scheduled the meeting for a few days later. Susan left that meeting still very unhappy.

Soon, the staffing plan for the next year became public knowledge among staff members. Susan grew belligerent and distant. She avoided making eye contact with me. During the day, other than to complete her assigned duties at recess, she refused to leave her classroom.

Tension among staff members grew. Another teacher, Jaclyn, expressed an interest in taking on Susan's Grade 2 classroom in September. Some staff members told me that the decision to move Susan was a good one for the division. Gossip around the issue continued. I reminded everyone about ethics and that it was inappropriate to discuss a colleague.

Now, only a few days remained before the end of June. I wanted to resolve the feelings around Susan's new assignment. I asked Susan to meet me after school in my office.

"Please sit down Susan," I began. "Would you mind sharing with me exactly how you are feeling and explain why you have so much concern over this particular assignment?" She paused and then sighed. She seemed to be collecting her thoughts. Then she quietly began her list of reasons.

"First, I have to tell you how absolutely miserable I've been for the last year. My marriage is on the rocks and I am very worried about the debt that we've accumulated. I know that the stresses in my life have been compromising my health." She looked up. The anger had vanished. She seemed grateful to finally explain the reason behind her behaviour. "I know that everyone in the school thinks I've been abusing my sick leave because I have more absences than anyone else. You know that there have been years when I was respected and appreciated for doing a great job in my primary class. You know that I love the little ones." She paused, trying to keep her composure.

"I beg you to please put me back in the primary class. I promise to do a better job next year. I know that a change may be good for me, but I can't leave with my self-esteem being so low. I want to finish on a good note." She was barely holding herself together now. The tears were spilling over her cheeks.

"I need to feel successful in my job. I want my colleagues to see that I am capable of succeeding in my old position and that it's my choice to move into a new situation. Then I could go forward with pride and confidence to try the new assignment another year. I just can't tolerate more stress and change in my life right now."

We sat silently for several moments. I began to compose my response.

PROFESSIONAL INQUIRY

The Professional Inquiry section is intended to support reflection, dialogue and the development of new understanding and insights. Engagement in the following processes can occur individually or collaboratively with colleagues. These processes are designed to facilitate new or revised interpretations of the leadership experience described in the case Life Changes. This additional knowledge may guide the subsequent leadership actions, thinking and decisions of the reader.

Vision and Influence

1. Explain the vision of education held by the principal of this school.

2. Identify actions that could be employed to support the development of a shared vision for this school.

3. Explore the references to "test scores" made by the principal and discuss how these comments reveal the principal's philosophy of education.

4. Critique the possible influence the principal may have on the staff's vision for the school, teacher autonomy and democratic teaching approaches, given her/his attitude as reflected in the following statements.

   Test scores would rise. The parents would be happy.

   My anxiety grew. I realized that our testing scores would probably remain low for the second year in a row.

Instructional Leadership

1. Discuss the principal's professional knowledge and practices as an instructional leader.

2. Explore the possible impact of the principal's reference to "test scores" for instruction and pedagogy in this school.

Culture of Professionalism

1. Identify the areas of professionalism that need to be addressed and enhanced in this case.

2. Describe the approaches you would employ, as an educational leader, to the issues of professionalism identified in this case.

Leadership Practice

1. Describe the leadership style of the principal.

2. Ascertain the values that might be guiding the professional actions and judgments of the principal in this case.

3. Critique the processes used by the principal to influence change in this school.

Decision Making

1. Identify the values that appear to guide the decision making of the principal.

2. Analyze the decision making processes used by the principal.

Professional Efficacy

1. Consider the impact of the situation on the professional identity of Susan. Describe the possible implications for her sense of self-efficacy as an educator.

2. Identify strategies that could be used to support the efficacy of Susan, the primary division teacher.

Reflective Practice

1. Reflect on the dilemmas in this case and write a commentary in response to the issues.

2. Think about and identify the possible assumptions, beliefs and values that seem to be guiding the thinking, actions and decisions of the principal.

3. Contemplate how a more reflective stance may have assisted the principal's professional practice.

CASE COMMENTARY CRITIQUE

1. Read the commentary(ies) written about the case.

2. Record your reflections regarding the commentary(ies) using the framework below:

   a. Identify the key points, perspectives or issues in the commentary.

   b. Analyze the key points, perspectives or issues identified in the commentary.

   c. List the new insights you gained from the commentary.

Commentary Critique			
Case Commentary Writer	Identification *What key points, perspectives or issues are identified in the commentary?*	Analysis *What is your analysis of the perspectives identified in the commentary?*	Synthesis *What new insights have you gained from the commentary?*

CASE COMMENTARIES

CASE COMMENTARY 1

Case: Life Changes

Alice Collins
Dean of Education, Memorial University of Newfoundland

The principal has done a stellar job. She has met with Susan, considered all options, reflected on the situation for other teachers and the students, has met with the superintendent, and had further conversations with Susan. This while doing the thousands and thousands of other things a principal does in the run of a day and a year. The principal is thoughtful, not reactive, not judgmental, and has shown care for Susan and others. Now she has to make a decision.

Susan has made clear what her preference is – to stay in the primary division. Does the principal order Susan to move to Grade 5 where she will be really unhappy (as though she were not unhappy enough)? Does she acquiesce to Susan's request and allow her to remain teaching Grade 2 despite languishing problems there and discontent from other teachers and parents about her return? Does she consider whether Susan should be teaching at all at this time?

Schooling is complex and the role of the principal is a test case for decision making that impinges on pedagogy, ethics, parental and community concerns, and teacher rights and responsibilities. Those interests, often differing and sometimes in conflict, converge around what is best for students, although lines blur as they do in this case. Teachers have hopes about the resolution of this case that may not be directly student centred, but we can easily infer that the impact of the decision on teachers can in turn impact the students. Parents have a right to be concerned about their children and to advocate in their best interests. The disconsolate teacher, Susan, somewhat isolated in this situation, must also be considered and cared for by the principal.

I have great confidence in this principal's ability to make a good decision given the thoughtfulness, concern and attention she has demonstrated already. However, there is no obvious right solution. The principal must take the information she has gathered and use her knowledge and experience to go forward. Not everyone will agree. If she moves Susan to Grade 5, teachers in the junior division and parents will applaud her. Susan will be angry at her. Problems may start in Grade 5. If she allows Susan to remain in Grade 2, there will be discontented parents and teachers but Susan will be gratified, at least, for the moment. Other possible solutions will also result in mixed reception.

When the principal has finished considering all of the circumstances and choices, has communicated with those who need to be heard and those who can advise, she must then make what she considers the best possible decision in this context. She needs to reflect on why she made that decision and its possible ramifications, communicate to those who should be informed, implement the decision and move on to the hundreds of other complex issues on her desk today. I would invite people to consider this: While this is a very important issue, it did not occur in isolation. What else was happening in the school as the principal addressed this situation?

CASE COMMENTARY 2

Case: Life Changes

Pat Rogers
Dean, Faculty of Education, University of Windsor

Lara Doan
Assistant Professor, Faculty of Education, University of Windsor

Migraines. Discontent. Stress. Unhappiness. Tension. Gossip. Testing scores. Belligerence. Absenteeism. Dismay. Anxiety. Fear of failure. Life Changes tracks the reverberations of one teacher's challenges with acute everyday stressors on the ecological well-being of a school and instructively illustrates the delicate interdependencies and interactions of relationships alive in school ecologies. Though it is sometimes expected that teachers should have the capacity to somehow *invisibilize* (Maracle, 2007) their own experiences of the human condition from the work they do as teachers, Life Changes underscores relationships between the emotional well-being of teachers and the healthy functioning of school life.

To help us think through the dilemmas posed in Life Changes, we take a closer look at the set of three formal meetings between Susan and the school principal. It is instructive to observe how differently Susan responded in each of these meetings. In the first meeting, the approach taken by the principal was to propose a resolution, which in effect assumed advance knowledge of the root causes of Susan's unhappiness. Though the resolution – to change Susan's teaching assignment to the junior division – may at first glance appear to provide a way to address the parents' concerns and the principal's consternation about test scores, such a move may only serve to transfer the difficulties expressed presently in the classroom from the primary to the junior grades. In fact, the move from primary to junior grades may exacerbate some of the many stressors, and it is difficult to envision how the students or the school community would benefit from this particular change in teaching assignment.

The second meeting, which was set to address Susan's concerns about the proposed reassignment, served only to announce the principal's intentions for Susan's professional career trajectory, seemingly without providing space for Susan to express her own aspirations or voice her concerns and views about the challenges she was currently facing. The first two meetings in a sense constrained the possibilities of Susan and her principal relating in a more holistic way. For example, while it was a positive development that Susan opted to enrol in a wellness program to help lessen and prevent her migraines, one wonders what other options might have been proposed had the stressors contributing to her migraines been acknowledged?

It was in the third meeting, when the principal expressed an interest in hearing how Susan was feeling and in listening to her concerns, where we, the readers and the principal, were able to form a more fulsome understanding of Susan's challenges and gain access to her sense of emotional well-being and what would be helpful to her professional growth. The difference in listening position of the principal appears to have been critical to Susan being able to share more of her personal life and the factors that were contributing to her physical, mental and emotional distress during this particular year. Additionally, in this third meeting Susan was able to articulate her own sense of self, highlighting her capacities, her commitments as they relate to her teacherly identity and her achievements in the years preceding this trying year. With the principal listening and Susan telling her story, new understandings can be made and new alternatives explored. From this listening stance, the principal is better able to inquire and make suggestions for professional and personal supports responsive to Susan's needs. For example, the principal might have suggested a half-time Grade 2 and half-time rotary music schedule for the classes in the primary division. This alternative takes greater account of Susan's life circumstances (financial worries, pressing uncertainty) and her teaching strengths and commitments (to fine arts, to the primary division).

Additionally, the part-time quality of the proposed position would allow another teacher to be involved in the teaching of the youngsters, thereby addressing parents' understandable concerns about consistency and meeting curriculum expectations. Finally, and perhaps as importantly, the point being made here is that insights made possible through listening to *more* of Susan's story might have given rise to resolutions that offer Susan agency in participating as a co-creator of a workable solution.

What also fascinates in the circumstances presented in Life Changes (as described by the principal), are the questions about the role of the arts and how such questions intersect with dilemmas about the well-being of school life. In her explication of the role of the arts in everyday life, simultaneously Maxine Greene also offers guidance to the questions raised about the arts and the human dilemmas presented in Life Changes. Greene says:

> Encounters with [the arts] frequently do move us to want to restore some kind of order, to repair, and to heal. Participatory involvement with many forms of art does enable us, at the very least, to *see* more in our experience, to *hear* more on normally unheard frequencies, to become *conscious* of what daily routines, habits, and conventions have obscured (Greene, 1995, p. 375).

CASE COMMENTARY 3

Case: Life Changes

Katherine Merseth
Director of Teacher Education at the Harvard Graduate School of Education

Educational practitioners in general, and school heads in particular, often feel that their role is to resolve challenging situations where there is a gap between what is and what should be. Whether the issue is one of a disgruntled parent, a shortage of textbooks, student misbehavior in the lunchroom or as in this case, the questionable performance of a staff member, school heads and the cultures in which they operate place a high value on quick and relatively easy solutions. Because we live in a 'can do' culture, the pressure on a leader to address a perceived problem, especially one that is visible to many other individuals in the organization, is enormous. Sometimes this pressure to act, and to act quickly, results in taking insufficient time to analyze or frame issues before jumping to action.

However, the framing of a problem is critical to its successful solution. As Albert Einstein once said, "The formulation of a problem is often more essential than its solution." A poorly framed analysis of a situation invariably leads to an unsatisfactory solution and sometimes to an even greater complication or complexity.

In *Life Changes*, the school head faces a vexing situation because of the performance of a teacher named Susan. While the head's focus is on Susan, there are several other stakeholders involved in this situation. These stakeholders include the children in her classes, the children at the intermediate level of the school, the other teachers at Susan's grade level, the Superintendent and parents. And beyond individuals, the situation with Susan raises questions about the purpose of education. This situation can trigger several broader conversations and considerations about the place and value of arts education in an elementary school, the merits of interdisciplinary approaches utilizing the arts to explore academic subjects and the social and emotional needs of children.

The case can also be seen, not as a problem where a technical solution of either re-assigning staff or changing responsibilities, could solve it, but rather as a *dilemma*. The vast majority of conflicts faced in school situations are "dilemmas" which, according to Larry Cuban, a Professor at Stanford University, "are messy, complicated, and conflict-filled situations that require undesirable choices between competing, highly prized values that cannot be simultaneously or fully satisfied." Different leaders might place different values on an individual staff member's mental health, student learning, team cohesion, the importance of standardized test scores and school culture or climate. In contrast to a dilemma, "A problem", Cuban writes, "is a situation in which a gap is found between what *is* and what *ought to be*. To close the gap, obstacles must be overcome."

In terms of framing this situation, it appears that the head has determined that this is a problem by deciding that the cause of the staff member's lackluster performance relates to her current grade level and content matter assignment. As a result of this framing, the head offers two alternative grade level and content placements. The first offer would move Susan from the primary division to the fifth grade and from being a generalist to a music specialist. This possibility is problematic because it would remove Susan from her preferred primary level and also would limit her ability to use all of the arts including dance, visual arts and music in her instructional practices. The second proffered solution also moved Susan from the content of the primary division to a grade five position, yet offered her continued work with music (but again not in drama or visual arts) in grade two. Susan's response to the proposed move is unsurprising as it doesn't seem to take into account her perceived skill and enjoyment of integrating the arts into the standard curriculum at the primary level.

Rather than frame this problem as one of mis-assignment, the school head would do well to step back and consider several alternative framings of the problem. For example, the difficulty that Susan was experiencing could result either from the stress of her job or more likely, from personal stress outside of school. Rather than turn to structurally-based solutions, if the head had discussed the situation with Susan to gain *her* perspective prior to offering a new assignment, the solution might have become more palatable to Susan. The head may have learned sooner about the family turmoil in Susan's life and therefore have gained valuable information that would lead to a human resources solution possibly including a short-term leave. Further re-framing and investigation might have uncovered tensions in the second grade team that were making Susan uncomfortable or other changes about which the head was unaware.

In working to resolve issues within schools, leaders must work against the instinct to quickly resort to structural and technical solutions and force themselves to frame and re-frame problems using multiple perspectives Situations can be complicated problems, while others are messy dilemmas. Knowing the difference between the two by carefully framing and re-framing an issue is essential because as Cuban wisely notes, problems can be solved with hard work and creativity, but dilemmas are never solved. Instead, dilemmas are managed and managing a dilemma begins with identifying competing sometimes conflicting values.

REFLECTION ON THE COMMENTARIES

The commentaries highlight the complex and interrelated nature of educational leadership. Reflective practice assists school principals to consider the implications of their decisions prior to implementing actions that impinge on pedagogy, ethics, student learning and teacher responsibilities.

The commentaries also reveal the impact of leader isolation and lack of affective wisdom in responding to highly complex educational dilemmas. The multi-dimensional aspects of these challenges are also highlighted. The issues that this school principal is responding to have components of political, legal, ethical and relational elements all intertwined. Reflect on and identify the forms of professional knowledge, the skills and the qualities you would need as an educational leader to effectively deal with these issues.

ADDITIONAL READING

DuFour, R. (1991). *The principal as staff developer*. Bloomington, IN: National Educational Service.

This book provides practical illustrations of how school principals can support teacher development. The seven main sections cover school improvement, principals as leaders, linking cause and commitment, and effective staff development practices.

Ladson-Billings, G. J., & Tate, W. F. (Eds.). (2006). *Education research in the public interest: Social justice, action, and policy*. New York, NY: Teachers College Press.

The authors address issues such as teaching for social justice, education inquiry, curriculum, assessment, school reform, language – minority students, and democratic education practices.

Mezirow, J. (1990). *Fostering critical reflection in adulthood: A guide to transformative and emancipatory learning*. San Francisco, CA: Jossey-Bass.

Critical reflection that can facilitate transformational learning is examined. The author illustrates how educators can use life histories, journals and computers as tools for guiding adults toward positive goals and increased awareness.

Shapiro, J. P., & Stefkovich, J. A. (2005). *Ethical leadership and decision making in education: Applying theoretical perspectives to complex dilemmas* (2nd ed.). Mahwah, NJ: Lawrence Erlbaum Associates.

Models for ethical decision making are presented and applied in this book as educational leaders analyze and respond to moral dilemmas encountered in practice.

Sleeter, C. (2008). Teaching for democracy in an age of corporatocracy. *Teachers College Record, 110*(1), 139–159.

The author explores the profiles and actions of teachers who are democratically minded and face two author-identified challenges: negotiating increasingly undemocratic systems, and critically examining the gaps between ideal and actual practice.

Whitehead, A.J., & McNiff, J. (2006). *Action research: Living theory.* Thousand Oaks, CA: Sage Publications.

The authors provide background and a vision regarding the growing methodology of action research. They explore with the reader the philosophy of action research and ways of conducting it.

CASE 9

The Principal in the Middle

The school has recently experienced a series of retirements and maternity leaves. There are new custodians and education assistants. There is one teacher on sick leave. The September election has brought an almost entirely new school council and a new chairperson. I am also new to the school as principal. My challenges during the first three weeks of September seem endless.

By the end of September, my desk is piled with a mountain of paper. Finally, I find an opportunity to tackle my in-basket. The secretary appears at my door. "We have a new student registering. I think you should speak to the mother. Her name is Mary Ham."

The school secretary, Janette, is experienced with standard registration procedures. I realize there must be a reason for her request that I meet with this mother. I smile at her reassuringly and respond, "I'll be right there. Please ask her to wait a moment."

Janette introduces me to Mary Ham. I invite her into my office and begin asking the usual questions about address, birth date and transfer forms. I casually mention that our Grade 7 teacher has the same last name as she does. "Yes," she says, lips barely moving, "Frank was my husband. We have recently divorced. I have sole custody of our daughter."

I indicate that I was not aware that Frank was divorced. I ask, "Do you both live in our school area?"

She replies, "He doesn't. I moved into the school area after we separated."

She tells me that her husband has only limited access to their child. I find this arrangement a bit surprising and somewhat worrisome. "Do you have the custodial papers with you?"

"No," Mary responds. "I will get them to you as soon as they are finalized. There should not be any problem though. "Frank teaches the older students. My daughter, Josie, is only in Grade 2. They are not likely to run into each other."

Now I am really beginning to become concerned. "Are there any other issues I should be aware of?" I ask.

Mary pulls herself up straight. She is obviously annoyed with what she considers to be my intrusive questions. She responds abruptly, "Are you going to register my child or not? I'm tired of all this questioning. My daughter has every right to attend this school. I expect you to make sure that her father has nothing to do with her while she is here. Frank is not involved with Josie. I never see him. Just register her and let me get back to work."

She turns and is halfway out the door before I continue. "I'm sorry. I don't mean to add to your worries. I do, however, need to know if you have a school transfer form and if there are any health issues, safety concerns or special needs before I register your daughter. This is normal information that we request for any of our new students."

Mary strides toward my desk, taking papers out of her bag. "Here is the transfer form. There are no other concerns. This transfer form is from one of your own schools and the principal told me to just come in and that I would be able to leave Josie here today." She turns again toward the door.

I quickly review the papers she has handed me – a transfer form and a letter from the other principal indicating that Josie had been registered in her school and had been doing well.

"We'll be pleased to register Josie at this school," I say. "However, I will require a copy of the custody papers before you clarify any specifics regarding Josie's contact or her teacher's contact with Frank."

Unexpectedly, Mary apologizes. "I'm sorry if I come on strong. You need to know that this has not been easy. Frank is being very difficult. I'm at my wit's end. I didn't mean to take it out on you. I'll arrange to have the papers sent by the end of this week. There are other issues, but you don't need to be aware of them. The only thing that you need to know is that the teacher at the last school thought that Josie might have some learning problems, but she said they weren't serious and there was no need for special programming. Josie also has some follow-up tests for headaches she's been having. The tests are scheduled for next month."

I reassure Mary that we are available for help or support. I ask that she inform us if there are any test results that we need to know about. She thanks me and reiterates that the custody papers will arrive in the next day or two.

After Mary Ham leaves my office, my thoughts turn to Frank. Frank has been absent several days already this term. I remember seeing him earlier this week in the hall. He was talking to a number of the young female staff members and had his arm around one of them. I pull out the staff committee list and examine it. Frank has volunteered to coach the basketball, volleyball and baseball teams.

I call the superintendent to inform him of the situation. He suggests that I discuss registration alternatives with the family. I tell him I want to talk to Frank first since I haven't had a chance to really get to know him yet. I will also try to see if we can arrange a joint meeting with both of Josie's parents to reach some common understanding. He agrees and tells me to keep in touch.

The following day, Frank swings open my office door and demands, "What did my wife tell you?" I'm on the phone with another parent and ask Frank to wait outside my office for a moment while I finish my conversation. Frank ignores my request. "My wife was in here and registered my daughter. What did she tell you? She has no business telling you any of our personal information!"

I quickly conclude the telephone conversation. "Frank, I think you should calm down. Your former wife registered Josie here. I assumed that you knew. I have asked her to arrange for the school to have a copy of the custody papers. Then I think you and Mary should meet with me and try to work out some arrangements for the school situation."

"Of course I knew," he answers rudely. "What I want to know right now is what else she shared with you. You have no right to know anything about my business."

I make eye contact and reply, "Frank, I have no intention of prying into your personal affairs. Josie has the right to attend our school. My role is to provide her with an appropriate program. I suggest that the two of you need to sit down and figure out how you are going to handle the issues that will arise while Josie is at school. I understand that your custody papers indicate that you have no access to your daughter on weekdays. I need to know how you are going to manage that arrangement with both of you now at the same school. We can sort out what the issues are for each of you and agree on how we will each proceed."

Frank rises and says, "There is no such order. I can see my daughter whenever I want. Neither you nor Mary is going to interfere with me doing whatever I want to whenever I want to. I'm going to file a grievance against you for interfering in my private business." Frank stomps out of my office.

Over the next six weeks, meetings are set and then cancelled by both Frank and Mary. Frank is offered a teaching job at another school. He indicates that he will not be run out of the school and launches another complaint. Frank refuses to acknowledge or accept the interpretation of the custody papers shown to him during a meeting in my office with the superintendent. He declines to consult his lawyer.

Another Monday comes. During a walk down the hall, I see Frank giving Josie a hug outside his classroom door. She looks embarrassed to be out of class and blurts out to me, "My class is in the gym. I went to the washroom and decided to come and talk to my Dad. I hope that is okay."

"Well, Josie, it is important that you do what your teacher gave you permission to do and then go immediately back to class. It is also import-ant that you not disturb your Dad when he is at work." I smile.

"Bye Daddy," she says. Josie walks slowly down the hall. Her eyes are downcast.

"Frank, you should be inside your class at this time. This is only going to confuse your daughter. Wouldn't it be better to set up your visits outside of school hours?"

Frank mutters under his breath and re-enters his classroom.

I call Mary and report the contact made between her daughter and Frank that morning. I request again that the two parents meet with me to discuss how the custody and access order should be enforced at the school. She responds, "I will try to get Frank to meet. You will have to be the referee for us. I can't get anywhere in any of my discussions with him."

After school, a group of four intermediate teachers comes into my office. They are obviously uncomfortable. One teacher begins by saying, "We were in the library and overheard a conversation." Another teacher interrupts, "We weren't listening. We were working on our reports during planning time. Frank was in another part of the library." A third teacher continues, "He was on a cellphone. He was talking very loudly and he was swearing abusively. We couldn't help but overhear. We think he was talking to Josie's mother." The teachers are clearly humiliated to be telling me this story. They are also very concerned.

To exacerbate the situation, increasing numbers of parents report dissatisfaction with the way that Frank is running the sports teams. They claim he yells at the students and that he does not give all of the students opportunities to play. When Frank meets with me about these concerns, he seems receptive to suggestions for improvement. The parent feedback, however, just adds to my growing unease about Frank.

I review the issues. There are concerns regarding the custody arrangements and court orders, the needs of Josie and both her parents, issues related to professional ethics, the grievance that Frank has lodged, and the complaints of parents about Frank's involvement in extracurricular activities. I worry about how he conducts himself in the classroom. I continue to wonder why Frank is so concerned about what Mary has shared about his personal life. Are there any risks for the staff and students at the school? My sense is that I'm missing an important piece of information.

PROFESSIONAL INQUIRY

The Professional Inquiry section is intended to support reflection, dialogue and the development of new understanding and insights. Engagement in the following processes can occur individually or collaboratively with colleagues. These processes are designed to facilitate new or revised interpretations of the leadership experience described in the case The Principal in the Middle. This additional knowledge may guide the subsequent leadership actions, thinking and decisions of the reader.

Tensions

1. Explicate the tensions in this case using the following framework:

Understanding the Tensions of the Case						
List the *Facts* in the case	Identify the *Interests* of the following individuals and groups:		List the *Tensions* that exist for the following individuals:			
	Individual Interests	In the Interest of the Common Good	Parent (Mary)	Staff	Teacher (Frank)	Principal
	Student (Josie)	Staff				
	Teacher (Frank)	Students				
	Parent (Mary)	Other (s)				

(Adapted from Duignan, 2006)

Ethical Practice

1. Describe the ethical challenges and issues encountered by this educational leader.

2. Identify the implications of these challenges and issues for this learning community.

3. Explore how the interests of the learner, Josie, are being served in this case.

Leadership Practices

1. Identify the leadership capabilities of the principal in this case.

2. Analyze the leadership style of the principal.

3. Identify the influences that may impact on the decision making processes of the principal.

Implementing Policy

1. Discuss the role that school or board policy might play in a case scenario such as this one.

Culture of Professionalism

1. Identify the strategies that could be employed to enhance professionalism in this school.

Reflective Practice

1. Discuss the principal's ability to think reflectively and strategically.

2. Critique the professional judgment and action of the educational leader in this case.

3. Analyze the tensions in this case from the perspective of the individual good and the pursuit of the common good.

4. Reflect on the impact of this situation on the professional identity of Frank as a teacher in this school community.

5. Generate alternative responses and strategies to the issues, tensions and challenges in this case.

CASE COMMENTARY CRITIQUE

1. Read the commentary(ies) written about the case.

2. Record your reflections regarding the commentary(ies) using the framework below:

   a. Identify the key points, perspectives or issues in the commentary.

   b. Analyze the key points, perspectives or issues identified in the commentary.

   c. List the new insights you gained from the commentary.

Commentary Critique			
Case Commentary Writer	Identification *What key points, perspectives or issues are identified in the commentary?*	Analysis *What is your analysis of the perspectives identified in the commentary?*	Synthesis *What new insights have you gained from the commentary?*

CASE COMMENTARIES

CASE COMMENTARY 1

Case: The Principal in the Middle

A.G. Rud
Associate Professor, Educational Studies, Purdue University

I am struck immediately by how isolated this leader is from his staff, his mentors, even a helpful family member. I assume that this leader is a man, though that is only my intuitive hunch, because I know few women who would operate in such a conceptual and affective vacuum and not think it crazy to go it alone in a situation fraught, not with bureaucratic knots and conundrums, but human needs, passions and desires. He receives little help when he calls the superintendent, who suggests a bureaucratic solution of "registration alternatives with the family" and offers some easy moral support ("tells me to keep in touch").

Yet I may be too harsh in my quick assessment of the scene. I need to return to the beginning of the case to realize how existentially fragile this leader is. We get clues right away that he is struggling to understand, and to lead, in a difficult situation: "The school has recently experienced a series of recent retirements and maternity leaves. There are new custodians and education assistants. There is one teacher on sick leave. The September election has brought an almost entirely new school council and a new chairperson. I am also new to the school as principal. My challenges during the first three weeks of September seem endless." In other words, he had barely located the drawer for the paper clips when in walks Mary Ham.

Had the setting been more stable and the principal a veteran, the scenario could very well have developed differently. A seasoned leader would no doubt have experienced similar situations and could draw on background knowledge and previous decisions. He might even have a cadre of veteran teachers from whom he could ask advice, or perhaps a district personnel officer who could mediate the parties and their concerns from the beginning.

This principal does not have this advantage of background knowledge and site-specific lore, or the bad or good decisions he made in other parent/student cases from years past. He is new and thrust right into the middle of a hornet's nest of anger and betrayal not of his making. His problems are compounded by his teachers, who are understandably alarmed by the father Frank's abusive cellphone conversations, which they overheard, and want the principal to address this issue too.

While it may not seem so, this principal is on the cusp of an extraordinary leadership moment with his teachers. They are looking to him to solve the problem, which they perceive as Frank's potentially explosive relationship with his ex-wife and the custody issues surrounding his daughter. The principal cannot fully and definitively solve this problem. He can't get Frank and Mary to love one another again and there is not much beyond a kind word he can offer to heal the emotional wounds of their daughter Josie. But he can show compassion for the situation by patiently listening to all parties and then acting based on what he has learned. The ensuing actions, though unlikely to result in any accord between the warring parents, will do much to establish a procedure for difficult situations. In other words, the school culture will be enriched as the principal's own values are writ large in how this school is a place for a particular set of norms and processes. This leader has the chance to be a moral exemplar, even if he stumbles and does not succeed in healing this particular sorrow.

CASE COMMENTARY 2

Case: The Principal in the Middle

Julie Mueller
Assistant Professor, Faculty of Education, Wilfrid Laurier University

Abbreviating an extended situation into a short case study seems a bit like taking a snapshot from a motion picture. We need to be cautious in our interpretations to ensure that we consider the scenario as a developing scenario rather than assuming that all of the information was available at one time to the actors in this motion picture. In this picture, the hesitation of the principal may at first glance present as indecision, but on closer examination it appears to be careful consideration of the facts and setting of priorities. In writing the case study, the principal indicates a search of several sources of information that are considered and weighed before action is taken. This attempt to get the whole picture is a prominent theme in the principal's handling of the situation and encourages fair and ethical treatment of all actors.

In each frame of the motion picture, however, the student's rights and needs are held as priority. The first request made by the principal is for the custody papers that would clarify any court orders. The principal returns the focus from the ex-marital relationship back to the student again when she/he inquires about health issues, safety concerns and special needs. Requests are also made for additional information and ongoing communication regarding Josie's tests. The principal accepts and disseminates information from and to several sources within the board (Josie's past school, the superintendent, the staff of the school). Meetings with the two parents (Mary and Frank) are scheduled and the principal makes observations in the school. There is a consistent path of inquiry and summary without judgment.

The title suggests that the principal is caught in a situation that has competing sides. There appears to be a melee, with the principal as referee. There is an ongoing struggle on the principal's part to consider the rights and needs of various players: Josie (the student), Mary (the mother), Frank (the husband and staff member), student athletes, parents and other staff members. I can hear the conflict in the principal's reporting of the case – presenting information from all sides and seeking information on which to make decisions – and the uneasiness that lingers at the conclusion of the case study.

The complexity of the situation is increased by the multiple roles of the players. That is, Frank is in the role of parent, teacher, and coach, with competing priorities and differing rules. Mary is a parent of a new student but also the ex-wife of a staff member. The principal must identify what is best for Josie as a student but must also consider her/his role in supporting the staff under her/his supervision. Staff members are acting as agents for their students but may be leery of prying into the personal life of a fellow teacher. These relationships are unfolding in a less-than-stable context. The staff at the school has had a great deal of turnover. The principal, who is also new to the school, has not had the opportunity to develop relationships with the staff and is already facing "endless" challenges. The tension of a custody battle could have a severe impact on the school culture. The principal is in the position of evaluating which roles take priority and must also consider the impact of any decisions on the school culture.

The pressures from the other players in the scenario can pull the focus away from the overarching objective – safe and secure learning for all students. According to the *Ethical Standards for the Teaching Profession* in Ontario, students must be treated with care and respect. Teachers must use integrity and develop trust in their relationships with students, parents and other professionals. The trust of the principal and other staff members in regard to Frank comes into question. Frank's trust in his principal is also at risk, evidenced by the grievance he has filed. Trust must be forged between Frank and his daughter, the school and Josie's family, amongst staff members and with the principal, through a well-thought-out, collaborative plan. The principal must consider the information available and investigate further to develop relationships among all of the players in the real-life drama of the school.

CASE COMMENTARY 3

Case: The Principal in the Middle

Denise E. Armstrong
Assistant Professor, Brock University

This case study illustrates the increasingly complex nature of the management roles and the depth and breadth of the political, legal and ethical challenges that principals face as they negotiate the organizational landscape. Within the hierarchical structure of education, principals are located in an ambiguous professional middle zone between school staff and district superintendents. Their front-line role as organizational buffers and boundary spanners also pulls them into the epicentre of the school community where they are expected to adjudicate issues, respond to crises, and protect their school from real and potential threats. This administrative middle zone is fraught with unpredictability and conflict because of the number and variety of demands that converge on them from inside and outside of the school. Like the principal in this case, organizational newcomers often feel caught in the middle as they attempt to balance competing interests and priorities while adhering to their personal and professional values.

My research shows that administrators experience tension and ambiguity when resolving middle-zone issues, particularly when they involve multiple organizational actors, competing issues, and layers of obligation. In this particular dynamic, the principal is required to interact with five different stakeholders who represent different levels of the organization and levels of accountability: the secretary, superintendent, students, parents and teachers. The principal is pulled into the middle of the custodial dispute by her secretary and the parents. Her involvement deepens when Mr. Ham, the non-custodial parent who is also a teacher, violates the court order. The situation is further complicated by Mr. Ham's grievance and the teachers' and parents' complaints regarding his unprofessional behaviour.

The principal is also caught between intersecting legal and professional accountabilities that emanate from her fiduciary duty of care to students, her responsibility to parents and the community, and her obligation to ensure due process in dealing with staff. At the core of these tensions is her desire to act in a fair and judicious manner and her unfamiliarity with the school culture and the teachers' background. As she reflects on this situation, she identifies at least five interconnected issues that will require immediate and long-term action and thoughtful resolution. As in most situations of this sort, a wide range of options exists, each with its own peculiar legal, political and ethical ramifications.

The principal's legal obligation to act *in loco parentis* requires her to uphold the duty of the law by enforcing the custody order. In light of the ongoing conflicts between Mr. and Mrs. Ham and between the principal and Mr. Ham, the principal should extricate herself from this middle zone and involve a third-party mediator. Since the teacher is receptive to suggestions for improvement, the principal should provide alternate sources of support while continuing to monitor his progress. The legislation also requires principals to ensure physically and emotionally safe learning environments. In order to allay her fears about potential risks for staff and students and to address her knowledge gaps, the principal should contact her predecessor and her superintendent for additional information. In order to reduce potential political fallout, the principal also needs to monitor this situation carefully while ensuring that the relevant district and union protocols are followed.

REFLECTION ON THE COMMENTARIES

The commentaries highlight the complexity involved in the situation and the challenges encountered by an educational leader who is trying to mediate and resolve the issues that emerge in this case scenario. Consider Rud's comment regarding the opportunity of the educational leader to be a "moral exemplar" and Mueller's comments regarding the significance of trust in this case. Reflect on your responses to both of these leadership concepts.

ADDITIONAL READING

Davis, S., Darling-Hammond, L., LaPointe, M., & Meyerson, D. (2005). *School leadership study: Developing successful principals (review of research)*. Stanford, CA: Stanford Educational Leadership Institute, Stanford University.

Administrative responsibilities can often exceed leaders' capabilities. The authors discuss the challenge of finding qualified individuals for the role of principal. They suggest that some school leaders are not adequately prepared for the position and do not receive the type of support needed. Elements of effective leadership programs are outlined.

Furman, G. C., & Shields, C. M. (2005). How can educational leaders promote and support social justice and democratic community in schools? In W.A. Firestone & C. Riehl, (Eds.), *A new agenda for research in educational leadership* (pp. 119–137). New York, NY: Teachers College Press.

Theories of democracy and social justice pertaining to school communities are outlined in this article. The authors contend that democracy that places value on participation, friendship and solidarity is required for schools in the 21st century. They show how social justice and democracy are interdependent and necessary in areas such as pedagogy and leadership practices.

Hermond-Prairie, D. (2005). Ethical leadership is not optional: How LPPs can help. *International Journal of Scholarly Academic Intellectual Diversity, 8*(1).

The author discusses the need for school leaders to exercise ethical behaviour and focus on creating moral learning communities. He argues that Leadership Preparation Programs (LPPs) provide effective training in ethical management for school leaders.

Jones, B. D., & Egley, R. J. (2006). Looking through different lenses: Teachers' and administrators' views of accountability. *Phi Delta Kappan, 87*(10), 767–771.

The study explores the implications of different perceptions of the effects of test-based accountability programs. The findings suggest that the views of teachers and administrators are based, in part, on how a testing program affected their own particular roles and responsibilities within a school. The authors propose strategies for creating a climate in which teachers and administrators can move forward on improving student learning.

Palmer, P. (1998). *The courage to teach: Exploring the inner landscape of a teacher's life*. San Francisco, CA: Jossey-Bass.

The author invites educators to explore the vocational call to become a teacher. He discusses the inner landscapes of teachers' lives and stresses the importance of a teacher's presence and heart in creating communities of learning.

SECTION IV

Leaders as Models of Professionalism

LEADERS AS MODELS OF PROFESSIONALISM

Being a consistent and positive model of professionalism is a necessary element of effective educational leadership. A strong unwavering commitment to student learning is a hallmark of professionalism. Such leaders strive to make a difference in the lives of students and recognize that a professional learning community can be a valuable resource in accomplishing this objective. The importance of cultivating and exercising informed professional judgment is clearly understood as a necessary requirement of professionalism by effective educational leaders. These individuals actively work to embody and encourage the integration of all dimensions of professionalism in learning communities: commitment to students, engagement in ongoing professional learning, ethical practice, collaboration, instructional leadership and knowledge creation.

CASES FROM PROFESSIONAL PRACTICE

The four cases in this section of the book invite further inquiry into the role educational leaders play as models of professionalism. Issues that impact on educational leaders' ability to effectively model and support cultures of professionalism can include things such as the professional identity of the leader, relationships with staff, professional responsibilities, the level of the leader's ethical knowledge, decision making approaches employed by the leader and the leader's vision of leadership. Leaders who engage in ongoing reflective practice may benefit from the additional insight this form of professional learning can provide. Disciplined forms of reflection can help educators become more conscious of the level of congruence between their espoused beliefs and values and their actual lived actions. The more congruent a leader's actions are with her/his articulated beliefs, the more likely the leader's practice will serve as an exemplary model of ethical professionalism.

> ### *Cases*
>
> *Choosing Sides*
> *An Occasional Dilemma*
> *Samantha*

CASE COMMENTARIES

Practitioners and educational scholars with experience in the areas of ethics, leadership, ethical standards, narrative, case methods and teacher education wrote commentaries in response to the cases in this section. The commentary writers raise issues related to trust, responsibility, relationships, reciprocal feedback, mutual respect, inclusivity, communication, best interests of the student, pedagogical duties, policies, community, transparency, open-mindedness, and the ethics of care, justice and critique.

Commentaries

Choosing Sides
John Wallace
Anthony H. Normore
John Lundy
Pierre Toussaint

An Occasional Dilemma
Lindy Zaretsky
James Heap
Jules Rocque

Samantha
Richard Shields
Michel Saint-Germain
Tom Russell

CASE 10

Choosing Sides

Despite a long season of bitter losses and player injuries, Eric and I had managed to transform a group of individual secondary school basketball stars into a smoothly functioning team. The rookie players were gradually becoming more highly skilled and learning to function as productive team members. Eric Gloucester's summer basketball camp had not only proven effective in promoting Gardner High's basketball program, but had also succeeded in recruiting new and gifted athletes. However, all the exhilaration I felt following today's win over the much-heralded Salmon Stingers was gone. Eric, my coaching partner and also a teacher on my staff, had told me on the drive home about a troubling incident involving another staff member.

Eric was furious. His comments about Rita, the head of English, were shocking. I wondered, "Could it be possible that Rita had acted so unprofessionally?" It was not uncommon to have teachers disagree on a classroom program. It was, however, not a common occurrence for a member of my staff to publicly question a colleague's competence in front of students. Apparently this is what had happened.

What would I say to Rita the next morning? As her vice-principal, should I confront her about her comments? Should I discuss the alleged incident with our principal first and get his advice?

As I walked into my office, the principal's administrative assistant handed me three pink pieces of paper. Even on a good day I hate those pink phone messages! The administrative assistant didn't ask if the team had won. I asked myself, "Did she even care? Shouldn't everyone in the school community be interested in the team and the game outcome? Why was everyone becoming so apathetic?"

I remember six years ago when I began my role as vice-principal. I felt passionate about teaching and wanted to create a school where staff and students could broaden their knowledge and experiences. I longed for a school where teachers really cared and were willing to take risks for their students. I wanted a school that was a learning community.

Six years later, I felt that these goals had not become a reality. A chasm existed between teachers. Some were quick to acquiesce to central office policies. They believed in maintaining a baseline standard that all students must meet or be deemed unsuccessful. Others were more ambivalent about standardized tests and felt uncomfortable promoting what they considered to be an arcane and myopic view of student achievement.

I glanced down at the messages in my hand, fearing they were all complaints from parents of students in Eric's classes. They were. I decided not to call back immediately. I would speak with Rita first.

I knew the parents were just going to repeat their demands. They wanted an explanation of how the administration was going to handle the final-exam dilemma for Eric's students. Eric's students had been complaining that his teaching was so bad they would end up performing miserably on the final exam. Recently, parent and student concerns had escalated because, as team coach, he had been frequently absent this semester.

I had overheard disparaging remarks about Eric while supervising students at lunch. The president of the student council had asked, "How do they expect us to get into college with marks like this? How are we supposed to study for the final exam when he hasn't even given us back our last three assignments? My dad is prepared to go to the board office to complain. Let's start a petition."

I could no longer deny that a groundswell of dissatisfied students had begun to rally their parents to complain about Eric's lack of class preparation and unmarked assignments. I wondered if Rita had fuelled these attacks. Rita had told her students, "If Mr. Gloucester was your teacher last year then you will be at a disadvantage. You won't have covered the work that you need to do well in my class."

I also wondered if Eric's frequent absenteeism was indicative of a deeper crisis. Maybe Eric's stress level had gone way up because of Rita's ongoing bullying tactics and unprofessional comments. I remembered the last English department meeting. Rita repeatedly ignored Eric's pleas for direction regarding the assessment of students with special needs. Eric had left the meeting very angry.

The morning after that meeting, Eric had been absent. Rita had marched into the principal's office to announce that Eric had again failed to leave lesson plans for the supply teacher. As Rita turned to leave she added, "Oh well, it doesn't really matter. All he does is show videos to his kids anyway."

I also remembered the first time Rita chaired one of our in-school committees. Several teachers left the committee after she humiliated them in front of colleagues. Her despotic style created tension among the committee members that almost led to a grievance. Helen, an experienced teacher nearly twice Rita's age, had cried in my office. She asked, "How does Rita get away with treating people like this? Doesn't she ever make a mistake? What is the administration going to do about her?"

Lately, I'd felt that Eric was depending on me to be supportive. We had coached together for years. We had also been teaching colleagues at another school. Eric had even asked me to be the godfather of one of his sons. Now I was Eric's vice-principal. I was determined that Rita would not undermine Eric's professional credibility at the school.

I realized that I would eventually need to involve my principal in this situation. To some degree, I relished the idea of finally getting something done about Rita. I knew that several other staff members would show little sympathy for Rita if Tom, our principal, put a stop to her ruthless behaviour and criticism of Eric.

Suddenly Rita was standing in my office doorway. "Oh, Hello Bill." She paused momentarily. "By the way, Tom has asked me to fill in for you this Friday while you're out at the board office at your meeting. Anything special I need to know? I'm really looking forward to being acting vice-principal in your absence. Tom has endorsed my application for the leadership pool."

Rita left the office smiling.

On Friday, she was going to be sitting in my chair. She would use my computer and my telephone. This was the last straw.

PROFESSIONAL INQUIRY

The Professional Inquiry section is intended to support reflection, dialogue and the development of new understanding and insights. Engagement in the following processes can occur individually or collaboratively with colleagues. These processes are designed to facilitate new or revised interpretations of the leadership experience described in the case Choosing Sides. This additional knowledge may guide the subsequent leadership actions, thinking and decisions of the reader.

Vision and Influence

1. Describe the vice-principal's vision of leadership.

2. Identify actions that the principal and vice-principal could employ to foster an authentic collaborative community of inquiry.

3. Explore the impact of the vice-principal's role modelling on this school community.

4. Analyze the influences the vice-principal has on teaching and student learning in this school.

5. Use the framework below to begin to develop your action plan for enhancing this school community in the best interests of learners.

Fostering a Collaborative Community of Inquiry				
Action Plan				
School Mission and Vision *What do we collectively believe? What do we want our school to look like in three years?*	**Commitment to Students and Student Learning** *How will we collectively demonstrate our commitment to students and student learning?*	**Professional Knowledge and Practice** *What are our collective plans for fostering our professional knowledge and practice on an ongoing basis?*	**Teacher Professionalism** *How will we interact with our colleagues? How will we support shared leadership with students and teachers?*	**Relationships with Parents** *How will we interact with parents?*

Instructional Leadership

1. Identify the vice-principal's responsibilities related to instructional leadership. Use the following framework to specify the instructional responsibilities the vice-principal has toward students, teachers and parents:

Instructional Leadership	
Responsibilities	
Students	
Teachers	
Parents	

Decision Making

1. Evaluate the decision making capacity of the vice-principal.

2. Critique the beliefs and values that appear to be guiding the thinking, actions and decisions of the vice-principal.

Professionalism

1. Identify the dilemmas associated with teacher professionalism in this case.

2. Identify the messages that are conveyed in this case scenario regarding teacher professionalism.

3. Generate strategies that the administrative team might use to foster a culture of professionalism in this school community.

Professional Identity

1. Describe the professional identities of the vice-principal and the two teachers, Rita and Eric.

2. Consider the impact of each educator's (Eric, Rita, Bill) professional identity on their professional practice and judgment. Identify the possible implications of their professional identity on their actions and practice.

Ethical Practice

1. Identify the ethical issues and tensions in this case.

2. Discuss how the *Integrity* of the school administrator was challenged.

3. Examine the professional judgment of Eric, Rita and Bill.

4. Identify the messages that are conveyed in this case scenario about:

   a. the culture of this school

   b. responsibility toward students.

Ethical Knowledge

1. Analyze the ethical knowledge of the educators in this case using the following framework:

Ethical Awareness and Knowledge			
Case Participants	Limited Ethical Awareness and Knowledge	Moderate Ethical Awareness and Knowledge	High Ethical Awareness and Knowledge

Trust

1. Use the framework below to identify how the ethical value of *Trust* was apparent in the actions of the participants in this case:

Trust		
Case Participants	Value of *Trust* Apparent in Actions	Value of *Trust* Not Apparent in Actions
Eric		
Rita		
Bill		

CASE COMMENTARY CRITIQUE

1. Read the commentary(ies) written about the case.

2. Record your reflections regarding the commentary(ies) using the framework below:

   a. Identify the key points, perspectives or issues in the commentary.

   b. Analyze the key points, perspectives or issues identified in the commentary.

   c. List the new insights you gained from the commentary.

Commentary Critique			
Case Commentary Writer	**Identification** *What key points, perspectives or issues are identified in the commentary?*	**Analysis** *What is your analysis of the perspectives identified in the commentary?*	**Synthesis** *What new insights have you gained from the commentary?*

CASE COMMENTARIES

CASE COMMENTARY 1

Case: Choosing Sides

John Wallace
Professor, Ontario Institute for Studies in Education,
University of Toronto

It's not about choosing sides. It's about establishing accountability relationships.

The author of this vignette, a school vice-principal, appears to be caught in the middle of a troubled relationship between Eric, an apparently underperforming staff member, and Rita, Eric's unpopular and somewhat overbearing subject head. This scenario is complicated by the author's developing friendship with Eric, leading to a more sympathetic portrayal of Eric than Rita. Consequently, the author interprets his role as "getting something done about Rita," rather than confronting Eric about his classroom performance.

A vice-principal's role is ill defined and all encompassing. Vice-principals are frequently called on to solve a myriad of school problems, typically involving relationships between and among teachers, department heads, students, parents and community members. Sorting out one's role in this complex web of relationships is often tricky and fraught with dilemmas. Without wishing to trivialize these difficulties, here are some suggested ways forward based on what I call accountability relationships. It might be helpful to explain a few general principles behind these kinds of relationships.

Focus on performance. Establishing accountability relationships means recognizing that the relationship between leaders and teachers is primarily about improvement in performance – the performance of leaders and the performance of teachers. This means establishing a climate where leaders and teachers work together to learn from each other, establish clear standards, expose and solve problems, and face ongoing and meaningful reviews of each other's practice. With this principle in mind, I suggest that the author needs to refocus his energies on Eric's performance as a teacher (and by association his own performance as a leader). Rita's performance as a leader is of secondary importance in this vignette, although I also believe that the author has a responsibility to model good leadership practices for Rita. The vice-principal's role is not to sort out the relationship between Eric and Rita, but to individually build sound accountability relations with each person.

Establish a climate of trust. Accountability relationships must be based on trust. Leaders and teachers are entrusted with the responsibility to carry out their own work and to account for their performance. Trust, built over time, must be exercised by leaders and teachers. One of the encouraging features of the relationship between the author and Eric is that they have already developed a sense of mutual trust – it is understood and accepted by both parties that each is responsible for doing her/his job as teacher, leader, coach and so on. What appears to be missing, for the most part, is the accountability dimension. While Eric may well routinely account to the author for his performance as a basketball coach (game stats, best players, player attendance at practice and so on), he clearly does not do so in the role for which he is primarily employed (as a classroom teacher). For Eric's sake (and for the sake of the students in his care), this situation clearly needs to change.

Accept responsibilities. Leaders have responsibilities in a professional culture to actively and explicitly help colleagues to improve their performance by developing trusting collaborative relationships that focus on improvement. Leaders also help colleagues by modelling their own accountability and a commitment to their own improvement. In this vignette, I believe that the vice-principal has a responsibility to help Eric understand his classroom responsibilities, allow him choice in meeting those responsibilities, help him account for the ways he is meeting those responsibilities, and provide measured and appropriate feedback on areas for improvement.

Seek, give and receive feedback. Accountability relationships are built between people. How relationships develop depends on the way people talk to and treat each other. The kinds of questions leaders ask their colleagues can help or hinder the development of professional accountability relationships. In informal or formal conversations with Eric, for example, the author could ask questions such as: What are you aiming to achieve in the classroom? How well are you doing? How do you know? What do you want to get better at? What would help you get better? How can I help you get better? How would you know if you are improving? and When will we meet again to talk about how you are doing? In a reciprocal manner, the author should ask Eric about her/his own performance: How am I doing as a leader?

To reiterate, I believe that the author's primary goal in this scenario should be to establish a professional accountability relationship with Eric (we will leave the author's relationship with Rita for the time being). Building on a pre-existing foundation of trust and mutual respect, the author should deliberately and gradually shift the basis of the relationship to focus on and nourish improvement (of his performance as a leader and Eric's performance as a classroom teacher). This is not to say that either party should assume responsibility for the other's duties, but to assert that each should provide an account to the other of his work in an environment where seeking, giving and receiving feedback is the norm. It is the author's responsibility as the leader to take the initiative here.

CASE COMMENTARY 2

Case: Choosing Sides

Anthony H. Normore
Associate Professor of Educational Administration in Graduate Education, California State University, Dominguez Hills

While reading Choosing Sides, several familiar issues resonated with me. Although the author presents some common complexities all too familiar in schools (accountability, responsibility and communication), inevitably, and as in any case, there are several omissions. The three characters in this narrative are people who seem to be at odds about what proven best practices they consider to be in the best interests of the students (Shapiro and Stefkovich, 2005). Essentially, vice-principal Bill struggles with ways to address these issues, which emerge through the recent unprofessional behaviour trends of two of his faculty members.

This school is in turbulence. Evidence throughout the case indicates that due to unaddressed past issues, ambivalence and apathy are rampant in the current climate. Examples include: (a) the office administrative assistant shows little to no interest in the recent win by the school's basketball team, (b) the school community oozes with apathy, (c) many teachers "acquiesce to central office policies" and believe in "maintaining a baseline standard that all students must meet or be deemed unsuccessful," (d) other teachers are "more ambivalent about standardized tests" and feel "uncomfortable promoting what they consider to be an arcane and myopic view of student achievement," (e) one bullying teacher publicly humiliates other teachers during committee meetings, (f) one teacher undermines the professional competence of another teacher in front of students, (g) parents and students incessantly complain about the instruction and absenteeism of one teacher, and (h) personal relationships have derailed the professional responsibilities of the school administration, resulting in preferential treatment of one teacher over another. To summarize, we are left with the feeling that the school climate seems to unintentionally foster practices that researchers have repeatedly identified as negatively impacting effective teaching and learning (Blasé and Blasé, 2003; Jazzar and Algozzine, 2007).

Vice-principal Bill finds himself at a crossroads of hope and despair. He is now confronted with a festering dilemma caused by two teachers – Rita and Eric. Judging from the facts presented in this case, one can safely surmise that this is not the first time that Rita has behaved unprofessionally. Her despotic style of publicly humiliating Eric and other teachers has wreaked havoc on several occasions. Eric's disdain for Rita's behaviour has created a ripple effect that has catapulted the school community into chaos and turbulence (Shapiro and Gross, 2008; Normore, 2004a). Although Bill will get no argument from most educators about the need to deal with Rita's behaviour, he will likely receive much criticism around "professional negligence" and "gender bias" if he chooses to ignore Eric's behaviour. Over time, we have learned a great deal about "modelling behaviour" and how teachers and administrators are constantly put under the microscope – especially by students, parents and the general public. Vice-principal Bill will need "to do the right thing" (Sergiovanni, 2005).

Due to the minimal reference to principal Tom in this case, it seems that he may be unaware of the current situation. Bill has already decided that Rita won't get sympathy from many colleagues if Tom puts a stop to her behaviour. What Bill doesn't know yet is that principal Tom has assigned Rita as acting vice-principal for the day – while Bill attends a board meeting. Furthermore, Tom has also endorsed Rita's application in the leadership pool. Although Bill is angered by these two actions, he seems to not realize that he is partially responsible. This is an example of an unintended consequence of vice-principal Bill's behaviour.

Turbulence and toxicity are prevalent in schools where lateral, horizontal and vertical communication is weak. This case is not specifically about Rita or Eric or Bill. We can do little more than share the author's disappointment and frustration about their behaviours and practices. Instead, the issue is far greater – one that requires us to become proactive in improving awareness by setting the example of friendly and respectful interaction and implementing consistent standards of professional ethics. This case is a prime example of the complexities of education leadership and reminds us of the constraints inherent in leadership positions. As asserted by Blasé and Blasé there is a comprehensive connection between sound school administrator practices, effective teaching and student learning:

> Collaboration is successful when school principals build trust in their schools ... trust, in turn, serves as a foundation for open, honest, and reflective professional dialogue ... problem solving; innovative initiatives; and, more directly, the development of the school as a powerful community of learners willing to take responsibility for success and capable of achieving it ... all principals need to work toward this end, and all education scholars need to willingly confront the kinds of mistreatments that, most assuredly, undermine such possibilities (Blasé & Blasé. 2004, p. 3).

CASE COMMENTARY 3

Case: Choosing Sides

John Lundy
Director, Laurentian University (English Language)
School of Education

Taking Sides is a really interesting case that involves lots of past history, role ambivalence, central task confusion and a nasty work environment. Bill, a six year vice-principal, is confronted by a seemingly clear incident of teacher-to-teacher unprofessional conduct. His feelings obviously favour his long-time colleague, Eric, a good co-coach but likely less than stellar teacher, and run contrary to Rita, a no-nonsense English department head who has made damning remarks about Eric's pedagogical qualities on this occasion and others. The issues seem to focus on professional conduct, staff relations and role clarity but are much more complex.

The key players are not new to education. It is obvious that Rita has overstepped her ethical and professional boundaries by making disparaging remarks to students about Eric's classroom performance. Leaving aside legal issues pertaining to specific state/provincial jurisdictions, Rita has erred significantly and her actions warrant administrative action in terms of reprimand but also in terms of professional development, especially given her nascent steps on the administrative ladder.

Her obvious nasty and unprofessional behaviour, as evidenced by previous unchecked incidents involving other school faculty, hides a significant administrative dilemma. Her basic criticisms of Eric's classroom practices do seem to warrant administrative attention. The role of a department head is fraught with role ambivalence, since heads are often part of teacher unions but are also expected to act in a quasi-administrative fashion with the teachers in their departments. Specific, concrete knowledge of the pedagogical practices of departmental teachers is typically not available to administrators and they rely on the headship role for information and advice. Rita's information to Tom, the school principal, may have rewarded her well with a recommendation for administrative advancement. She has highlighted shortcomings of teachers like Eric, and the complaints of parents, while they may be fuelled by her negative statements to students, do strike a responsive administrative chord. Eric has been frequently absent from school, substantially late returning assignments to students and, from the standardized testing focus, very lax in preparing his students for impending exams, the results of which are deemed potent success capital by many parents, students and administrators alike.

One's support or rejection of standardized testing is not the central issue; not performing one's pedagogic duties is. Rita has brought Eric to task on his classroom performance and her inappropriate manner of doing so has clouded the situation. Both Eric and Rita are in need of appropriate guidance, an ethical imperative on the part of school-level administration. Bill has had some evidence for a long time (student complaints; previous comments by Rita) that Eric's classroom performance has been inadequate or at least lacklustre. As vice-principal, he has not intervened by communicating privately or officially with Eric about these complaints and possible remedies. Furthermore, Bill has not had a serious chat with his principal, Tom, about Eric's problems or Rita's inappropriate behaviour on this and other occasions. Working on role clarity, especially in terms of responsibility for faculty management and professional development, appears as an important internal administrative agenda item. The school administrative team has a duty to ensure both that the central task of teaching-learning is actually occurring in their school and that department heads operate in a judicious and ethical fashion. A healthy and productive work environment, as well as restored parental confidence in the teaching profession, need to be the foci of this school for some time to come.

One might be tempted to psychologize this situation and concentrate on Bill's rather narrow notion of a learning community. He was somewhat taken aback when an office administrator was not elated at their basketball team's win; he conceptualized faculty as dividing into two fairly distinct camps, wherein one was acquiescent to "central office policies" while the other camp was "more ambivalent about standardized tests" seen by this group as an "arcane and myopic view of student achievement." Since he is recounting this administrative story, we are tempted to concentrate on his perspective, which tends to favour the latter group. Thus, one is tempted to see the administrative problem as uniquely belonging to Bill, his lack of appropriate action and his reluctance to respect contrary pedagogic views.

However, this situation is circumscribed by the legal and ethical school-system context. Policies and procedures for a safe, healthy and productive work environment need to be in place and senior school-system management needs to oversee the professional development of administrators and teachers alike in these policies and procedures. If the government of the day has mandated specific activities like standardized testing, then administrators and teachers have a duty to carry out these policies. Aside from ethically odious policies (enacting policies contrary to human rights legislation, etc.), there is not much choice. Students deserve the best education possible, while teachers and all other school-system persons deserve a safe and healthy work environment. Administrators have an ethical mandate to ensure that this happens.

CASE COMMENTARY 4

Case: Choosing Sides

Pierre Toussaint
Professor, Faculty of Education, Université du Québec à Montréal

To illustrate the complex ethical dilemmas that are part of the day-to-day work of today's leaders in education, we consider it important to suggest reflection on some of the situations that will confront education administrators. This is known as informed leadership. There are many such dilemmas and they can develop into full-blown disputes. Administrators must use their leadership and experience to turn these difficult situations into living and learning opportunities. Such reflective practice is an opportunity for administrators and teachers to progress beyond self-interest. An administrator must exercise leadership to foster her/his staff members' social cohesion, team spirit and professional ethics.

The Choosing Sides case study presents a specific situation: an ethical problem involving a teacher's lack of professionalism toward one of her colleagues. The problem is that Rita, a member of the teaching staff, is publicly questioning a colleague's competency in front of students. Anyone would agree this is an intolerable situation, but what is the response in such situations?

A vice-principal cannot fail to respond to such an incident, but the response must be made tactfully, without infantilizing Rita. She is an adult who must be made to acknowledge her ethical and professional responsibilities. The discussion must be firm but courteous. The vice-principal must exercise convincing leadership, since a good leader must be able to set out the facts without "losing it." In this case, the vice-principal must ensure that Rita apologizes to her colleague for her action concerning him. Public apologies are not necessary, but she must make some form of reparation and, most importantly, she must acknowledge the harm she has caused her colleague and take steps to avoid making such remarks in future.

A school must be a place of teaching and learning, but it is also a living environment with social cohesion that favours collective living.

But what is social cohesion in the modern school environment? In a school context of tension and even upheaval, the first challenge facing an administrator or any member of the education community is to create an atmosphere conducive to work, through communication and universal respect.

The administrators in this case study need to reassure those parents who are asking questions about their children's academic success. They need to create an atmosphere conducive to learning, but also conducive to work, one that encourages co-operation among staff, administrators and parents – what some writers refer to as "willing togetherness." At the same time, in response to legitimate anxieties and concerns on the part of parents or some staff members, they must demonstrate transparency and open-mindedness. What is involved here is "leadership of profound change," in the words of Peter Senge (Senge et al, 1999). The school is heading or should head in the direction of an ecology of leadership, a new kind of leadership that calls on the co-operation of everyone concerned. For James MacGregor Burns (1978), however, leadership is a skill expressed in terms of a transactional or transformational approach (quoted in French in Langlois, 2002, p. 79). In this context, how does a high school encourage team spirit and professional ethics?

First, in a high school, a sports team can act as a catalyst for bridging the gap between students, administration, staff and parents, but it must never become an impediment to students' academic success. Maintaining a sports team is demanding for those who take part in it, but it is an excellent education tool. A school sports team must be an education project for the school. The teachers who become involved in it must do so with competence and also with professionalism. Morally speaking, professional ethics or willing togetherness are engaged.

This willing togetherness in the modern school community is an essential aspect of any attempt to create an education community, which consists of the students, the school team and the parents, as well as community youth agencies and external partners.

REFLECTION ON THE COMMENTARIES

The commentaries emphasize the importance of trust, communication, feedback, pedagogic responsibilities and collaboration in the cultivation of communities of learning where professionalism reigns. Reflect on your own experiences as an educator and identify conditions and strategies that support the development and sustenance of these communities.

ADDITIONAL READING

Fullan, M. (2003). *The moral imperative of school leadership*. Thousand Oaks, CA: Corwin Press.

This is an in-depth exploration into principalship and the importance of school leaders in facilitating change and growth in professional learning communities. Some of the topics include the context of change, barriers to the principalship, and ethical leadership.

Leithwood, K., & Beatty, B. (2008). *Leading with teacher emotions in mind*. Thousand Oaks, CA: Corwin Press.

The authors examine teachers' emotional well-being in five key areas. They suggest that mental wellness has an affect on teachers' daily practice and that educational leaders are responsible for school environments that enhance teachers' well-being.

Murphy, J. (2006). A new view of leadership. *National Staff Development Council, 27*(3), 51–53.

A broader understanding of leadership for the 21st century is based on empowerment, entrepreneurship and environmental sensitivity. This educational and ethical core is presented by the author based on. this model of leadership that focuses on education and the moral aspects of schooling and calls on leaders to use a new lens for looking at the leader's role.

Tschannen-Moran, M. (2004). *Trust matters: Leadership for successful schools*. San Francisco, CA: Jossey-Bass.

This book focuses on developing and repairing trust in school environments. The author presents a variety of elements that influence most trust decisions. The educational leader is highlighted as someone who helps to facilitate trusting relationships with all community partners.

Williams, R. B. (2006). Leadership for school reform: Do principal decision making styles reflect a collaborative approach? *Canadian Journal of Educational Administration and Policy*, 53, 1-22.

The author explores a collaborative approach to school leadership and calls for a redefinition of principal-leadership knowledge, skills and responsibilities. The various styles of leadership used by principals in New Brunswick schools are also investigated.

CASE 11

An Occasional Dilemma

Main Street Elementary School in Inglis Falls is busy. Students are straggling into the building, brushing off snow and chattering excitedly. In the staff room, teachers work at their laptops and enjoy their morning coffee.

George, a veteran Grade 8 teacher, appears anxious. Ken, his colleague and fellow Grade 8 teacher, asks, "What's up George? An experienced teacher like you isn't stressing about report cards are you? After all, there's one more week before they're due!"

"You know why I'm stressed. You know who is teaching my class right now," sighs George.

Heads rise. Knowing and empathetic glances tell the staff story. Leah Cooper, the long-term occasional teacher, is teaching French first period in George's class and then second period in Ken's.

Someone whispers, "Maybe Leah Cooper should receive a report card. Under Learning Skills, her report card could indicate that learning skills are not an issue in her classes because no one ever learns anything!" There are a few guffaws. People turn their heads uneasily to see if Leah Cooper is in the staff room or if anyone else has overheard the comment.

As vice-principal, I am the focus of their gaze. I silently contemplate what to do. It's evident that the problems with Leah Cooper are worse than I had realized. The difficulties are so widespread and well-known that staff members are discussing them openly and within earshot of school administration.

George complains, "The teacher who has the bad luck to teach the class the period after Leah Cooper's French lesson really has a job to do. You need to apply every trick in the book about classroom management to get the kids back to work!"

George has seen me in the staff room but he continues to list his concerns. I am uncomfortable and incredulous. Are staff members expecting a reaction from me? Do they want me to respond to their concerns? I'm at a loss about how to react. I can relate to why these teachers who, after just a few months of working with Leah, refuse to believe that she has been successful in any of her previous efforts at employment.

I begin to reflect on Leah's first few months at the school. Leah Cooper is a new teacher. Although she is in her early thirties, she's already tried several careers. Her resumé indicates that she worked as a registered nurse in Ottawa for four years. When she left that position she went back to college and earned her Child and Youth Worker Diploma. She then worked in a Pembroke group home for kids 10 to 16 years of age. After nine months there she took the summer off to reflect on whether she wanted to stay in the child and youth worker role. She decided against returning and pursued a teaching career. She received her master of science in education from Brown University and then applied for the French teaching position at our school.

Leah did not hold the specific qualifications for teaching French as a second language. She did, however, come to our school with recommendations from several prominent people in our small town of 3,000. During her hiring interview, we learned that she had four undergraduate French credits from the local university. She had also coached baseball, was active in the community, and indicated a willingness to learn the French-language curriculum. We hired her. Her contract extended from the start of the school year until the beginning of April when the regular French teacher, Madame Lafarge, was scheduled to return from maternity leave.

In September, Leah seemed to be a competent beginning teacher. She was enthusiastic about implementing a new series of French-language lessons purchased by the board. I soon heard comments, however, indicating that she had difficulty controlling her emotions. I also heard rumours that she easily became exasperated with students' difficult questions. She was reported to have repeatedly muttered under her breath, just loud enough for the class to hear, "Why did I ever take this job?"

In early October, Leah had confided to me that she was nervous about managing Peter, a challenging student who openly questioned her and regularly ignored her instructions. During another conversation she related with anger how Henry refused to respond in French to her questions and turned his chair to face the back of the class.

At this point my silent reflections abruptly stopped. Leah Cooper burst into the staff room to pick up some forgotten handouts. It was clear that she had overheard her colleagues discussing her. She was furious.

I followed her out and down the hall. She was sniffling and holding back tears. When she whirled around and saw who was behind her, she tried to pull herself together. She asked if I had overheard the conversation in the staff room. "Yes," I replied.

I asked, "Have you had an opportunity to meet with the other French teacher, Pierre Foucault?" Pierre was a vivacious man who was always singing in the halls. He didn't seem to have any problem captivating and motivating his class. I knew that he would be glad to offer her a pointer or two. Leah Cooper reluctantly agreed to arrange a meeting soon.

A few days later, I heard that Pierre and Leah had met. I made it my business to find Pierre and follow up on his meeting with Leah. Pierre told me that he had recommended to Leah a class management strategy that provided for first one, then a second, warning. These warnings would be followed by an appropriate consequence for a third infraction. I was glad he was willing to be a mentor and felt confident that Leah would receive appropriate support from a talented teacher like Pierre Foucault.

But only a week later, Pierre sought me out. "I have serious concerns about Leah Cooper," he began. "She had difficulty thinking of appropriate consequences for student misbehaviour. When I suggested that students stay in for recess, she replied that she was unwilling to give up her own free time to supervise these students. Her reasoning was, 'Why should I have to pay a penalty when it wasn't me who was out of line?'"

A few days later, a frustrated Leah complained to another teacher, Tom Martin. "What am I doing wrong? Joyce ignores my pleas to stop talking during the lesson. I followed Pierre's advice, but Andrew only smirks." Leah Cooper was not blind. She observed students mimicking her warnings and stopping just short of making faces at her. Leah told Tom Martin, "I'm at my wit's end."

Tom Martin confided to me that he didn't know what else to suggest except that Leah talk to me. He assured her that I would help her in any way I could.

So I sat through both Grade 8 classes, occupying a desk much too small and observing Leah's French lessons. My "help" meant occupying this desk every day for two periods to assist with classroom management.

A few days later, I received a phone call from a normally supportive parent. "Good day, Mr. Franklin. I'm calling to express my concern about an assignment in Mrs. Cooper's French class. The students have been asked to write, in the French language, a 100-word summary describing a trip that they have enjoyed with their family. I really think that is unreasonable! Could you look into the matter?"

When I invited Leah Cooper into my office to discuss the assignment, she bluntly replied, "If the class had been paying any attention at all, they would have no difficulty completing the work." I suggested that she review the criteria for the assignment, consider adapting the requirements to meet the needs of the class and telephone the parent.

Leah was livid. "If I don't have the right to develop my own class work, why am I here at all?" She continued to vent her feelings. "I'm sure other schools don't have these kinds of problems. Maybe I should take a position back in the city and get out of this small town where country bumpkins and their parents seem to run the show!"

After a few more outbursts, Leah looked up from her tissue, wiped her eyes again and apologized, "I'm so sorry, Mr. Franklin. I will follow your instructions to the letter." She hurried out of my office. I breathed a sigh of relief.

The next day, the regular Grade 8 teacher, George, sat in the room at the back of his class completing his student evaluations during Leah's French lesson. He was astounded when he heard her explain, in a broken, stuttering voice, that due to the complaint of a parent, the assignment had been reduced to 50 words. She added sarcastically, "Surely this class is capable of doing that."

Laughter and boisterous cajoling went on for the remainder of the period, until George couldn't bear to see the French teacher humiliated any longer. He stood up, glared at the students, and asked them to take out their assignments and work quietly. Leah Cooper rushed from the room, mumbling under her breath between sobs.

Leah Cooper did not make it to her next class.

The following morning my principal commented, "We really must do something to help Leah Cooper when you're not here to supervise her classes." A meeting with Leah was set for four o'clock that afternoon.

The principal, Leah and I gathered in the meeting room. There wasn't much discussion. There were no flippant comments about the community and there were no more exasperated cries about the loss of her teaching creativity. The principal expressed our commitment to Leah that the school administration would continue providing support for her classroom management.

I grudgingly continued to sit in on the classes with Leah Cooper and the Grade 8 students. I also tried to suggest positive remedies and teaching strategies. I even recommended that she use French-language comic books to bring a little humour and fun into her lessons. She was as dry as a pine forest in August. The kids groaned at her attempts to win them over. We planned telephone conversations to enrich their oral French. The first time she tried this activity I left the classroom for a few minutes and returned to discover the students talking in English to friends on their cellphones. The worst part was that she hadn't even noticed!

Finally, April arrived. Madame Lafarge, our regular French teacher, resumed her duties. The Grade 8 classes returned to normal for the remainder of the school year.

Imagine our concern, however, when the following September, Madame Lafarge told us that she would be on leave from January until the end of June that school year. A long-term occasional position for teaching French at our school was advertised. The only applicant was Leah Cooper.

PROFESSIONAL INQUIRY

The Professional Inquiry section is intended to support reflection, dialogue and the development of new understanding and insights. Engagement in the following processes can occur individually or collaboratively with colleagues. These processes are designed to facilitate new or revised interpretations of the leadership experience described in the case An Occasional Dilemma. This additional knowledge may guide the subsequent leadership actions, thinking and decisions of the reader.

Values

1. Compare the principal's and the vice-principal's strategies for communicating to Leah Cooper that she was a valued member of the school community.

2. Explore the role of professional trust and respect in this case.

Professional Identity

1. Identify the possible impact of the various influences on the professional identity of Leah Cooper using the following framework:

Professional Identity	
Influences	Impact on Professional Identity
Public comments made about her practice by colleagues	
The vice-principal's perception of Leah	
Responses of learners to Leah's teaching	
Responses of parents to Leah's teaching	

Professional Responsibilities

1. Describe the vice-principal's professional responsibilities related to this case.

2. Identify and discuss the professional responsibilities of other teachers toward their colleague (Leah) and toward students in this case.

Decision Making

1. Critique the actions and decisions employed by the vice-principal using the following framework:

Actions/Decisions	Critique

Ethical Awareness and Knowledge

1. Analyze and discuss the level of ethical awareness and knowledge demonstrated by participants in this case using the following framework:

Ethical Awareness and Knowledge			
Case Participants	Limited Ethical Awareness and Knowledge	Moderate Ethical Awareness and Knowledge	High Ethical Awareness and Knowledge
George			
Vice-principal			
Pierre Foucault			
Tom Martin			

CASE COMMENTARY CRITIQUE

1. Read the commentary(ies) written about the case.

2. Record your reflections regarding the commentary(ies) using the framework below:

   a. Identify the key points, perspectives or issues in the commentary.

   b. Analyze the key points, perspectives or issues identified in the commentary.

   c. List the new insights you gained from the commentary.

Commentary Critique			
Case Commentary Writer	Identification *What key points, perspectives or issues are identified in the commentary?*	Analysis *What is your analysis of the perspectives identified in the commentary?*	Synthesis *What new insights have you gained from the commentary?*

CASE COMMENTARIES

CASE COMMENTARY 1

Case: An Occasional Dilemma

Lindy Zaretsky

Superintendent of Instructional Services, K–12 and Leadership,
Simcoe County District School Board

This case explores the consequences of a vice-principal's attempts to support an occasional teacher's understanding of what makes effective teaching and learning possible with adolescent learners in core French classes. It examines the professional challenges for school administrators and teachers as they confront what are fundamentally social and critical questions. These questions involve issues of effective performance, authentic engagement with students and colleagues, critical connections between professional learning structures and cultures within a school, and authentic coaching and mentoring embedded within new teacher induction programs. Education issues such as the one presented here cannot be adequately addressed or understood by practitioners and scholars in merely technical how-to solutions. School leaders are articulating significant tensions associated with ethical dilemmas of practice that nevertheless require definitive responses from them. The aim here is to contribute further to healthy deliberations that are defined by identity politics, collective norms, and moreover, by the profession.

I am applying a multi-dimensional paradigmatic framework (Starratt, 2003) with which to approach the particular dilemma of practice confronting the vice-principal and principal. They must decide whether to re-hire the occasional teacher, Leah Cooper, as the sole applicant, to the same position as core French teacher in which she apparently demonstrated less than adequate performance. In his seminal work on building an ethical school, Starratt (2003) identifies three interdependent ethics: the ethics of critique, justice and care. The ethic of critique involves challenging the status quo by asking questions that look toward the removal of barriers to fairness. It involves the critiquing of policies, practices and structures that might be advantaging some over others. The ethic of justice has us interrogate critical issues of fairness and equal treatment. The ethic of care demands the preservation of the dignity of each individual and the valuing of uniqueness and diversity. The ethic of the profession, introduced by Shapiro and Stefkovich (2005), has indicators placing students' best interests at the forefront. The ethic of community (Furman, 2004) centres the community over the individual as the moral agent.

Ethic of Justice

Whitmore (2002) refers to coaching as a means of unlocking individuals' potential to maximize their own performance. It helps them to learn as opposed to teaching them. Lipton, Wellman and Humbard (2002) talk about learning-focused interaction with planning, problem solving and reflective conversations as part of this coaching activity. The vice-principal and principal need to more effectively support the teacher by helping her to learn how to provide evidence of goal setting, the planning of next steps, and reflection and assessment of her own learning as well as her students' learning. The school administrators need to guide her in setting high yet achievable expectations. This will assist in the identification of learning outcomes that are broader than a lesson or unit, developing action plans, prioritizing tasks, and identifying resources for achieving the goals. They should be enlisting the support of other staff within and beyond their school (and certainly beyond the other French teacher in the school, although this is a beginning!). The vice-principal and principal must reflect together on the links they might be trying to build in their school between professional learning structures and cultures. They must also consider the mentoring/coaching activity and structures of a new teacher induction program, in which this occasional teacher could and should be participating, and from which she would without a doubt profit!

Ethic of Care

It is apparent that Leah Cooper has had many varied professional experiences that have shaped her person and who she is as a professional, yet it appears that neither the administrators nor the teaching staff have made any significant attempt to get to know her. We have only heard about the disrespectful dialogue in which some staff members engaged and that Leah overheard. However, what do we really know about this person outside of a perceived lack of personality and humour, and an inability to manage a classroom of adolescents? The staff should be getting to know more than just her overt weaknesses. What are her strengths and talents as a person and a professional? With this knowledge in hand, staff can support her much more effectively in improving her teaching and management skills. It is also essential that greater value be placed on the role of the French teacher if students, teachers and parents are to view French as a valuable and valued academic subject. It may be that greater valuing of her role might lead to greater valuing of her person.

Ethic of Critique

The school district as a whole must be committed to improving instruction through the provision of more intensive and ongoing professional development for French teachers. The research suggests that French teachers feel undervalued as "specialist literacy" teachers, which in fact, by virtue of their professional training, they are – and they need to be recognized for their expertise. Many French teachers believe that many others view them as "prep relievers" and not as literacy specialists in a core area of the academic curriculum. Moreover, a significant number do not perceive themselves to be part of any teaching team or professional learning community within the school or across schools. If schools are to attract and retain French teachers, it is critical that French teachers view themselves as valued and valuable contributors to improving student achievement in literacy and the learning of an additional language. There needs to be a more integrated and co-ordinated leadership team approach at both the system and school levels in order to advance this particular agenda.

Ethic of the Profession

With respect to this case, we need to consider both the students' learning as well as the individual rights of this occasional teacher. The teaching of core French to students in Grades 7 and 8 has often been thought of as a near-impossible task. Because of the emphasis on the oral component in the second-language classroom, the teacher must find new and innovative ways to remain faithful to the goal of communicative and experiential teaching while keeping in mind the curriculum and the adolescent learner. New teachers cannot do this alone, nor should they be expected to! Furthermore, classroom management cannot be separated from effective teaching practice. Effective teaching practice is most certainly a blend of targeted teaching methodologies and interventions alongside classroom management practices that together create a positive teaching and learning environment. Teachers need to create classroom climates that serve to re-engage an increasingly diverse and disengaged student body that is finding the current curriculum irrelevant to their lives and identities. When students are actively engaged in learning that meets their interests and individual needs, classroom management may not appear to be as much of an issue. Effective classroom management is much more complex than having a fixed set of classroom expectations and consequences, as suggested by the other French teacher in this case. In fact, elements of effective classroom management are threaded throughout all the domains in the more formal teacher-performance appraisal system in Ontario.

If French teachers are to be respected and valued as teachers, then they also need to become active participants in cross-curricular literacy initiatives. They need to be provided with professional learning opportunities that heighten their own and their colleagues' sensitivity to learning differences in the FSL classroom and support them with practical strategies to meet individualized needs. There are a significant number of appropriate, language-rich resources and technologies on literacy instruction and assessment in French that could be explored. Through such a targeted intervention approach, the school administrators would more effectively be able to monitor improvement, not only in teaching performance, but in teacher satisfaction as well as student attitude, engagement and achievement in French. This particular teacher may also wish to incorporate suggestions into an annual learning plan or create a growth/improvement plan to target areas of strength and improvement.

Ethic of the Community

There is no strategy for classroom management that will overcome student behaviour problems if the teacher is not well prepared to provide an engaging program that welcomes each student's active participation based on their needs and strengths. The development of authentic partnerships with students, other teachers and parents is also critical to the success of this teacher. School administrators and their staff need to explore ways (through assemblies, parent evenings, literacy events, student and school council meetings, and so on) to highlight the importance and relevance of learning another language. There is no mention of this type of school activity. Moreover, there is little evidence presented that the vice-principal and principal have established a sense of a professional learning site where there is commitment to supporting one another in situating themselves as co-learners and partners in this process. More specifically, this type of connectivity to a professional learning community requires ongoing nego-tiation in shared planning around interventions to re-engage learners in meaningful and purposeful learning. In his description of authentic teach-ing and learning, Starratt describes this type of interactive learning as:

> … involving an explorer in a foreign land. The explorer has to learn her/his way in a much more dialogical fashion, taking time to listen to the inhabit-ants of the foreign land, acquire their language, let their customs speak to him of their values, slowly infer the patterns of their relationships with one another and with their environment. In this dialogical relationship, the intel-ligibility inherent in the evidence talks back to the explorer's intelligence (Starratt, 2006, p. 7).

This also implies that the school leadership needs to model the valu-ing of the nurturing of relationships that focus on such interactive pro-cesses. Given that all of these professional learning processes and structures have been put into place to support *all* teachers' learning and growth, and there is still no evidence of growth over a considerable period of time for Leah Cooper, it may be in her best interests as well as the best interests of the students that she reconsider the teaching profession as the right one for her.

CASE COMMENTARY 2

Case: An Occasional Dilemma

James Heap
Dean, Faculty of Education, Brock University

I see this as a case about the transformation of the teaching profession and its anchoring value, responsibility. From the watershed of the 1968 Hall-Dennis Report in Ontario, through to the founding of the Ontario College of Teachers in 1997 and the establishment of Ontario's *Ethical Standards for the Teaching Profession* (Ontario College of Teachers, 2006a) and *Standards of Practice for the Teaching Profession* (Ontario College of Teachers, 2006c) we have seen a move from the teaching profession as a focus on silo performers to a focus on teachers as co-performers in com-munities of practice. With this move, the sense of responsibility in the profession shifts.

When teaching is seen as a silo performance, the teacher can be said to be "on stage" when she/he is in front of the class (in the silo). The staff room is "back stage," a place where performers rest, relax and prepare for their next solo/silo performance. Back stage is also where criticism and mentoring occur. Within the context of teaching as a siloed performance, only department heads and administrators have responsibility for mentoring. Administrators, like the vice-principal, are interlopers back stage, allowed, and some times set up, to overhear things, like complaints about Leah. For the teacher who is now an administrator, a visit to the staff room can produce reminders that the administrator is always on stage.

With the development of what I'll call communitarian professionalism, the nature and lines of responsibility change, as in the ethical standards. When the ethical standards are juxtaposed with the standards of practice, we see that the responsibility of the teacher is not only to the students, for their learning, but to other teachers within learning communities. Indeed, we see that leadership is expected of teachers in learning communities.

Applying the leadership frames formulated by Bolman and Deal (2003), we see that the profession is redefining the structural responsibility of teachers. Putting the structural frame of roles and the human-resource frame of employment policies together in the context of communitarian professionalism, we see that the standards of practice apply to occasional teachers, and therefore to the members of the learning communities that they join (if only on an occasional basis). This means that George, Ken and the other teachers in the staff room can now be expected to mentor and support a newcomer like Leah, no matter what her employment status is. Not to do so has political and symbolic consequences for how they and the school will be seen and judged in relation to the standards of practice. The staff room is no longer back stage. It is a secondary stage; whoever is there can be taken to be on stage and available to co-perform, for example, to mentor.

In this new scheme of professionalism Mr. Franklin, the VP, is expected to carry out the usual activities of a silo supervisor, but now he's a curriculum leader. Within the scheme of communitarian professionalism, Mr. Franklin has a right to expect that teachers will exercise leadership (take responsibility) to acculturate and mentor occasional teachers like Leah into school learning communities.

What about Leah? She's faced dilemmas in two prior professional careers, and now faces another one as she seeks another OT position at Main Street Elementary. If she reflects on the first standard, "Commitment to Students and Student Learning," will she rethink her application?

Can you see how the dilemma for the administrative team at Main Street – about whether to rehire Leah – is actually reduced, if only the administrators orient to the standards of practice rather than to silo management?

CASE COMMENTARY 3

Case: An Occasional Dilemma

Jules Rocque
Professor, Collège universitaire de Saint-Boniface

My thoughts concerning action the vice-principal might consider are identified in this commentary. Of course, a case presents only some of the components of a situation, therefore the possible actions taken by the vice-principal may vary depending on the specific content.

Comments in the Staff Room

If the vice-principal can identify the person who made the "whispered" remark, he should meet privately with that person right away to go over the facts, refer to the ethical standards and, if needed, emphasize the policies, bylaws and administrative guidelines that refer to teachers' professional obligations. There is no need for a reprimand, especially if this is the first time, but this is an opportunity to emphasize the importance of having respect for everyone affected by the remark and to review professional obligations. If the vice-principal himself did not overhear the person making the remark but was told about it by someone else, he should still proceed in the same manner, calling the person into his office and letting her/him know what he has been told. He could begin by saying, "I have been told that you made a remark about Ms. Cooper in the staff room at such-and-such a time, concerning such-and-such. I would like to go over the incident with you."

Since George provoked the incident with his comment, the vice-principal should also broach the matter with him, in the manner suggested above.

Since other staff members were in the staff room at the time the comments were made, not to mention Ms. Cooper herself, the vice-principal should review the incident with the principal, who could take the opportunity – at a staff meeting, for instance – to review the administrative expectations and ethical standards with all staff. The principal could emphasize desired behaviour in the staff room, thereby avoiding any awkward situations in the future.

The vice-principal must also provide follow-up by speaking with Ms. Cooper. Since she appears to be dealing with several challenges, the vice-principal needs to be empathetic while informing her about the planned follow-up concerning the comments (as suggested above). It is important to discuss only the follow-up at this meeting, making an appointment with her at a later date to discuss the matter of possible support in the classroom. Discussing the matter in the hallway outside the staff room immediately after the incident is neither the right place nor the right time.

"An ounce of prevention is worth a pound of cure!" Setting out the expectations of the administrative team at the beginning of the year concerning appropriate conversation in the staff room will probably cut down on the number of such incidents. That said, the reality of human nature is such that a principal must always manage behaviour and cannot turn a blind eye to such situations.

REFLECTION ON THE COMMENTARIES

The commentaries address concepts such as ethical standards, the ethic of care, the ethic of justice, the ethic of critique, the ethic of the profession, the ethic of the community and a principal's responsibility to act. Contemplate the meaning of these concepts for your own professional practice.

ADDITIONAL READING

Northwest Regional Educational Laboratory (NWREL). (2005). *Leadership practices of successful principals: Retaining strong leaders.* Portland, OR: Author.

Findings from NWREL's 2004 Regional Needs Assessment survey suggest that a high percentage of principals do not have the time or resources to handle the leadership roles and responsibilities presented to them. This article offers supportive suggestions, including increased collaboration with school staff and the community, and the implementation of leadership training programs.

Schultz, B. (2005). Finally a superintendent: Now what? *School Administrator,* 62(6), 10–13.

Encountering unexpected hazards while running a school system made the author reflect on measures that a superintendent might consider: Be ready to take decisive action, make the local education system work, communicate potential concerns, control and build trust by empowerment, learn from previous mistakes, and be a reflective, lifelong learner. These calls to action in schools or districts are groundwork for effective administrators.

CASE 12

Samantha

"This is not the end of things!" exclaimed Samantha as she stormed down the hall, clutching her performance appraisal. Her outburst marked the culmination of a challenging school year.

This had been my first year as principal. It had also been my first experience as an administrator working with a hard-to-place teacher.

I had heard the name Samantha Davis in June, prior to my arrival at Blue Lake School as principal. Samantha had applied for the Senior Kindergarten position at the school. I called Brian, one of my vice-principal colleagues who had worked with her, and mentioned that Samantha Davis had applied for a teaching position at my new school. There was a long silence. Finally, Brian calmly said, "Perhaps you might want to ask the human resources department if there were any other applicants."

I set up a meeting with my superintendent and two human-resource staff members. After a long and at times difficult discussion, Samantha was assigned to Blue Lake for September. The superintendent had asked for my co-operation and support regarding this experienced but hard-to-place, teacher. He ended the meeting by saying, "Keep me posted and be sure to carry out a performance appraisal for Mrs. Davis prior to the end of the next school year."

On June 28th, just prior to my first meeting with the teachers at Blue Lake School. I sat down at my desk and read my first telephone message. The school secretary had neatly written out Samantha's recorded message:

"Unable to attend orientation meeting this afternoon. See you in August."

I decided to begin a documentation file for Samantha Davis even before the school year began. The message was the first item to be put in her file. Entry two went in on August 14th. It was another telephone message left at my home number: "Going on vacation. See you on the first day of school."

Samantha did arrive the first day of school on September 3rd. Her kindergarten children began arriving the same day. Her classroom walls and bulletin boards were bare. There were boxes everywhere. I realized that the documentation file was likely going to become thicker as time went on.

In spite of my concerns, I decided to wait until the end of September to meet with Samantha officially. This would give her time to become comfortable with her students and adjust to her new school. In the interim, I was determined to keep a close eye on her. Several times, I intended to talk to her informally during her planning time, but it was often difficult to find her. When I asked her about this, she said, "Oh, I was in the storage room and didn't hear your page," or "Sorry, I had to pop out to get some lunch." She always had an excuse.

Toward the end of September, the Junior Kindergarten teacher summoned me impatiently at the end of the day. "Just look at the tricycles and scooters strewn in the hallway. Someone is going to trip over them." I knew they were all from Samantha's classroom. When I found Samantha she said, "They must have been left there by one of the education assistants using the equipment for the students with special needs."

I questioned the Special Education assistant about the tricycles and scooters. "No, I didn't use them," she said. "We haven't used them with the students with special needs." I made another entry in Samantha's file.

The following week, the vice-principal discovered Samantha's Senior Kindergarten class watching a movie in the library with only a lunchroom supervisor present. Samantha was working on her report cards in the computer room. She sputtered, "Well, it was only for a few minutes. I really have to get my work done, you know." He curtly responded, "That's what your planning time is for. Your responsibility right now is to be with your students." She just shrugged and continued working on her report cards.

The vice-principal and I recorded this incident and added it to Samantha's growing file. We decided it was time to initiate Samantha's formal performance appraisal process. We reviewed our calendars and determined a number of potential dates for the initial meetings with Samantha, as well as three classroom observation sessions.

During one of the meetings, I asked Samantha to identify areas for her professional growth. She paused and then replied, "Well, I can't really think of any areas for growth. I guess I could join more committees. That's about it."

During the process, I provided her with many documented examples of her absence from class during instruction time. A record of her excuses accompanied each incident. "I was just walking down the hallway … I was getting a snack in the staff room … I was helping a Grade 2 student look for his lost coat … I was talking to the caretaker in the foyer." The list went on.

I reminded her of the report card incident. She didn't see anything wrong with abandoning her class during scheduled instructional time. The issue with her report cards, however, did not end there.

Samantha, like most staff members, needed to make adjustments to the comments on her student report cards. After reviewing her set of report cards, I attached detailed instructions and examples that she could use to improve the comments. She also needed to correct a number of spelling errors and to write the comments in complete sentences. I explained that comments like, "Serena did a poor job in math" provided insufficient detail. I had given all staff a written set of expectations for both the content and the format of student report cards. Samantha's effort did not even come close.

Samantha returned the report cards to me in record time. I hoped for the best. However, there was little evidence of substantive changes. She had made spelling corrections on a handful of reports. I hurried down to her room.

As I spoke to her about her lack of attention to my request for changes, her body tensed and she curtly responded, "I made the corrections. There must be a computer problem."

I decided to follow up. Many calls and visits to the central-office computer services department revealed that Samantha had not, in fact, made any changes other than the few spelling corrections. I firmly informed her, "I have verified that there have been no technical difficulties that would have had an effect on your report cards." I began to explain again my expectations for school report cards. She just rolled her eyes. I felt ready to explode.

One of the more compassionate teachers on staff spent the afternoon working with Samantha. At the end of the day, I had a note from Samantha that said, "Your reports are done." I was lucky to have a supportive colleague like Beth, who had taken the time and initiative to work with Samantha Davis. I made a mental note to write Beth a word of appreciation.

In June, at a meeting with Samantha regarding her performance appraisal, I detailed my concerns and outlined my expectations for her growth during the following year. She responded vehemently, "The appraisal is unfair and also unsubstantiated." She refused to sign her performance appraisal report.

This was the last day of school. I turned off my office light for the summer. I hoped that Samantha would reflect on her year at the school and return in September prepared to meet the expectations outlined in her performance appraisal.

When September began again with fresh, smiling faces, I looked forward to a better year with Samantha Davis. Hope quickly faded. Staff and parents brought new concerns to my attention.

Throughout all of the challenges with Samantha over the past year, the staff had demonstrated support over and over again. They did their utmost to take her under their wing. They planned with her, shared their resources, worked late to provide mentoring, and accommodated her requests for assistance. Now, in late September, the staff had reached a breaking point.

The day before, Samantha had declared in the staff room, "I hope someone knows how to use an EpiPen because I brought a peanut butter sandwich for lunch. You all know how allergic that new student Alex is."

The vice-principal ran into my office, exclaiming, "Samantha has gone too far this time!" He recounted the story. I knew he was right.

I went to speak with Samantha immediately. She turned red and retorted, "Can't they take a joke? Who ratted on me? They had to know I was just kidding. People get offended so easily! What a closed clique. They have never accepted me. No wonder you continue to check on me and believe their gossip." I stressed that such humour was neither appropriate nor appreciated. Samantha pouted and mumbled something under her breath. After that, she began avoiding the staff room.

Complaints from parents were surfacing daily in spite of Blue Lake School's reticent and generally complacent parent community. Within a period of one week, two parents contacted me to express concerns regarding Samantha's treatment of their children and her classroom management. One parent, Ms. Allen, brought one of our kindergarten students into my office at lunchtime, claiming that Samantha had abandoned her in the playground. As usual, Samantha was nowhere to be found.

Ms. Allen also noticed that, while volunteering in the classroom, students often argued over supplies and toys while Mrs. Davis worked at her desk. There was pushing and name-calling, and supplies were left all over the floor. Ever apologetic, Ms. Allen commented, "I don't want to get Mrs. Davis in trouble, but one of these children might get hurt."

Another parent volunteer, Mrs. Emerson, noticed a child hitting her son, Shawn. Trying to stay out of it, she watched Shawn push the other boy away. All Samantha saw was the end of the altercation. She sent Shawn for a time out without allowing him to explain what had happened. She then consoled the child who had been hitting Shawn.

Mrs. Emerson spoke to me about the incident. I asked Samantha to join us in my office. Unruffled, Samantha said to Mrs. Emerson, "You just observed one incident. You should be here every day. Shawn gets himself into trouble on a regular basis. If he didn't start it this time, he's been the instigator on numerous occasions. In fact, I think Shawn might have psychological problems. I don't think he's ready for school, either. Perhaps it isn't such a good idea for you to be volunteering in my classroom."

Mrs. Emerson was shocked and offended. I assured Mrs. Emerson that I would look further into the situation.

Negative parental input continued to pour in. When I raised the subject with Samantha, she retorted angrily, "What do you expect me to do? The class is large and there are behaviour problems. Some of the kids aren't ready for school. I need help. I can't do it on my own." Some of

Samantha's explanations and complaints were, I must admit, at least partly justified.

Samantha returned the next day, demanding, "You really have to provide assistance for me. You need to get another teacher or at least an education assistant. My friend is a teacher and she has an education assistant because her class is large."

I assured Samantha that I would speak to the superintendent but added, "However, Samantha, you are going to have to learn the skills necessary for dealing with a large kindergarten class with challenging students." I offered to contact the primary consultant and arrange for Samantha to have help with her classroom management skills.

Initially, she refused. Samantha said, "I've been teaching primary students for 15 years. I don't need to be observed or helped." I explained that the consultant could provide her with a wealth of ideas and resources. Samantha grudgingly agreed to no more than one demonstration lesson. "I'm totally fed up with all these intrusions and check-ups on my teaching," she yelled.

She stormed out of my office. I pulled out my documentation file and dialled the superintendent's telephone number.

PROFESSIONAL INQUIRY

The Professional Inquiry section is intended to support reflection, dialogue and the development of new understanding and insights. Engagement in the following processes can occur individually or collaboratively with colleagues. These processes are designed to facilitate new or revised interpretations of the leadership experience described in the case Samantha. This additional knowledge may guide the subsequent leadership actions, thinking and decisions of the reader.

Professional Identity

1. Describe Samantha's professional identity and efficacy as an educator.

2. Describe the principal's professional identity and efficacy as an educator.

3. Identify factors that may have influenced or shaped the professional identity of both the principal and Samantha.

Responsibilities

1. Identify and discuss the responsibilities the principal, vice-principal and Samantha display toward teaching and learning within this school context.

2. Critique the ways in which the principal, vice-principal and Samantha enact their professional responsibilities as educators.

Decision Making

1. Analyze the decisions the principal made prior to meeting Samantha.

2. Identify the assumptions and values that might have guided the initial decisions the principal made regarding Samantha.

3. Critique the subsequent decisions the principal made in response to Samantha during the first and second school years.

Relationships

1. Consider Samantha's relationships in the school community from the perspectives of empathy, care, trust, respect, authenticity and presence. What insights can be gained about the situation from these perspectives?

2. Review Samantha's relationships with her students, colleagues and supervisors. Isolate relational factors that could be considered in the construction of a plan to support teachers who are experiencing similar challenges in their profession.

Professionalism

1. Reflect on the role of the principal and vice-principal as models of professionalism. Analyze their actions and decisions from this perspective.

2. Explain the possible impact of both the principal's and vice-principal's observable actions on the culture of this school.

3. Develop a professional growth plan for the principal in this case.

CASE COMMENTARY CRITIQUE

1. Read the commentary(ies) written about the case.

2. Record your reflections regarding the commentary(ies) using the framework below:

   a. Identify the key points, perspectives or issues in the commentary.

   b. Analyze the key points, perspectives or issues identified in the commentary.

   c. List the new insights you gained from the commentary.

Commentary Critique			
Case Commentary Writer	Identification *What key points, perspectives or issues are identified in the commentary?*	Analysis *What is your analysis of the perspectives identified in the commentary?*	Synthesis *What new insights have you gained from the commentary?*

CASE COMMENTARIES

CASE COMMENTARY 1

Case: Samantha

Richard Shields
Teacher, Hamilton-Wentworth Catholic District School Board
and Sessional Lecturer in Education and Ethics,
University of St. Michael's College and McMaster University

Clearly, Samantha presents serious challenges. Her outsider persona sends a "stay away" message that makes meaningful communication difficult. Samantha's professional behaviour suggests an indifference to students' learning and safety, and disinterest in the staff community. It raises questions about her ability and willingness to practise according to the *Ethical Standards for the Teaching Profession* (Ontario College of Teachers, 2006a) and the *Standards of Practice for the Teaching Profession* (Ontario College of Teachers, 2006c). It is difficult not to ask, "Should Samantha be a teacher?"

If effective learning environments and professional communities of teacher practice are the goals, education requires leaders who understand and enact their ethical responsibilities. The responsibility facing the principal is daunting. She/he must lead – set a course that not only manages a situation effectively, but also embodies and models ethical relations among colleagues, students and the community. The pressure to perform effectively can be stressful to a new principal, especially when one teacher's attitude and practice seem to threaten that goal.

It is curious that Samantha has remained in the school system, given the concerns about her performance. Is she someone who doesn't belong in the profession? Has she been adequately mentored, supervised and supported? Ethical leadership strives for a big-picture perspective. It acknowledges, as much as reasonably possible, the role that betrayals, failures or losses in the career or personal life of this "hard to place" teacher play in her performance.

How can the ethical standards of *Integrity, Trust, Care* and *Respect* guide the principal's actions?

Integrity requires that the principal recognize the ethical demands of the situation and define for herself the appropriate ways to approach Samantha. Instead of letting Samantha set and control the terms of (non-)

encounter, integrity informs choices that avoid the reactive escalation of frustration described in the story.

How does *Trust*, which supports fairness, openness and honesty in our professional relationships, inform the principal's decisions and actions? Was the principal's professional relationship with Samantha compromised by the prior phone calls? Has the process begun on a false note, putting the reputation before the person? The principal acknowledges that Samantha's presence in her school evokes feelings of uneasiness and a concern that Samantha will present problems for the administration. Honest reflection on how those feelings might influence her/his relationship to Samantha seems like a necessary condition for building trust.

Given the difficulty of the situation and the principal's need to act decisively, one still must ask how building a case against an already weak colleague will contribute to a good outcome. The value of *Care* calls for a commitment to Samantha's well-being. Instead, mechanisms of control seem to determine the approach taken. Considering Samantha's history, the issue seems larger than the incidents cited. And the kinds of help offered are more apt for documenting failure than enabling success.

The value of *Respect* can also inform the principal's actions. How would the story unfold if the principal had told the teacher from the start that she/he was compiling a documentation file and carrying out a performance appraisal prior to the end of the school year? How does withholding that information honour Samantha's dignity? A frank discussion of why the principal wants to follow this formal process and the possible consequences for Samantha would be painful, perhaps, but solid evidence of willingness to build a relationship based on respect.

Samantha is a human being, a colleague, and a professional, whose attitude and behaviours raise questions about her suitability for the teaching profession. She is a woman with a career that has somehow gone off the tracks. Documenting what is already known and repeating the need to do what she is already not doing may be a good way to get rid of her. However, it does not seem compassionate. Nor does it offer probable roads to professional improvement. And that does not seem just.

Although the case study focuses on the principal's relation to Samantha, responsibility to students, staff and community are never far from the centre of what is happening. Teachers have an obligation to build a school community imbued with care, respect, trust, and integrity. Supporting or confronting an underperforming colleague requires prudence and courage.

Protecting students and fostering learning in a difficult situation poses an ethical challenge to staff. Samantha is not just a problem for the principal.

The *Ethical Standards for the Teaching Profession* (Ontario College of Teachers, 2006a) can guide and support a principal on the journey to becoming a strong ethical leader. Living the ethical standards is not simply an individual responsibility, and teaching is participation in a profession, a shared practice. Learning to lead will be easier when the principal sees the ethical standards as lived values, animating the school community and embodied in the actions and attitudes of superintendents and school staff.

CASE COMMENTARY 2

Case: Samantha

Michel Saint-Germain
Professor of School Administration, Faculty of Education,
University of Ottawa

This case study highlights three key aspects: selective perception, integration into a new school, and difficult personalities.

From the outset, the principal defines her/himself as an administrator, and this informs the management approach she/he will take. The principal's call to Brian initiates a process of selective perception: she already has a negative perception of Samantha, as proven by the fact that before even meeting her, she/he is already trying to get rid of her, after a long and tedious discussion with a superintendent and two HR employees. Selective perception, a perceptual error, is a tendency to discriminate in favour of an interpretation of reality that corresponds to what we ourselves believe to be true, leading us to see only those aspects that confirm our belief. On the other hand, it is normal for a principal to inquire about new staff members who are joining the school – in order to find out how to approach them and welcome them, and not be surprised by their behaviour. This begs an ethical question: what chance do new staff members have if the information that is obtained, which is context-dependent, paints an unflattering picture? This is the case with Samantha.

The missed meeting on June 28 is a catalyst that prompts the principal to open a file before even meeting Samantha. Given that the school year was not yet over for teachers, might Samantha have had a meeting at her own school as well on June 28, which prevented her from attending the meeting at Blue Lake? Or might she have had to "close up" her classroom or pick up her materials?

The incident on August 14 is telling. Samantha, who (surprisingly) has the principal's home phone number, tells her that she will be at the school on the day classes resume. This point must be dealt with from a legal perspective. If a date for the start of school is set out in the collective agreement or a board policy, Samantha is at fault and the principal must place an official memorandum in her record (including salary or any other implications). The principal, however, did not contact her concerning this matter after the call on August 14, even to leave a message on her voice mail or send a letter. The process of selective perception is again evident when the principal correlates the untidiness in the hallway with the fact that the "documentation record seems to be expanding *rapidly* (my emphasis)." This is a self-fulfilling prophecy.

Samantha's welcome at the school poses the problem of the integration of an experienced new teacher into a school. In spite of Brian's warnings, the missed meeting on June 28 and the lack of preparation for the start of the school year, the principal does not meet formally with Samantha until late September. During the month of September, Samantha had to "fly by the seat of her pants" to set up her classroom routines. There was clearly no integration or welcome, either because the principal was afraid of a confrontation with Samantha or because she/he wanted to watch her acting "freely" so as to get an idea of her potential and initiative. In view of Samantha's actions, it would have been better to set the tone as soon as school started by giving her some guidance at that time.

Samantha appears to be someone who ascribes external causes to her actions and refuses to take responsibility for them: excuses for failing to meet with the principal, excuses about the tricycles, excuses concerning the report cards and spelling, a refusal to sign her performance appraisal. She is not aware of the consequences of her actions, especially in the way she manages her classroom. In addition, she is unresponsive to the help she is offered by others, such as the principal, colleagues and parents. She is incapable of assessing her behaviour in accordance with the standards of practice for the teaching profession.

A distinction needs to be made between idiosyncrasies (individual ways of doing things that are related to personality and an individual's theory of teaching) and professional misconduct. This case includes both.

Samantha undoubtedly has her own way of responding to authority. She can be insubordinate without being unlawful, but she commits illegal actions (a collective agreement is a legal document) by her refusal to report to the school at the beginning of the year, by leaving her class unsupervised, and by failing to supervise students. Disciplinary action should have been taken against her during the school year for her disobedience, especially to the vice-principal, who reminds her that she is responsible for her students.

The principal and vice-principal did not know how to be firm at the outset, so the situation got worse. The principal appears more concerned with her/his documentation file than with taking concerted steps that would have gone beyond attempts to meet informally about Samantha's planning times. She/he was probably ill-equipped to deal with this type of personality.

Since Samantha has alienated both parents and colleagues, she clearly cannot stay either at the school or in the teaching profession.

CASE COMMENTARY 3

Case: Samantha

Tom Russell
Professor, Faculty of Education, Queen's University

The story of Samantha poses several significant challenges for the thoughtful reader seeking to learn from the ethical dilemmas raised by this case. My biggest challenge involves understanding how adults could persist for so long, apparently caught up in the same highly unproductive patterns of behaviour. At the outset, we learn that the superintendent of human resources and many others are aware that Samantha Davis is a "hard to place" teacher; the superintendent seems to be asking the principal for a favour. The superintendent also asks for a performance appraisal in the coming year, but we never see the superintendent playing a constructive role later in this case.

Samantha's complex patterns of behaviour begin with messages that she is unable to attend an end-of-year meeting in June and a start-of-year meeting in August. When Samantha does arrive on the first day of school, the principal's reported thought focuses on anticipation of documenting a large number of problems over the school year. Does it ring true that one would wait until the end of September to meet officially with

Samantha? My personal concern is that waiting provides Samantha with a period of time in which to become accustomed both to pretending that her reputation has not preceded her and to operating on her own without clear indication of what is expected of all teachers in the school.

Samantha is hard to find during planning time and always has excuses. Problems arise and there are more excuses. Never is there any indication of a firm expectation being declared. Then formal appraisal begins. The principal is ready to explode over the issue of comments on report cards, but is this a productive response? Another teacher helps to resolve the report card problem, but this is hardly a strategy for resolving what appears to be a long-term personnel problem.

The first year ends with disagreement over Samantha's performance appraisal and reference to expectations for Samantha's growth in the coming year. Why would any of these behaviour patterns be cast as a problem of growth? A year has gone by and there has been no involvement of the superintendent or representatives of the teachers' federation. In the second year, predictably, more problems arise as parents and teachers alike experience frustrations. Near the end of this case, when the primary consultant is to be called in to assist Samantha, the issue is largely unrelated to the patterns of behaviour that form the heart of this professional dilemma.

While it is difficult to give credence to Samantha's behaviours as those of a teacher with 15 years of experience, I elected to side with Samantha in the preceding comments because there never seems to be a moment when issues are put to her clearly and directly. How can a principal expect to bring about changes in a professional's behaviour without being clear and explicit and without turning to external consultation? Hope and platitudes are not enough. What is the value of building a file of documentation if it only serves to confirm that there are problems? How did more than a year pass without involving the superintendent and representatives of the federation? As incredible as Samantha's behaviours and excuses may be, the behaviours of the principal are even less credible.

REFLECTION ON THE COMMENTARIES

The commentaries reveal alternative perspectives regarding the responsibilities of both the principal and the teacher in this case. The issues raised in the commentaries invite reflection on induction processes and the principles that guide these practices. Reflect on your own experiences supporting the induction of educators new to a school. Consider how well your experiences modelled a collective responsibility and shared practice toward induction.

ADDITIONAL READING

Euvrard, G. (2006). The values manifesto project. Namibian students ponder which values are worthy of their fledgling democracy. *Educational Leadership, 63*(8), 43–46.

A project called Values Manifesto was launched after its pilot success within a teacher education program. Students in Grades 1 to 12 participated in discussions regarding what values were most important to them. The author discusses the values identified by the students and the positive changes and long-term effects that occurred in the classroom and in the teachers' professional lives after the study was completed.

Knapp, M. S., Copland, M. A., & Talbert, J. (2003). *Leading for learning: Reflective tools for school and district leaders.* Seattle, WA: Centre for the Study of Teaching and Policy.

This well-organized article is based on published and ongoing research. Storytelling is used to provide a context for the reader. The authors supply tools to enhance student learning.

Leithwood, K., Seashore, K., Anderson, S., & Wahlstorm, K. (2004). *Review of research: How leadership influences student learning.* University of Minnesota: Center for Applied Research and Educational Improvement.

This report is the first in a series that seeks to establish how leadership promotes student achievement and to summarize the basics of successful leadership. The author discusses three leadership strategies: setting a clear vision, supporting and developing a talented staff, and building a solid organizational structure to meet the challenge of school reform.

Reyes, P., & Wagstaff, L. (2005). How does leadership promote successful teaching and learning for diverse students? In W.A. Firestone & C. Riehl (Eds.), *A new agenda for research in educational leadership* (pp. 101–118). New York, NY: Teachers College Press.

The authors examine how shifts in diversity are perceived in society. As diversity increases in schools across the United States, in terms of race, gender, physical ability, age and religion, schools find they must consider and set new student boundaries. The article focuses on the difficulty that educators have in teaching such a diverse student population.

SECTION V

Leaders as Educational Partners

LEADERS AS EDUCATIONAL PARTNERS

The important role educators play as educational partners is an essential ingredient of effective school leadership. Developing positive relationships with all members of a community significantly contributes to the optimization of student learning and success. Effective school leaders develop partnerships through employing inclusionary practices, implementing transparent communication and decision making approaches, modelling communal processes (Furman, 2004), and consistently embodying ethically guided actions.

CASES FROM PROFESSIONAL PRACTICE

The two cases in the section illustrate the importance of relational encounters based on trust, transparency and mutual respect between parents and educators. Effective partnerships are developed when the diverse voices and perspectives of all partners are authentically included, heard and understood. The cases invite reflection regarding the role of parents in the education of their children; the role of communication; the importance of a shared vision regarding the role of the school; and the implications of a vision of education that enables the voice of test scores to dominate, to silence the voices of learners and parents, and to shape the actions of educators.

> ### Cases
> #### Blindsided
> #### The School Supper Club

CASE COMMENTARIES

The case commentaries in this section are written by educational scholars in the fields of ethics, leadership, case methods, narrative and teacher education. In the first case, Blindsided, the commentators identify that the teachers acted in the best interests of Billy, the learner. Despite the efficacy of the teachers in this case, the limited government funding of schools and an overly dominant focus on test scores tragically impacts Billy's future and the future of many other students with similar life experiences and learning profiles.

The second case, The School Supper Club, is viewed differently by each commentator. The commentators' diverse perspectives, reactions and understanding invite considerable dialogue and critique. Issues discussed by the commentators include leadership models, the transition of a vice-principal to principal in the same school, the difference between a conflict and an ethical issue, discrepancies in expectations and outcomes between the school and the parent community and the impact of working conditions on teachers' ability to endlessly respond to community requests.

Commentaries

Blindsided

Cheryl J. Craig

Carolyn Shields

Pam Bishop

Anne Phelan

The School Supper Club

Robert Stake and A. Rae Clementz

Vivienne Collinson

Linda Grant

Laura C. Jones

CASE 13

Blindsided

Even on the calmest days, you never know what surprises will challenge your expertise.

Today is a bright June afternoon during my third year as principal of Jones Street School. The school population is made up of about 500 students from Junior Kindergarten to Grade 8. The school is located in an older, established area of the city. The building is a little worn in appearance but the feeling inside radiates the school motto of "tradition, school spirit and excellence."

This year is providing me with numerous challenges that tap my repertoire of knowledge, skills and values. I continually strive to meet the combined needs of students, staff and parents. The last three years have presented me with many opportunities for personal growth. I sometimes wonder if I have made the right decisions, but I try to make choices that uphold my professional and personal ethics and values.

Today, everything is going well and it feels good to be a leader at one of the more challenging schools in Elmville. I breathe a sigh of relief that the last Special Education Identification Placement Review Committee (IPRC) meeting will soon be over. I feel reinforced by the fact that my team at this school is confident, relaxed and supportive of students who are being identified for special programs. The earlier IPRC meetings have gone like clockwork. I expect this last one will be the same.

It is 2:15 in the afternoon. The yearly IPRC review is slated to start for Billy McGee. He is a red-haired 14-year-old Grade 8 student previously identified as intellectually challenged in the area of language. I am delighted to note, however, that this relatively mature young man has had a fairly good year.

I recall Billy's first day at Jones Street School. He was a stocky 11-year-old who caught my attention when I saw a tear in the corner of his eye. The tear, I thought, was probably due to his trepidation at entering yet another new school in his short life as a student. But slowly, he made friends. He joined the Scrabble club. He developed confidence in both his spelling and his courses. In Grade 7, Billy grew like a beanpole and became a star player on the school's basketball and track teams. In Grade 8, his accomplishments continued. Maybe it was being selected as vice-president of the student council that launched Billy into possibly his best year yet. He was proud of himself and I championed his success in both the social and the academic arenas.

Suddenly, my silent reminiscing is over. The click of a binder signals the start of the meeting. The IPRC meeting involves Mrs. Miller, Billy's classroom teacher, Mr. Olsen, the Special Education resource teacher, Billy's mother, a single parent who works out of town, Billy's aunt with whom Billy resides, and myself, as principal.

After a brief review of last year's minutes, Mrs. Miller lists Billy's strengths over the course of the year. Mrs. Miller is as meticulous in her classroom as she is in her appearance. She is observant, careful and precise in the way she has documented Billy's progress. She comments that Billy is extremely co-operative. He often stays after school to clean blackboards and distribute materials for class use the next day. Mrs. Miller is exacting, thorough and thoughtful as she describes Billy's achievements in her classroom. She also highlights Billy's burgeoning confidence and how he has taken a more active role in small group discussions. Now, she says, he even presents orally to the entire class. This would have been unheard of in early September.

"His assignments are always completed on time, despite frequent errors in spelling and grammar," says Mrs. Miller. She comments that Billy's participation in class is still limited, but that he continues to improve. She reads from his report card: "While his oral expression has seen some improvement, his word-decoding skills, spelling and grammar need constant monitoring. He is presently on a modified spelling and reading program."

She continues on to add that subjects such as social studies and science do give Billy extra anxiety. She explains that she must make minor modifications to content and allow for some accommodations with regard to the work that is assigned to Billy. She adds, "I believe that Billy has demonstrated success that is consistent with his Individual Education Plan."

Mrs. Miller concludes her presentation. "Billy is working very well in class and he appears to be doing his best. However, he will require constant monitoring with respect to oral and written work next year in secondary school. Overall, however, I am satisfied with his progress." She ends by smiling, unable to conceal the fact that she is very proud of Billy's success.

We all listen intently. There is silence. No questions are asked. This surprises me because I'm accustomed to parental requests for clarification or a personal desire on a parent's part to build on or extol the successes of their offspring. But Mrs. McGee says not a word. I cannot read her face.

I follow protocol and continue on. I thank Mrs. Miller for her comments and the work she has done with Billy's program. Billy's teachers nod and acknowledge one another. They share a moment of pride in his accomplishments.

Unexpectedly, Mrs. McGee suggests that we revisit Billy's report card to review his marks over the school year. She points out that he displayed consistent progress, with all his grade averages in the mid 50 to mid 60 per cent range, with the exception of the 44 per cent in French. She points out that the marks were consistent over the year in spite of comments such as, "Billy shows steady progress" and "Billy appears to be putting forth his best effort." I realize that Mrs. McGee's focus is on the grades, not the comments.

Mrs. McGee asks a few questions about Billy's Individual Education Plan. Then, suddenly, she remarks, "I'm not sure if you are aware, but in September Billy will be moving with me to Ironwood, 90 minutes west of Elmville. He will have a fresh start at the new school in Ironwood."

I thank Mrs. McGee for this information. I wonder what is on her mind. I tell her that I personally know the principal in the new school and would be glad to communicate with him directly. Still unsure about her tone, I try to be supportive. "Don't worry, Mrs. McGee, the principal at the new school and I will be in contact as soon as Billy's records are transferred."

Mr. Olsen, the Special Education teacher, must also feel some tension in the air because he states emphatically, "Billy has grown over the past two years. I know that he's not at grade level yet, but his work habits have improved and his self-image has blossomed." Determined to reassure Mrs. McGee, he explains, "Billy sees me in the morning before class when he has a test in social studies or science and feels that he needs specific help." Mr. Olsen reiterates Billy's achievements, but balances them with the reality of Billy's daily support by adding, "Although great strides have been made, careful monitoring and strategic intervention in specific subjects are necessary to continue to build on his present successes."

Again, I thank all participants for their comments. I begin to summarize the discussions and suggest a potential transition plan for Billy to his new school situation. Mrs. McGee interrupts me. I stop speaking. I listen to Billy's mother.

Mrs. McGee begins to describe Billy's early years of schooling and reflects that it was in Grade 3 that her son began to experience difficulty. She mentions that his teacher at that time had noticed "language" issues. However, neither the Grade 3 teacher nor the principal at the time were willing to fail Billy.

Mrs. McGee continues, "Now, here he is in Grade 8 not able to do Grade 8 work. If he can't do Grade 8, he will most certainly not be able to do Grade 9 work. Therefore, I do not want Billy to pass. I want him to fail Grade 8." Mrs. McGee is adamant. She goes on to add, "Billy will be moving to a new community with me over the summer. There, no one will know Billy. He can have a fresh start and he can use next year to catch up on all the work that he has missed."

The teachers' eyes freeze on me, begging for a response.

I am speechless. What should I say? How do I support my staff? How do I respond to Mrs. McGee? What is in the best interests of the student? My mind races as I search for the right thing to say to this parent.

I stall for a few minutes by paraphrasing the meeting discussions. I review all the comments made by the committee and by Mrs. McGee. I remind Mrs. McGee that Billy is doing his best. I also add that we felt that to fail Billy at this time might have long-lasting negative effects on his self-image and on his achievement in the future. I assure Mrs. McGee that we would recommend a modified program for Billy next year and that our staff will be in close contact with his new high school to ensure that Billy's transition is a smooth one.

I want desperately for Billy's mother to really hear the progress that he has made and not insist on her plan to keep him in Grade 8. I want her to build on the strides Billy has made this year.

My colleagues all nod their heads in agreement. However, my fears are realized. Calmly, Mrs. McGee reaffirms her position. "I do not agree with your recommendations. I want Billy to fail and repeat Grade 8. That is final."

PROFESSIONAL INQUIRY

The Professional Inquiry section is intended to support reflection, dialogue and the development of new understanding and insights. Engagement in the following processes can occur individually or collaboratively with colleagues. The processes are designed to support the creation of new or revised interpretations of the leadership experience described in the case Blindsided. This additional knowledge may guide the subsequent leadership actions, thinking and decisions of the reader.

Vision

1. Describe the principal's vision of educational leadership.

2. Assess the perspectives that each case participant had regarding Billy.

Case Participant	Perspectives of Billy
Classroom teacher	
Mr. Olsen (Special Education teacher)	
Principal	

Case Participant	Perspectives of Billy
Billy's mother	
Billy's aunt	

Leadership Practice

1. Discuss the ways in which formal meetings designed to enhance student learning and empower students and families can fail to meet goals.

2. Critique the ways in which the members of this school team enacted their practice in a collaborative, inclusive, caring and just manner.

Instructional Leadership

1. Analyze the demonstrations of instructional leadership revealed in the practices of the classroom teacher, Special Education resource teacher and principal.

Professional Knowledge

1. Identify the forms of professional knowledge apparent in the practices of the educators in this case.

2. Develop a professional growth plan for each of the educators.

Ethical Practice

1. Assess the level of ethical practice embodied by each educator.

Educational Partnerships

1. Critique the principal's ability to be an authentic partner in responding to the best interests of Billy.

2. Analyze the classroom teacher's (Mrs. Miller's) and the Special Education resource teacher's (Mr. Olsen's) ability to be authentic educational partners in responding to the best interests of Billy.

3. Describe the ways in which Billy and his mother are *positioned* in this case.

4. Identify the impact of *power, position* and *influence* in this case scenario.

Reflective Practice

1. Reflect on your own professional practice and share a case in which students' and parents' voices and perspectives were not *privileged* in the education conversations and decision making.

2. Identify insights you gained about your own education leadership by examining the thoughts, feelings and actions you experienced in that situation.

CASE COMMENTARY CRITIQUE

1. Read the commentary(ies) written about the case.

2. Record your reflections regarding the commentary(ies) using the framework below:

   a. Identify the key points, perspectives or issues in the commentary.

   b. Analyze the key points, perspectives or issues identified in the commentary.

   c. List the new insights you gained from the commentary.

Commentary Critique			
Case Commentary Writer	**Identification** *What key points, perspectives or issues are identified in the commentary?*	**Analysis** *What is your analysis of the perspectives identified in the commentary?*	**Synthesis** *What new insights have you gained from the commentary?*

CASE COMMENTARIES

CASE COMMENTARY 1

Case: Blindsided

Cheryl J. Craig

Professor and Co-ordinator of the Teaching and Teacher Education
Program, University of Houston

When I read this case, three thoughts immediately struck me: one
having to do with each of the parties/perspectives gathered around the
table, although some individuals were present whose voices were not
heard.

One reflection concerned Mrs. Miller, Billy's classroom teacher, and
Mr. Olsen, the Special Education resource teacher, who had obviously
worked hard to assist eighth-grader, Billy McGee. They clearly had taken
their *in loco parentis* roles seriously and had acted in the child's best interests, as a parent or principal caretaker would do. I could only imagine
their chagrin when their recognition of Billy's significant growth was
seemingly ignored by Mrs. McGee, who chose to privilege academic
achievement understood in terms of test scores above all other indicators
of growth.

This brings me to my second reflection. It is easy to cast Mrs. McGee,
the parent, in a villain role in this case, particularly since Billy is not living
with her but with an aunt who is present at the meeting, yet remains
strangely silent. After all, Mrs. McGee is not quietly accepting of the
professional opinions offered her, nor does she engage in helpful discussion
that would shed light on Billy's situation. In fact, she appears to hold the
school at fault because the comments on Billy's report card do not reflect
the grades he received. This was presumably because the anecdotal comments assessed Billy's growth in relation to his Individual Education Plan,
whereas the marks Billy was assigned had to do with the grade-level standard set by the province and his achievement compared to that of all other
eighth-grade students.

However, when I stepped back from the case, I wondered, "Was Mrs.
McGee a villain? A victim? Both? Neither?" Peeling back layers, it seemed
to me that she was only giving back to the educators the dominant story
of schooling, the one commonly understood by all members of society.
This was a plot line that had shaped the course of her life and one she

knew would ultimately shape her child's life, particularly since Billy was about to enter secondary school. Knowing that story and her son's difficulties with language, she knew Billy needed to conform to its plot lines. Thinking of her son's future and society's expectations of him, she felt she needed – as a caring parent – to bring forward the age-old story that test scores matter above all else because test scores can be used to compare the achievement of one student to that of another.

Thinking of Mrs. McGee's response also caused me to think of parent education. If teachers such as Mrs. Miller and Mr. Olsen and principals such as the one narrating this case want parents like Mrs. McGee and the public in general, for example Billy's aunt, to know other versions of academic excellence besides the test-score version, awakenings to the broad plot lines of these alternate versions of schooling most certainly need to happen in face-to-face meetings when the stakes are not so high, roles not so clearly demarcated, and the spotlight not turned on one's own child who has already been deemed deficit by virtue of the kind of meeting that has been called. For Mrs. McGee and Billy, the deck appears already stacked against them. And was not Mrs. McGee's move to another community and school a way to restore her family unit and an attempt to carve a fresh start for Billy and for her? But, was it not also her way of letting the Jones Street educators know that she was indeed awake to the dominant story of schooling and that she knew the perils of those who did not pay attention to it?

Then, I thought about the third perspective, that of the principal/narrator of the case and his sense of helplessness in dealing with the complexities that arose in the meeting. Clearly, his desire was to make everything right for everyone involved, particularly Billy, although Billy was not given the opportunity to participate in the meeting. Most certainly, the principal was attentive to the responses of Mrs. McGee and the teachers involved. But when Mrs. McGee became concerned about growth and achievement understood only in numerical terms, she took the script of the Identification Placement Review Committee meeting off course. Her statements added new twists and vulnerabilities to the situation. Not only was her child perceived as failing, his teachers understood as failing him (through academic achievement as narrowly defined) and the parent as failing her child (because she had not parented him right/given him the right genes/was not presently living with him, or whatever), the principal was now failing in the meeting because he could not meet everyone's needs and interests in a manner expected of principals in their leadership roles.

This would be doubly true if he felt his gender role concurrently urging him to arrive at a definitive ruling as the father figure in the school. When Mrs. McGee used power to mask her powerlessness, she challenged the teachers – but even more so the principal – to use power, which would also reveal his sense of powerlessness, which was palpable in this case.

I can only imagine how defeated everyone around the table must have felt that particular day with each person attempting to find another – or the school generally – at fault. Just below the surface, however, the academic horse race of education understood only in the language of test scores continued on, potentially losing yet another child well in advance of the finish line.

CASE COMMENTARY 2

Case: Blindsided

Carolyn Shields
Professor of Leadership, Department of Educational Organization and Leadership, University of Illinois at Urbana-Champaign

This case raises a number of important questions about the purposes of education and how we communicate them to members of our school communities. In this instance, Billy had gained self-confidence and the respect of his peers, although he still struggled academically. Nevertheless, the goals and perceptions of Billy's mother and the educators in his school came into conflict. The case thus raises the question of who has the right to make a final education decision in a democratic society. What is the role of expertise and are there boundaries to parental choice? Moreover, how do we resolve conflicts to accomplish what all parties clearly desire: the best outcome for the child?

As I reflected on the case meeting, I wondered how it might have been possible to better communicate Billy's strengths, to emphasize the wider education goals of citizenship, and to explain how the school could continue to support him as he made the transition to high school. To what extent must the school take responsibility for his mother's single-minded focus on test scores and grades? How can we promote a more complete and complex understanding of achievement, learning, and growth? The question does not simply relate to Billy's case but to all children whose parents (for many reasons, perhaps related to student ability/disability or to elements of cultural background such race, class, ethnicity, language (

religion) may hold values that seem inconsistent or incompatible with those of the school. Who decides and on what basis?

Perhaps most important in this case is the desire on the part of Billy's mother to have him held back — and this at a time when his adolescent development might be most harmed by such a decision. Do Billy's consistent grades really indicate a lack of progress or are there alternate possible interpretations? In other words, what do the grades really mean? How can we communicate that research indicates that retention rarely promotes increased learning, but often has a detrimental impact? Billy's school attendance had been good, he had been learning to take responsibility for his learning; and he had been exerting considerable effort, despite some challenges. How can educators assist his mother to understand that retention may negatively affect his new-found self-confidence and that changing to a new school will not really mitigate the impact for Billy?

Here, the teachers were silent, begging the principal to intervene. Despite the element of surprise in this case, might it have been possible for the principal to have helped them, through the year, to develop the skills to engage in dialogue with Billy's mother? The educators listened to her and then tried to convince her of their perspective; might a more meaningful dialogue have promoted deeper understanding? Could dialogue among the staff throughout the year have led to a different focus and different kinds of reporting that did not create the dichotomy between civic responsibility and academic achievement? Indeed, could the principal have facilitated a wider dialogue about the democratic purposes of education with the parent community and the students as well?

Here, the case clearly illustrates some of the detrimental effects of a narrow focus on tests and grades to the exclusion of other social, emotional and citizenship goals and raises the critically important question of the role of educators in helping the public to understand both the multiple goals of education and the complex constructions of success required for participation in a democratic society.

CASE COMMENTARY 3

Case: Blindsided

Pam Bishop
Associate Professor and Co-ordinator of Educational Leadership, Graduate Division of Educational Research, Faculty of Education, University of Calgary

In this case, the conflict between Mrs. McGee and the principal and teachers at Jones Street School ultimately turns to the issue of whether Billy will (or will not) fail and repeat Grade 8.

Neither course of action is ideal for Billy. If he has to repeat Grade 8, it is likely to come as an unwelcome, bewildering shock to him. Yet, if he is to simply proceed into successive grades in the next few years, it is likely he will struggle with much of his learning.

However, given the circumstances, the mother's right to decide her son's grade (at Ironwood school) should be privileged over the Jones Street school's stance on the matter. The individuals most involved and/or likely to be affected in this situation are Billy, Mrs. McGee, Billy's aunt, Mrs Miller, Mr Olsen, and the principal at Jones Street School.

Mrs. McGee's decision should be respected and implemented by the principal at Jones Street School. Were Mrs. McGee a mother who had considerable social and cultural capital, she, as a parent, may resort to a higher authority to ensure that Billy is able to repeat Grade 8.

The Jones Street principal and teachers should provide the Ironwood school with a detailed brief about this decision plus Billy's education needs, qualities, interests and achievements. The principal should explain to Mrs. McGee that, on the basis of experience and evidence, the decision is unlikely to achieve what she hopes it will.

Notably for Mrs. McGee, a former principal and teacher refused to allow Billy to repeat Grade 3. In Mrs. McGee's view, that decision has played a role in Billy's present learning difficulties. Thus, she now trusts her conclusion about what should be done (to help Billy) ahead of the current principal's and teachers' views. That Mrs. McGee's decision came as a surprise to the principal and teachers suggests there may have been insufficient communication between school and home.

The impressive efforts of Mrs. Miller and Mr. Olsen in particular should be acknowledged by the Jones Street principal, preferably in the presence of Billy's mother and in a later debriefing with those teachers. Mrs. Miller and Mr. Olsen's care and commitment to Billy have contributed to his social and education progress. Both teachers would likely be distressed by Mrs. McGee's demand, and fear the consequences for Billy. The principal could (and should) attempt to convince Mrs. McGee to change her decision, but the time for that to be effective seems to have passed.

Sadly, given the strong link between socio-economic status and student outcomes across the western world, and the demographic factors of Billy's family, plus his history of schooling, it is unlikely that he will dramatically improve academically in subsequent grade levels.

The Jones Street principal and teachers should not accept an unreasonable degree of responsibility for Billy's lack of social and academic progress. Despite the efficacy of Billy's teachers, schools such as Jones Street are ultimately limited in the support they can provide due to funding. If governments are unwilling to fund schools in ways that enable principals and teachers to properly attend to the experiences and needs of students from high-poverty backgrounds, the core responsibility must rest there. Tragically, Billy and disproportionate numbers of students like him from materially poor backgrounds will not prosper as they might while schools are so inadequately funded.

Reference

Canadian Psychological Association. (2001). *Guidelines for professional practice for school psychologists.* Retrieved February 26 2008 from, http://www.cpa. ca/documents/PsyTest.html.

CASE COMMENTARY 4

Case: Blindsided

Anne Phelan
Associate Professor, Department of Curriculum and Pedagogy
and Research Associate, Centre for the Study of Teacher Education,
University of British Columbia

Upon reading this case I was immediately returned to the dictionary to check my understanding of the word "blindsided." I learned that the term is often used in sports to describe how a player might be attacked "from the blind side," surprised and put at a disadvantage. I wondered at the negativity of the term, positing something to be avoided at all costs. I wondered about the use of the term in an education context. Why would educators think of being surprised as something to be avoided? Why would educators expect or hope that all would go "like clockwork"? When did a craving for predictability begin to shape encounters among students, teachers and parents? When did education become so uneventful?

Education, as lived in the institution of school, emerges in this case as a site of struggle between at least two sets of values. Ms. McGee's focus is on her son's grades rather than teachers' qualitative comments. She correctly points out the apparent inconsistency between the teachers' claim of progress and Billy's consistent achievement level of 50–60 per cent, with the exception of 44 per cent in French. Put simply, Billy is "not at grade level," and that he should repeat Grade 8 in order to "catch up" appears as an inescapable matter of logic. Consistent with the practices of the institution, Ms. McGee engages in determinative judgment – she uses predetermined criteria, reflected in ministry guidelines, to adjudicate her son's progress compared to that of other students at his grade level.

The teachers, on the other hand, although immersed in ministerial mandates themselves, engage in reflective judgment – they resist the application of generalized criteria and share their qualitative understanding of a particular child. As such, the teachers emphasize the growth of Billy's social skills: "extremely cooperative ... stays after school to clean blackboards and distribute materials for class use the next day ... self confidence" (evidenced by his more active role in small group discussions and oral presentations to the whole class, and his rise to vice-president of the student organization) and "diligence" (assignments completed on time). While the teachers mention Billy's ongoing challenges with language (frequent errors in spelling and grammar), social studies and science, they are taking measures (Billy is on a modified spelling and reading program) and they believe that he is progressing.

But how can Ms. McGee take her son's teachers seriously? How can the teachers persuade Ms. McGee to trust their point of view? All are caught in an education system that embraces the concept of normal distribution. The emphasis on "common curricula, homogeneous classrooms, uniform teaching methods, age-appropriate routines, and standardized achievement testing" rests on the assumption of a "normal child," and "all of them contribute to the entrenchment of that assumption within educational structures" (Davis, Sumara & Luce-Kapler, 2007, p. 46). This, of course, renders any attempt at counter-normative thinking difficult. The teachers' appreciation of individual progress and their attempts to create spaces for difference are always set against and within a normalizing discourse that drowns out that difference.

The principal seems curiously uncritical about the sense of normativity that pervades the struggle between teacher and parent. Confident that the teachers are "supportive of students," the principal assumes that all will go "like clockwork" in the IPRC meeting. The meaning of being "supportive" is hardly transparent or straightforward, however. The principal confronts a plurality of thought embodied in parents and teachers. Education encounters cannot proceed with the unvarying regularity of a clock; they always have the potential to unsettle. The promise of the teacher-parent interaction is its potential to redirect everyone's attention toward the very values that stage their encounter – normalization. A different kind of conversation can emerge as a result, one that refuses to dwell only on questions of how we can reach a particular end (meeting Grade 8 expectations) but invites questions about why that end is what we should aim for at all.

REFLECTION ON THE COMMENTARIES

The commentaries raise issues regarding the purpose of education and the significance of social justice. Craig suggests that testing can become the dominant story of schooling. Consider how educational leaders can help to collaboratively develop alternative narratives in schools so that social justice and teaching and learning that are democratic and holistic become the dominant story of schooling.

ADDITIONAL READING

Hord, S. (1997). Professional learning communities: What are they and why are they important? *Issues ...about Change,* 6(1).

This short article describes attributes of professional learning communities. It is organized under five headings: supportive and shared leadership, collective creativity, shared values and vision, supportive conditions, and shared personal practice. The author discusses possible outcomes for students and staff that might result from successfully creating professional learning communities.

Kochan, F. K., & Reed, C. J. (2005). Collaborative leadership, community building, and democracy in public education. In F.W. English (Ed.), *The Sage handbook of educational leadership: Advances in theory, research, and practice* (pp. 68–83). Thousand Oaks, CA: Sage Publications.

The authors suggest that leadership in schools should resemble a collaborative and democratic model. They examine school leadership trends with a focus on the disassociation of schools and the public. Through a review of literature, four ways in which collaborative leadership can be fostered emerge for discussion. These concern the role of values, issues of power, organizational factors and transcendent leadership.

Leithwood, K., Jantzi, D., & Steinbach, R. (1999). *Changing leadership for changing times*. Buckingham, PA: Open University Press.

This book's main focus is the success of schools in a changing world. The authors present a variety of leadership styles that might be effective when attempting to maintain or sustain education systems during constantly changing times. Their theories are informed by a long-term study on transformational leadership.

Maxwell, J. C. (2003). *There's no such thing as "business" ethics: There's only one rule for making decisions*. New York, NY: Warner Books.

Stories and examples from business, sports and government show that the Golden Rule can be applied to any difficult decision or situation. The author discusses the five most common reasons why people compromise their ethics and presents the many benefits, such as increased employee morale, of applying the Golden Rule.

Pellicer, L. (2003). *Caring enough to lead: How reflective thought leads to moral leadership* (2nd ed.). Thousand Oaks, CA: Corwin Press.

Concepts of leadership are illustrated by a series of questions, short vignettes, selected quotations and stories. The authors provide reflections at the end of each chapter to invite the readers to assess the meaning of leadership.

CASE 14

The School Supper Club

I knew that trouble was brewing. I remembered exactly what Rita Davidson, the council chairperson, had said at the meeting tonight.

"The reason we hold this dinner every year is so that the school staff and the community can help raise funds for the parish to build its own church. We've done this since the first year the school opened. Every year, fewer teachers are involved in the planning. Now hardly any of them even bother to attend. As principal, can't you do something about this?"

It was true. Many parents were disappointed about the lack of teacher involvement. The parish was currently working out of the local high school. The funds raised during this annual dinner went directly into the building fund for a new church. Parents viewed this event as an opportunity for the community and the school staff to work together for the well-being of the parish.

I realize that staff participation in community events outside of the regular school day is voluntary. Mrs. Davidson, and many other parents, feel differently. "It's the duty of teachers to support this event. They should all be there as part of their job," she exclaimed earlier this evening. Heads nodded around the council meeting table. All eyes turned toward me, silently asking, "What are you going to do about this?"

Our school community is a cross-section of subsidized housing and wealthy homes. The council members tend to be middle class. Most have served since the school's opening 11 years ago. The continuity on council is often a benefit because of the camaraderie established among members and the ease with which items are addressed.

At times, however, the council functions as a closed group, with little room for new ideas and spontaneity. In retrospect, I think it would have been a valuable exercise for the council to have deliberately encouraged new membership over time.

Eleven years ago, I attended the first fundraising dinner as the school vice-principal. During the first few years, a large contingent of staff eagerly participated in all fundraisers. We were a new school in a newly established area and there was a great deal of enthusiasm on the part of students, staff and parents. For several years, this annual dinner was the most successful strategy we had for building community partnerships. As well, the dinner allowed the school to make a significant contribution to the parish church building fund. The speeches, the laughter and the mingling of staff and parents created many positive memories. The community loved the fact that our students always waited tables at the event. The students were really motivated by the camaraderie between home and school. We were like a big family planning and celebrating an important stage in our life.

The school and community have faced numerous challenges. Most recently, the teachers have been required to implement new curriculum with minimal resources. They have worried about presenting this curriculum without enough time and professional development to master the content and teaching expectations. Teachers and support staff feel pressured and overworked. It saddens me to see that there is little understanding or compassion on the part of our community. Parents just don't seem to understand the impact that this curriculum is having on their children, educators at all levels and the education system as a whole.

During the same time that teachers were expected to deal with these curriculum changes, the population of the school ballooned to nearly 1,000 students. This rapid increase in numbers necessitated the placement of 23 portable classrooms on the school site to house the additional students.

In the midst of this whirlwind of change, during the middle of the school's seventh year of operation, I was asked to return to the school as principal. The previous principal, who had served the school for the first seven years, was an admired and respected educator. He was an outstanding professional and an effective administrator. Parents really liked him.

This tight little community, however, still seemed to view me as the vice-principal with whom they had worked years earlier. I was really getting tired of hearing, "That's not the way it was done in the past." These words seemed to lurk in the hallways and whisper to me whenever I took charge of a challenging situation.

These weren't the only problems I faced. Our 23 portable classrooms had to be inspected for mould, and those that were found to be contaminated had to be rebuilt. This meant that, on a monthly basis, portable classrooms were being relocated to the main school building. The repeated relocations necessitated the use of the library and gym for full-time classroom use. Staff members packed and unpacked entire classrooms. We had to count books, post new schedules, search for misplaced articles of children's clothing and check regularly for dangerous construction sites. It was a nightmare.

Things got worse. In September, the year after my return, we faced another disruption. The school population was split and two schools were housed in our one building. The new school would be ready for occupation in January. I was grateful that the other principal in the building was a generous and accommodating person. We worked well as a team and tried hard to minimize the disruption for the students and staff.

That summer, after half of the 1,000 students had relocated to their new school, construction began on a new addition to our school. The constant stop and start of renovation and construction added to the already full workload of the students, staff and administration. Somehow we managed.

This school community had dealt successfully with a number of changes and challenges in quick succession over a short period of time. I was proud that, during this difficult period, we experienced a steady increase in student test scores. In addition, athletic teams continued to win, place or show in the many sports events at the junior and the intermediate levels. The tone of the school stayed positive. Our motto during these stressful times remained, "What really matters is how we treat one another."

It was therefore a shock for me at the council meeting to hear staff members criticized for their apparent lack of support for the fundraising dinner. I was most disappointed in the comments made by the chairperson of the council meeting.

The following morning I held a staff meeting. I began the meeting by saying, "At the school council meeting, parents publicly expressed their disappointment at the low level of staff participation for the annual fund-raising dinner." I shared Mrs. Davidson's comments verbatim. I added, "I want you to know that I appreciate all the extra time and effort that you have given to our students and the school community. This effort has been particularly evident throughout the many changes that we have experienced during recent years. I have reminded the council members about your dedication and explained to them that your participation in a fundraising dinner is purely voluntary."

That night, I received an e-mail from Mrs. Davidson, the council chairperson, complaining that my meeting with the staff had been inflammatory and that she had been misquoted. Mrs. Davidson's e-mail included negative personal comments about me. She specifically mentioned my lack of integrity.

I sent a reply. "Could we please meet and develop a plan to address our difference of opinion." I wanted to heal this rift quickly.

Two weeks went by before we were able to meet. Mrs. Davidson maintained that parents just wanted to work together with staff for the common good of our students. I again reminded her that events such as the fundraising dinner were extracurricular. My final comment on the matter was, "Staff members view attendance at the dinner as an invitation, not an expectation."

I hoped that Mrs. Davidson and other members of the community would come to understand that the entire staff had been giving all they had to give. I wanted the chairperson to look at the broader picture in terms of what the staff had already volunteered.

The issue about staff attendance at the dinner seemed to die a natural death. However, in the aftermath, I definitely felt that the level of trust that we had built over the years was damaged. The relationship between Rita Davidson and myself was never the same. Perhaps she still thought of me as the vice-principal. Maybe she resented my strong support for the school staff. At least the school stand on staff participation in extracurricular activities was now clear.

PROFESSIONAL INQUIRY

The Professional Inquiry section is intended to support reflection, dialogue and the development of new understanding and insights. Engagement in the following processes can occur individually or collaboratively with colleagues. The processes are designed to support the creation of new or revised interpretations of the leadership experience described in the case The School Supper Club. This additional knowledge may guide the subsequent leadership actions, thinking and decisions of the reader.

Reading and Reflecting on the Case

1. Record the facts, issues/dilemmas, leadership style and ethical responsibilities of the educational leaders in this case using the following framework:

Case Reflection			
Facts of the Case *What are the pertinent facts of this case?*	**Issues/Dilemmas** *What issues or dilemmas are apparent in this case?*	**Leadership Style** *What leadership qualities, knowledge, skills and practices are evident in this case?*	**Ethical Responsibilities** *What are the moral and ethical responsibilities of the educational leader in this case?*

School Councils

1. Identify strategies to help foster a shared understanding of the role of a school council in contributing to the enhancement of the school and respecting teachers' autonomy.

2. Discuss the importance and benefits of having a plan for including new membership on a school council.

3. Explore the role and responsibilities principals have toward both teachers and school councils.

4. Identify characteristics that illustrate and contribute to authentic educational partnerships. Use the following framework to record the characteristics:

Characteristics of Authentic Partnerships
•
•
•
•

Working Conditions

1. Identify and analyze the possible impact of the working conditions teachers were exposed to in this school community. Use the following framework to record your analysis:

Working Conditions	Impact on Teaching and Learning

2. Critique the responsibilities the principal and the school district had regarding the conditions the teachers and learners were exposed to in this school. Use the following framework to record your thoughts:

Responsibilities	
Principal Responsibilities	**School District Responsibilities**

Professional Identity

1. Explore the professional identity of the principal in this case.

2. Consider the variety of perspectives presented in this case (teachers, parents, administration and students).

3. Analyze the factors that appear to influence the ongoing formation of the principal's professional identity.

CASE COMMENTARY CRITIQUE

1. Read the commentary(ies) written about the case.

2. Record your reflections regarding the commentary(ies) using the framework below:

   a. Identify the key points, perspectives or issues in the commentary.

   b. Analyze the key points, perspectives or issues identified in the commentary.

   c. List the new insights you gained from the commentary.

Commentary Critique			
Case Commentary Writer	**Identification** *What key points, perspectives or issues are identified in the commentary?*	**Analysis** *What is your analysis of the perspectives identified in the commentary?*	**Synthesis** *What new insights have you gained from the commentary?*

CASE COMMENTARIES

CASE COMMENTARY 1

Case: The School Supper Club

Robert Stake
Director of the Center for Instructional Research and Curriculum
Evaluation, University of Illinois at Urbana-Champaign

A. Rae Clementz
Doctoral candidate, Educational Psychology Department,
University of Illinois

Some Administrative Problems Are Not Ethical Problems

Ethical conflict is less often a matter of code violation or personal
discord; it is more often a choice between conflicting principles. This case
described a dispute between a principal and council chairwoman over the
obligation of school faculty to participate in an annual dinner to raise
funds for a new church. This is not intrinsically an ethical issue.

As narrator, the principal described being in a pickle. In short, the
chairwoman had expressed a need for the faculty to help with the fundraiser, with the opinion that "they should all be there as part of their job."
The principal conveyed that opinion to the faculty, assuring them that
they were free to participate or not. When the chairwoman expressed anger
at the principal's lack of support, they met and worked through the disagreement.

Instructional case studies are regularly incomplete. Their purpose is
to describe briefly a situation and focus on an issue. Their authors do not
want the reader to be bogged down in detail. But details are often important. Moreover, the clearest fact in this situation is that the facts are unclear.
The story is told by only one person. We hear the chairwoman's position
only from the principal. We hear, from her/him, that other council members felt the same, and that faculty members felt unappreciated and over-
burdened. The conflict centres around faculty obligation, but we do not
learn how members of the faculty responded. We do not know what in
their contracts might have obligated them to participate. We do not know
if their prior participation in the dinner and other events might have
established a precedent to continue. We do not know if present faculty

members are the same as or different from those who helped earlier. Should ethical questions be decided on such little information? Sometimes they have to be, but there is no indication from the principal that there might be important information she/he did not convey, important questions that might arise for the reader. The story deserves further clarification.

Failure to fulfill obligations can become an ethical matter, if it causes harm. The ethics of faculty non-participation and the principal's conduct need to be based not only on formal contracts and school rules, but also on mature expectation. Working relations were hurt, but it is not apparent that any rules, expressed or tacit, were broken.

Some readers may be dismayed at how the principal chose to communicate the council's expectations to the faculty. Some leadership models call for behaviour to head off conflict, and in doing so the position of either the council or the faculty might have been misrepresented in order to defuse the problem. But misrepresentation, however common and sometimes admired, is only a step toward ethical perdition. As far as we know, nothing unethical happened. Others will be dismayed by the stand taken by the council chairwoman, and might see her behaviour as unethical. Given her position, the opinion she expressed carries something of potential censure. But we have no reason to believe that it was intended to intimidate. Her e-mail, as described, was intemperate – but not unethical.

Ethics are high codes of conduct and principles; unethical behaviours are hurtful violations of pledges and values, not just bad manners or management. If the two of us were speculating as to possible ethical issues in this case, rather than on the conflict described, we would look to decisions made while sending students and teachers first to 23 temporary classrooms and later to a second building. These would have been times when unfairness threatened. Who got the best deals? Who was compromised? Ethics were a balloon stretched around this school. But we heard no punctures. The expansion we noted probably changed the composition of the faculty, and might have diminished historical sensitivity to norms on matters of fundraising and community building, but this case was a pickle, not a puncture.

CASE COMMENTARY 2

Case: The School Supper Club

Vivienne Collinson
Associate Professor, Michigan State University

This intriguing case raises many more questions than it answers: How difficult is it to move from vice-principal to principal in the same school? Are professional commitment expectations different for private school teachers than for public school teachers? What role does community size play? How was the invitation written or presented to the teachers? What was the pattern of declining teaching attendance for 11 years? Was the principal speaking for her/himself or for the teachers regarding "the school stand on staff participation?" Who on staff serves as a conduit to Rita Davidson? Were the other school's principal and teachers at the annual dinner? (Their involvement or lack of involvement is not indicated but could affect readers' understanding of the narrative.) Who learned what?

Many principals reading this case study can sympathize with the author, knowing how difficult it is to choose battles carefully, and understanding how one word or action can set many more in motion. Teachers reading this case study can empathize with the teachers who did not attend the annual dinner. An unknown number of those teachers had been through a curriculum change with few resources as well as huge upheavals, such as moving their classrooms from portables to the gym or library and back again, coping with an exploding student population and a split into two schools, and teaching to the din of building renovations. It is a tribute to the principal and teachers that throughout so many turbulent years, student scores steadily increased, enrolment increased, extracurricular athletic teams did well, and the school motto, "What really matters is how we treat one another," appeared to stay in focus. But did the school motto extend to adults outside the school?

The author's language suggests that relationships are very important to this leader (for example, "club … community partnerships … we were like one big family … saddens me … little understanding or compassion … really liked him … a generous and accommodating person … we worked well as a team … I wanted to heal this rift quickly … level of trust … death … aftermath … damaged … relationship"). However, wanting good relationships and developing the necessary skills to establish healthy social, ethical, intellectual and political environments are two different matters (see Collinson, in press, for a summary of necessary skills such as dialogue, inquiry, conflict management). For example, readers have little evidence of inquiry. Did the principal conduct an inquiry to find out which teachers did not attend the dinner (past regular attendees? new teachers who might not know the council's expectations? teachers who had suffered the most disruptions?) For what reasons did some teachers attend and others not?

Similarly, "hoping for understanding" does not replace communication skills that foster understanding (for example, questioning, dialogue, argumentation). The principal and chairperson each appeared to take a position immediately and then merely repeat it, instead of engaging in dialogue to understand the reasoning behind the other's position. Each appeared to have a Lone Ranger approach rather than collaborative skills that require "digging into an issue to identify the underlying concerns ... and [finding] an alternative that meets both sets of concerns" (Friedlander, 1983, p. 207). Instead, the protagonists resorted to defensive behaviours such as untested hypotheses ("perhaps she still thought of me as the vice-principal ... maybe she resented my strong support for the school staff"), difficulty hearing negative feedback (a "shock ... to hear staff members criticized"), generalizations ("inflammatory" comments, the "school stand" on participation) and personal attacks ("lack of integrity"). Did the supper club issue really die "a natural death" or merely go underground until the following year or until the next mismatch between expectations and outcomes?

CASE COMMENTARY 3

Case: The School Supper Club

Linda Grant
Education Consultant

Even the title of this case is classic film noir. This is a story about disillusionment, pessimism and desperation. The narrator, in this case an experienced school principal, shares a cynical perspective on life as an administrator in the publicly funded Catholic education system. The story unfolds in a dark and gloomy setting. The overcrowded school building and 23 mouldy portables make a perfect backdrop to showcase human weakness and moral ambiguity. Supporting characters in the story remain in a shadowy background. We get glimpses of a school council meeting and a staff meeting. The perspectives and reactions of the parents, teachers and students are never fully disclosed. The focus remains constantly on the perspective of the protagonist. The principal in this story wants to be the hero.

The principal begins by telling about how the school parents have held a fundraising dinner for the past 11 years to solicit money for the building fund for a new parish church. Then the story twists and turns while the administrator reflects about how the parents continue to think of him as the school vice-principal, even though he had been the principal for the last four years. The principal describes the challenges that over-crowding and the 23 portables have brought, the overworked teachers trying to implement new curriculum without enough time and profes-sional development, and how there are actually two schools with two principals housed in a single overcrowded building. How much bleaker could this story become?

The narration switches back to the school council and the disillusioned parent group. These parents want to know why the teachers are not sup-porting and attending the annual fundraising dinner. They want to know what the principal is going to do to rectify this situation. Will the hero rescue the dinner?

The next morning, the principal calls a staff meeting before the school day begins. This experienced administrator shares verbatim the parents' comments about the staff's perceived lack of support and involvement in the dinner. The principal, in desperation to remain the hero, ensures the teaching staff that the parents were reminded about how dedicated the staff was and how teacher involvement in a fundraising dinner was strictly voluntary.

Enter the tough-sweet female lead. Mrs. Davidson is the school coun-cil chair. She calls the principal's meeting with the school staff inflamma-tory. She claims that she was misquoted. She makes negative comments about the principal in an e-mail. The plot thickens.

In this oppressive atmosphere, anything can go wrong. And did. The principal did not realize that, for a school administrator, trust and respon-sibility in relationships with parents and teachers are paramount. Who would trust a principal who shared the informal discussions of frustrated parents at a meeting with colleagues the morning after? How do this principal's revelations to the teaching staff promote public trust and con-fidence in the teaching profession? Is this school leader modelling positive influence, professional judgment and empathy in practice? Whose human dignity did this principal respect? Is this principal modelling the spiritual values of the Catholic community that is the employer? Has this principal been honest or has this principal been manipulative? Has this principal acted in a way that demonstrates honesty, reliability and moral action?

Parents involved in the school council feel betrayed. Staff members worry about saying anything that might be passed on to the parents or anyone one else. This principal did it once and it could happen again. Cynicism and scepticism permeate this environment.

This principal has compromised the ethical standards for the teaching profession. As a result, the *Care, Respect, Trust* and *Integrity* of the teaching profession have suffered. The evidence of this principal's self-absorption and need for power remains subtle. However, the principal's behaviour serves to undermine the trust placed in every member of the teaching profession.

The protagonists in film noir are driven by their past mistakes and human weakness. So is this principal. The unfortunate aspect of this story is that the hero will most likely repeat these actions and continue to undermine the integrity of the profession. This principal is no hero.

CASE COMMENTARY 4

Case: The School Supper Club

Laura C. Jones

Associate Professor, Language, Literacy and Technology Department, Nazareth College

Words are powerful. Words like "duty … part of their job … what are *you* going to do … invitation not an expectation" all establish clear and distinct types of power relationships between the members of the organization. Even though the heat of the incident has died a natural death, the resentment is still there. Clearly the principal believes there is a permanent riff between the two groups and I wonder how effective any future collaborative projects will be.

If I was to offer suggestions to both the principal and the council president it would be to consider Wheatley's criteria for measuring change:

> To measure whether a change effort has been successful, we need to ask, Are people in the organization more committed to being here now than they were at the beginning of this effort? In terms of sustainability, we need to ask if, at the end of this change effort, people feel more prepared for the next

wave of change. Did we develop capacity or just stage an event? Do people feel that their creativity and expertise contributed to the changes? (Wheatley, 2000, p. 347)

Clearly, the people involved with this benefit at the start of this school community did not ask, "how can we sustain this commitment?" For example, as the years went by, there should have been a change in the membership of the council. At the very least, there should be one teacher at the meetings as well as the vice-principal or principal. Although this proposed solution provides only "representative access" to the council, at least it would be a start.

Furthermore, I am surprised by the council's complete lack- of sensitivity to the dramatic changes that have taken place at the school. From the details provided, it appears the work of the annual dinner was undertaken solely to benefit the parish, not the school or the teachers. Even though I do agree that in the beginning this fundraising dinner was probably a wonderful strategy for building community partnerships, the needs of the community were different at that time. Eleven years ago, it was easy for the teachers to give of their time, energy and talents to such a community project. However, when teachers are dealing with infectious mould, frequent moves between portables and the gym, lost schedules, lost instructional time and no resources, the school council should have realized that their request has become unreasonable and unmanageable.

In order to re-establish a shared commitment to this event rather than just "stage an event," I would recommend the council consider revising the focus for this benefit. The obvious suggestion for the immediate future would be to raise money directly for the school, rather than for the church. This alone would demonstrate to the teachers that the council feels an equal sense of "duty" and "responsibility" for the school organization. However, even if raising money for the church remains the primary fundraiser for the council, the council needs to explore ways to say thank you to the teachers for their commitment to the community effort. Unless the teachers feel that their "creativity and expertise" in the classroom are valued by the council, the council's expectations regarding the teachers' duty to support the community will never meet capacity.

REFLECTION ON THE COMMENTARIES

The commentaries encourage dialogue regarding the meaning of ethical codes, the significance of collaboration, the importance of teacher autonomy, the role of school councils, the development of leadership capacity, and the impact of school environmental conditions on student learning and teachers' ability to facilitate learning. Reflect on your own educative philosophy and personal response to each of these issues.

ADDITIONAL READING

Buskey, F. C., & Early, M. (2005). *A call to action: The moral imperative in school leadership.* Paper presented at the annual meeting of the Mid-Western Educational Research Association, Columbus, OH.

The authors demonstrate that moral leadership makes a difference. A case-study approach is used to examine how a principal's focus on the moral imperative of public education transformed her ethical actions and how her actions contributed to both students' and teachers' accomplishments. The study also reveals that an emphasis on student-centered decision making can facilitate a sense of community in schools.

Foster, W. P. (2004). The decline of the local: A challenge to educational leadership. *Educational Administration Quarterly, 40*(2), 176–191.

This article looks at schools as systemic, rule-bearing institutions that challenge the role of educational leaders. Are they virtuous and free or are they mere agents of the state? The author pits national/state narratives for disseminating rules and standards against the ethos of local communities. Can educational leaders work against the domination of the state to create communal narratives?

Giroux, H. A. (1994). Educational leadership and school administrators: Rethinking the meaning of democratic public cultures. In T. Mulkeen & N. Cambron-McCabe (Eds.), *Democratic leadership: The changing context of administrative preparation,* (pp. 31–47). Norwood, NJ: Ablex Publishing.

Giroux links the revitalization of democratic public life to the development of a theory of educational leadership. He postulates that schools should become democratic public places where students are prepared to play significant roles in reconstructing democratic communities by extending the principles of social justice to all aspects of economic, political and cultural life.

Johnson, C. (2005). *Meeting the ethical challenges of leadership: Casting light or shadow* (2nd ed.). Thousand Oaks, CA: Sage Publications.

This book illustrates a variety of ethical approaches and perspectives that apply to the diversity of ethical demands associated with leadership. The importance of values and shaping ethical contexts are highlighted.

FINAL REFLECTIONS

Exploring Leadership and Ethical Practice through Professional Inquiry offers practical professional learning support to educators responsible for developing, sustaining and leading school cultures that are ethical and student oriented, and that strive to contribute to improving a democratic society.

Educational leadership is a complex, multi-dimensional process that requires increasing knowledge and expertise. This book attempts to support educators in becoming more aware of the tensions, challenges and issues associated with leading schools. As educators inquire into their practice and engage in ongoing professional learning, their understanding and capacity to support ethical cultures and maintain the ethical integrity of public schools is enhanced.

Students and teachers thrive in school communities that have a collaborative, inclusive and trusting culture. The professional environment in these communities can promote relationships that are authentic, open and transformative. Inquiry becomes a preferred mode for both students and teachers in these communities. School leaders in these contexts consciously attend to the emotional, instructional and social justice aspects associated with democratic teaching and learning. Leadership grows as committed individuals foster the ethical agency of all members of the school community in partnerships that share a vision of education in which all children and teachers can learn and excel. The engagement in ongoing self-reflective processes enables these educational leaders to deepen their self-knowledge and understanding. The following leadership self-reflection instrument is one method that can assist educators in acquiring deeper insight into their own leadership philosophy, values and ethics.

LEADERSHIP SELF-REFLECTION INSTRUMENT

Self-Reflection

Reflect on your vision of leadership and ethical practice by completing the following statements:

The important values underlying my philosophy of leadership are...

The principles that I believe should guide my actions are...

The values and beliefs that should influence my decision making are...

I would describe my passion in education as being...

Others would say that in education I stand firmly for...

The things that influence me or guide me in my professional practice are...

For me, being an educational leader means...

For me, being an ethical educator means...

Self-Inquiry

Reflect on your responses to the above statements and then answer the following questions:

What themes emerge in your responses?

Do any of your responses surprise you?

Do your responses affirm the educator you want to be or do they invite you to consider change or further development?

Bibliography

Adalbjarnardottir, S., & Runarsdottir, E. M. (2006). A leader's experiences of intercultural education in an elementary school: Changes and challenges. *Theory into Practice, 45*(2), 177–186.

Arendt, H. (2005). *Responsibility and judgment.* New York, NY: Random House.

Argyris, C., & Schön, D. (1978). *Organizational learning: A theory of action perspective.* Reading, MA: Addison-Wesley.

Armstrong, D. (2004). Constructing moral pathways in the transition from teaching to administration. *Values and Ethics in Educational Administration, 3*(1), 1–8.

Arriaza, G., & Krovetz. M. (2006). *Collaborative teacher leadership: How teachers can foster equitable schools.* Thousand Oaks, CA: Sage Publications.

Awbrey, S., Dana, D., Miller, V. W., Robinson, P., Ryan, M. M., & Scott, D. K. (Eds.). (2006). *Integrative learning and action: A call to wholeness.* New York, NY: Peter Lang Publishing.

Ball, S. J. (2000). Performativities and fabrications in the education economy: Towards the performative society. *Australian Educational Researcher, 2*(27), 1–24.

Barkley, S., Bottoms, G., Feagin, C. H., & Clark, S. (2001). *Leadership matters: Building leadership capacity.* Atlanta, GA: Southern Regional Education Board.

Barth, R. S. (1990). *Improving schools from within: Teachers, parents, and principals can make the difference.* San Francisco, CA: Jossey-Bass.

Bass, B. M. (1985). *Leadership and performance beyond expectations.* New York, NY: The Free Press.

Bass, B. M. (1997). *Transformational leadership: Industrial, military, and educational impact.* Mahwah, NJ: Lawrence Erlbaum Associates.

Beatty, B. (2005). Emotional leadership. In B. Davis (Ed.), *The essentials of school leadership* (pp. 122–144). Thousand Oaks, CA: Sage Publications.

Beatty, B. (2007). Feeling the future of school leadership: Learning to lead with the emotions in mind. *Leading and Managing, 13*(2), 44–65.

Beatty, B., & Brew, C. (2004). Trusting relationships and emotional epistemologies: A foundational leadership issue. *School Leadership and Management, 24*(3), 329–356.

Beatty, B., & Brew, C. (2005). Measuring student sense of connectedness with school: The development of an instrument for use in secondary schools. *Leading and Managing, 11*(2), 103–118.

Beck, L. G. (1997). *Ethics in educational leadership programs: Emerging models.* Columbia, MO: University Council for Educational Administration.

Beckner, W. (2004). *Ethics for educational leaders.* Boston, MA: Pearson Education.

Begley, P. T. (1999). Guiding values for future school leaders. *Orbit, 30*(1), 19–23.

Begley, P. T. (2004). Understanding valuational processes: Exploring the linkage between motivation and action. *International Studies in Educational Administration, 32*(2), 4–17.

Begley, P. T., & Johansson, O. (Eds.). (2003). *The ethical dimensions of school leadership.* Boston, MA: Kluwer Academic Publishers.

Belenky, M. F., Clinchy, B. M., Goldberger, N. R., & Tarule, J. M. (1986). *Women's ways of knowing: The development of self, voice and mind.* New York, NY: Basic Books.

Bezzina, C. (2006). The road less traveled: Professional communities in secondary schools. *Theory into Practice, 45*(2), 159–167.

Blasé, J., & Blasé, R. (2003). *Breaking the silence: Overcoming the problem of principal mistreatment of teachers.* Thousand Oaks, CA: Corwin Press.

Blouin, P. (2006). A profile of elementary and secondary school principals in Canada: First results from the 2004–2005 survey of principals. *Education Matters: Insights on Education, Learning and Training in Canada, 3*(2).

Bolman, L. G., & Deal, T. E. (2003). *Reframing organizations: Artistry, choice and leadership* (3rd ed.). San Francisco, CA: Jossey-Bass.

Bronckart, J.P., & Gather-Thurler, M. (Eds.). (2000). *Transformer l'école.* Issy-les-Moulineaux, France: ESF.

Brooks, J. S., & Normore, A. H. (2005). An Aristotelian framework for the development of ethical leadership. *Values and Ethics in Educational Administration, 3*(2), 1–8.

Brooks, L. J., & Selley, D. (2008). *Ethics and governance: Developing and maintaining an ethical corporate culture.* Toronto, ON: Canadian Centre for Ethics and Corporate Policy.

Browne-Ferrigno, T. (2003). Becoming a principal: Role conception, initial socialization, role-identity transformation, purposeful engagement. *Educational Administration Quarterly, 39*(4), 468–503.

Browne-Ferrigno, T., & Muth, R. (2004). Leadership mentoring in clinical practice: Role socialization, professional development, and capacity building. *Educational Administration Quarterly, 40*(4), 468–494.

Brunet, L. (2003). La gestion des mouvements des ressources humaines: La mobilisation et la mobilité. In J. J. Moisset, J. Plante, & P. Toussaint (Eds.), *La gestion des ressources humaines pour la réussite scolaire* (pp. 267–290). Sainte-Foy, QC: Presses de l'Université du Québec.

Brunet, L., & Boudreault, R. (2001). Empowerment et leadership des directions d'école: Un atout pour une politique de décentralisation. *Éducation et Francophonie, 29*(2), 283–299.

Bryk, A., & Schneider, B. (2004). *Trust in schools: A core resource for improvement.* New York, NY: Russell Sage Foundation.

Buber, M. (1970). *I and thou.* (W. Kaufmann, Trans.). New York, NY: Simon and Schuster. (Original work published 1923).

Buber, M. (1965). Education. In M. Buber, *Between man and man* (pp.98-123). New York, NY: Routledge and Kegan Paul.

Burns, J. M. (1978). *Leadership.* New York, NY: Harper and Row.

Buskey, F. C., & Early, M. (2005). *A call to action: The moral imperative in school leadership.* Paper presented at the annual meeting of the Mid-Western Educational Research Association, Columbus, OH.

Camburn, E. M., Spillane, J. P., & Sebastian, J. (2006*). Measuring principal practice: Results from two promising measurement strategies.* Paper presented at the annual meeting of the American Education Research Association, San Francisco, CA.

Campbell, E. (2003). *The ethical teacher.* Maidenhead, UK: Open University Press.

Canadian Psychological Association. (2001). *Guidelines for professional practice for school psychologists.* Retrieved February 26· 2008 from, http://www.cpa.ca/documents/PsyTest.html.

Clandinin, J., & Connelly, F. M. (1995). *Teachers' professional knowledge landscapes.* New York, NY: Teachers College Press.

Collinson, V. (2008). Leading by learning: New directions in the 21st century. *Journal of Educational Administration, 46*(4), 443–460.

Connelly, F.M., & Clandinin, J. (1988). Studying teachers' knowledge of classrooms: Collaborative research, ethics, and the negotiation of narrative. *Journal of Educational Thought, 22*(2), 269–282.

Coombs, C. (2003). Developing reflective habits of mind. *Values and Ethics in Educational Administration, 1*(4), 1–8.

Darling-Hammond, L., Hammerness, K., & Shulman, L. (2002). Toward expert thinking: How curriculum case writing prompts the development of theory-based professional knowledge in student teachers. *Teaching Education, 13*(2), 219–243.

Davis, S., Darling-Hammond, L., LaPointe, M., & Meyerson, D. (2005). *School leadership study: Developing successful principals (review of research).* Stanford, CA: Stanford Educational Leadership Institute, Stanford University.

Davis, B., Sumara, D., & Luce-Kapler, R. (2007). *Engaging minds: Changing teaching in complex times.* New York, NY: Routledge Press.

Deal, T. E., & Peterson, K. D. (1999*). Shaping school culture: The heart of leadership.* San Francisco, CA: Jossey-Bass.

Dewey, J. (1929). *Democracy and education.* New York, NY: The Free Press.

Dewey, J. (1990). *The school and society and the child and the curriculum.* Chicago, IL: University of Chicago Press.

DuFour, R. (1991). *The principal as staff developer.* Bloomington, IN: National Educational Service.

Duignan, P. (2006). *Educational leadership: Key challenges and ethical tensions.* New York, NY: Cambridge University Press.

Duke, D. L. (1986). The aesthetics of leadership. *Educational Administration Quarterly, 22*(1), 7–27.

Elmore, R. F. (2000). *Building a new structure for school leadership.* Washington, DC: The Albert Shanker Institute.

Euvrard, G. (2006). The values manifesto project. Namibian students ponder which values are worthy of their fledgling democracy. *Educational Leadership, 63*(8), 43–46.

Fesmire, S. (2003). *John Dewey and moral imagination.* Bloomington, IN: Indiana University Press.

Forster, K. (1998). *Promoting the ethical school: Professional ethics for school administrators.* Discussion paper presented at the symposium on the Ethics of the Teaching Profession, Sydney, Australia.

Foster, W. P. (2004). The decline of the local: A challenge to educational leadership. *Educational Administration Quarterly, 40*(2), 176–191.

Freire, P. (2005). *Education for critical consciousness.* New York, NY: Continuum International Publishing Group.

Friedlander, F. (1983). Patterns of individual and organizational learning. In S. Srivastva (Ed.), *The executive mind* (pp. 192–220). San Francisco, CA: Jossey-Bass.

Fullan, M. (2001). *Leading in a culture of change.* San Francisco, CA: Jossey-Bass.

Fullan, M. (2002). The change leader. *Educational Leadership, 59*(8), 16–21.

Fullan, M. (2003). *The moral imperative of school leadership.* Thousand Oaks, CA: Corwin Press.

Fullan, M. (2005). Professional learning communities writ large. In R. DuFour, R. DuFour, & R. Eaker (Eds.), *On common ground* (pp. 209–223). Bloomington, IN: National Education Service.

Fullan, M. G. (1996). *What's worth fighting for in the principalship?* New York, NY: Teachers College Press.

Furman, G., & Gruenewald, D. (2004). Expanding the landscape of social justice: A critical ecological analysis. *Educational Administration Quarterly, 40*(1), 47–76.

Furman, G. C. (2004). The ethic of community. *Journal of Educational Administration, 42*(2), 215–235.

Furman, G. C., & Shields, C. M. (2005). How can educational leaders promote and support social justice and democratic community in schools? In W.A. Firestone & C. Riehl, (Eds.), *A new agenda for research in educational leadership* (pp. 119–137). New York, NY: Teachers College Press.

Giroux, H. (2001). *Theory and resistance in education: Towards a pedagogy for the opposition.* Westport, CT: Greenwood Publishing Group.

Giroux, H. A. (1994). Educational leadership and school administrators: Rethinking the meaning of democratic public cultures. In T. Mulkeen & N. Cambron-McCabe (Eds.), *Democratic leadership: The changing context of administrative preparation,* (pp. 31–47). Norwood, NJ: Ablex Publishing.

Goldblatt, P., & Smith, D. (2005). *Cases for teacher development: Preparing for the classroom.* Thousand Oaks, CA: Sage Publications.

Greene, M. (1995). Art and imagination: Reclaiming the sense of possibility. *Phi Delta Kappan, 76*(5), 378–382.

Gross, S. J. (2006). *Leadership mentoring: Maintaining school improvement in turbulent times.* Lanham, MA: Rowman and Littlefield.

Habermas, J. (1992). *Between facts and norms: Contributions to a discourse theory of law and democracy.* Cambridge, MA: The MIT Press.

Habermas, J. (1990). *Moral consciousness and communicative action.* (C. Lenhardt & S. W. Nicholsen, Trans.). Cambridge, MA: The MIT Press.

Halpern, B. L., & Lubar, K. (2003). *Leadership presence.* New York, NY: Penguin Books.

Hargreaves, A., & Fink, D. (2006). *Sustainable leadership.* San Francisco, CA: Jossey-Bass.

Harré, R., & van Langenhove, L. (Eds.). (1999). *Positioning theory: Moral contexts of international action.* Malden, MA: Blackwell Publishers.

Haynes, F. (1998). *The ethical school: Consequences, consistency, care, ethics.* New York, NY: Routledge.

Hermond-Prairie, D. (2005). Ethical leadership is not optional: How LPPs can help. *International Journal of Scholarly Academic Intellectual Diversity, 8*(1).

Hord, S. (1997). Professional learning communities: What are they and why are they important? *Issues …about Change, 6*(1).

Houston, P. D., & Sokolow, S. L. (2006). *The spiritual dimension of leadership: 8 key principles to leading more effectively.* Thousand Oaks, CA: Corwin Press.

Jazzar, M., & Algozzine, R. (2007). *Keys to successful 21ˢᵗ century educational leadership.* Boston, MA: Allyn and Bacon.

Johnson, C. (2005). *Meeting the ethical challenges of leadership: Casting light or shadow* (2nd ed.). Thousand Oaks, CA: Sage Publications.

Johnston, K. (2006). *Education for a caring society: Classroom relationships and moral action.* New York, NY: Teachers College Press.

Jones, B. D., & Egley, R. J. (2006). Looking through different lenses: Teachers' and administrators' views of accountability. *Phi Delta Kappan, 87*(10), 767–771.

Katz, M., Noddings, N., & Strike, K. A. (Eds.). (1999). *Justice and caring: The search for common ground in education.* New York, NY: Teachers College Press.

Knapp, M. S., Copland, M. A., & Talbert, J. (2003). *Leading for learning: Reflective tools for school and district leaders.* Seattle, WA: Centre for the Study of Teaching and Policy.

Kochan, F. K., & Reed, C. J. (2005). Collaborative leadership, community build-ing, and democracy in public education. In F.W. English (Ed.), *The Sage handbook of educational leadership: Advances in theory, research, and practice* (pp. 68–83). Thousand Oaks, CA: Sage Publications.

Kohlberg, L. (1981). *The philosophy of moral development: Moral stages and the idea of justice.* New York, NY: Harper and Row.

Kouzes, J. M., & Posner, B. Z. (2001). *Leadership practices inventory (LPI): The facilitator's guide* (2nd ed.). San Francisco, CA: Jossey-Bass.

Kouzes, J. M., & Posner, B. Z. (2003). *Encouraging the heart: A leader's guide to rewarding and recognizing others.* San Francisco, CA: Jossey-Bass.

Kouzes, J. M., & Posner, B. Z. (2007). *The leadership challenge* (4th ed.). San Francisco, CA: Jossey-Bass.

Ladson-Billings, G. J., & Tate, W. F. (Eds.). (2006). *Education research in the public interest: Social justice, action, and policy.* New York, NY: Teachers College Press.

Langlois, L. (2004). La résolution de problèmes complexes et le leadership de cinq femmes directrices générales de la province de Québec. *Éducation et Francophonie, 32*(2), 79–94.

Langlois, L. (2004). Responding ethically: Complex decision making by school district superintendents. *International Studies in Educational Administration, 32*(2), 78-93.

Langlois, L. (2008). *Can ethics be learned? Results from the TERA three-year research project.* Paper presented at the annual meeting of the American Education Research Association, New York, NY.

Leithwood, K., & Beatty, B. (2008). *Leading with teacher emotions in mind.* Thousand Oaks, CA: Corwin Press.

Leithwood, K., Jantzi, D., & Steinbach, R. (1999). *Changing leadership for changing times.* Buckingham, PA: Open University Press.

Leithwood, K., & Musella, D. (Eds.). (1991). *Understanding school system admin-istration: Studies of the contemporary chief education officer.* London, UK: Falmer Press.

Leithwood, K., Seashore, K., Anderson, S., & Wahlstorm, K. (2004). *Review of research: How leadership influences student learning.* University of Minnesota: Center for Applied Research and Educational Improvement.

Lipman, M. (2003). *Thinking in education* (2nd ed.). New York, NY: Cambridge University Press.

Lipton, L., Wellman, B., & Humbard, C. (2002). *Mentoring matters: A practical guide to learning-focused relationships.* Alexandria, VA: Association for Supervision and Curriculum Development.

Maracle, L. (2007). Toward a personal global feminist agenda. Speech presented at the Distinguished Visitor Community Dinner, Windsor, Ontario.

Margolis, D. (1998). *The fabric of self: A theory of ethics and emotions*. New Haven, CT: Yale University Press.

Marks, H.M., & Printy, S. (2003). Principal leadership and school performance: An integration of transformational and instructional leadership. *Educational Administration Quarterly, 39*(3), 370–397.

Maxwell, J. C. (2003). *There's no such thing as "business" ethics: There's only one rule for making decisions*. New York, NY: Warner Books.

McCay, L., Flora, J., Hamilton, A., & Riley, J. F. (2001). Reforming schools through teacher leadership: A program for classroom teachers as agents of change. *Educational Horizons, 79*(3), 135–142.

Mezirow, J. (1990). *Fostering critical reflection in adulthood: A guide to trans-formative and emancipatory learning*. San Francisco, CA: Jossey-Bass.

Miller, J. P. (1994). *The contemplative practitioner: Meditation in education and the professions*. New York, NY: Bergin and Garvey Publishers.

Miller, J. P. (1999). *Education and the soul: Toward a spiritual curriculum*. Albany, NY: State University New York Press.

Moxley, R. S. (2000). *Leadership and spirit*. San Francisco, CA: Jossey-Bass.

Murphy, J. (2006). A new view of leadership. *National Staff Development Council, 27*(3), 51–53.

Noddings, N. (2002). *Educating moral people: A caring alternative to character education*. New York, NY: Teachers College Press.

Noddings, N. (2005). *The challenge to care in schools: An alternative approach to education* (2nd ed.). New York, NY: Teachers College Press.

Normore, A. H. (2004a). The edge of chaos: School administrators and account-ability. *Journal of Educational Administration, 42*(1), 55–77.

Normore, A. H. (2004b). Ethics and values in leadership preparation programs: Finding the North Star in the dust storm. *Values and Ethics in Educational Administration, 2*(2), 1–4.

Northwest Regional Educational Laboratory (NWREL). (2005). *Leadership practices of successful principals: Retaining strong leaders*. Portland, OR: Author.

Ogawa, R. T. (2005). Leadership as social construct: The expression of human agency within organizational constraint. In F. W. English (Ed.), *The Sage handbook of educational leadership: Advances in theory, research, and practice* (pp. 89–108). Thousand Oaks, CA: Sage Publications.

Ontario College of Teachers. (2003). *Exploring ethical knowledge through inquiry: Standards in practice (resource kit 2)*. Toronto, ON: Author.

Ontario College of Teachers. (2006a). *The ethical standards for the teaching profession*. Toronto, ON: Author.

Ontario College of Teachers. (2006b). *Foundations of professional practice*. Toronto, ON: Author.

Ontario College of Teachers. (2006c). *The standards of practice for the teaching profession*. Toronto, ON: Author.

Ontario College of Teachers. (2008). *Exploring ethical practice through inquiry*. Toronto, ON: Author.

Ontario College of Teachers (Producer). (2009). *Living the Standards DVD (Education Video)*. Available from Ontario College of Teachers, Toronto, ON.

Orelove, F. P., Sobsey, D., & Silberman, R. K. (Eds.). (2004). *Educating children with multiple disabilities: A collaborative approach*. Baltimore, MD: Brookes Publishing.

Palmer, P. (1998). *The courage to teach: Exploring the inner landscape of a teacher's life*. San Francisco, CA: Jossey-Bass.

Pearce, C. L., & Conger, J. A. (2003). *Shared leadership: Reframing the hows and whys of leadership*. Thousand Oaks, CA: Sage Publications.

Peel, H. A., & Walker, B. L. (1994). What it takes to be an empowering principal. *Principal, 73*(4), 41–42.

Pellicer, L. (2003). *Caring enough to lead: How reflective thought leads to moral leadership* (2nd ed.). Thousand Oaks, CA: Corwin Press.

Reina, M. L., & Reina, D. S. (1999). *Trust and betrayal in the workplace*. San Francisco, CA: Berrett-Koehler Publishers.

Retelle, E. (2007). *The preparation and promotion of vice-principals to the principalship*. Paper presented at the annual meeting of the Canadian Society for the Study of Education, Saskatoon, SK.

Reyes, P., & Wagstaff, L. (2005). How does leadership promote successful teaching and learning for diverse students? In W.A. Firestone & C. Riehl (Eds.), *A new agenda for research in educational leadership* (pp. 101–118). New York, NY: Teachers College Press.

Schultz, B. (2005). Finally a superintendent: Now what? *School Administrator, 62*(6), 10–13.

Senge, P. (1990). *The fifth discipline: The art and practice of the learning organization*. London, UK: Random House.

Senge, P., Kleiner, A., Roberts, C., Roth, G., Ross, R., & Smith, B. (1999). *The dance of change: The challenges to sustaining momentum in learning organizations*. New York, NY: Doubleday Business.

Senge, P., Scharmer, C. O., Jaworski, J., & Flowers, B. S. (2004). *Presence: Human purpose and the field of the future*. New York, NY: The Doubleday Broadway Publishing Group.

Sergiovanni, T. J. (1995). *The principalship: A reflective practice perspective*. Boston, MA: Allyn and Bacon.

Sergiovanni, T. J. (1996). *Moral leadership: Getting to the heart of school improvement*. San Francisco, CA: Jossey-Bass.

Shapiro, J. P. (2006). Ethical decision making in turbulent times: Bridging theory with practice to prepare authentic educational leaders. *Values and Ethics in Educational Administration, 4*(2), 1–4.

Shapiro, J. P., & Gross, S. J. (2007). *Ethical educational leadership in turbulent times: (Re)solving moral dilemmas*. Mahwah, NJ: Lawrence Erlbaum Associates.

Shapiro, J. P., & Stefkovich, J. A. (2005). *Ethical leadership and decision making in education: Applying theoretical perspectives to complex dilemmas* (2nd ed.). Mahwah, NJ: Lawrence Erlbaum Associates.

Shoho, A. R., & Barnett, B. G. (2006). *The challenges of new principals: Implications for preparation, induction, and professional support*. Paper presented at the annual meeting of the American Education Research Association, San Francisco, CA.

Shulman, J. H. (Ed.). (1992). *Case methods in teacher education*. New York, NY: Teachers College Press.

Shulman, L. (1992). Toward a pedagogy of cases. In J. H. Shulman (Ed.), *Case methods in teacher education* (pp. 1–30). New York, NY: Teachers College Press.

Sleeter, C. (2008). Teaching for democracy in an age of corporatocracy. *Teachers College Record, 110*(1), 139–159.

Smith, D. (2003). *Discovering a methodology that reveals ethical knowledge*. Paper presented at the International Study Association of Teachers and Teaching, Leiden, The Netherlands.

Smith, D. (2007). *Exploring ethical practice through inquiry*. Toronto, ON: Ontario College of Teachers.

Stake, R. (1995). *The art of case study research*. Thousand Oaks, CA: Sage Publications.

Starratt, R. J. (1999). Moral dimensions of leadership. In P. T. Begley & P. E. Leonard (Eds.), *The values of educational administration* (pp. 22–35). London, UK: Falmer Press.

Starratt, R. J. (2003). *Centering educational administration: Cultivating meaning, community, responsibility.* Mahwah, NJ: Lawrence Erlbaum Associates.

Starratt, R. J. (2004). *Ethical leadership.* San Francisco, CA: Jossey-Bass.

Starratt, R. J. (2005). Responsible leadership. *The Educational Forum, 69*(2), 124–133.

Starratt, R. J. (2006). *The moral agency of educational leaders.* Paper presented at the Annual Conference of Leadership and Ethics in Education, Victoria, BC.

Stengel, B., & Tom, A. R. (2006). *Moral matters: Five ways to develop the moral life of schools.* New York, NY: Teachers College Press.

Strike, K. A. (2007). *Ethical leadership in schools: Creating community in an environment of accountability.* Thousand Oaks, CA: Corwin Press.

Strike, K. A., & Soltis, J. F. (2004). *The ethics of teaching* (4th ed.). New York, NY: Teachers College Press.

Strike, K. A., Soltis, J. F., & Haller, E. J. (2005). *The ethics of school administration* (3rd ed.). New York, NY: Teachers College Press.

Theoharis, G. (2006). *Woven in deeply: Identity, calling, and urban social justice.* Paper presented at the annual meeting of the American Education Research Association, San Francisco, CA.

Tschannen-Moran, M. (2004). *Trust matters: Leadership for successful schools.* San Francisco, CA: Jossey-Bass.

Weiner, B. (2004). Attribution theory revisited: Transforming cultural plurality into theoretical unity. In D. M. McInerney & S. Van Etten (Eds.), *Big theories revisited: Research on sociocultural influences on motivation and learning* (pp. 1–12). Greenwich, CT: Information Age Publishing.

Wheatley, M. J. (1997, Summer). Good-bye, command and control. In *The Jossey-Bass reader on educational leadership* (pp. 339-347). San Francisco, CA: Jossey-Bass.

Whitehead, A.J., & McNiff, J. (2006). *Action research: Living theory.* Thousand Oaks, CA: Sage Publications.

Whitmore, J. (2006). *Coaching for performance: Growing people, performance, a purpose* (3rd ed.). London, UK: Nicholas Brealey Publishing.

Williams, R. B. (2006). Leadership for school reform: Do principal decision making styles reflect a collaborative approach? *Canadian Journal of Educational Administration and Policy, 53,* 1-22.

Wilmore, E., & Thomas, C. (2001). The new century: Is it too late for transformational leadership? *Educational Horizons, 79*(3), 115–123.

Zubay, B., & Soltis, J. F. (2005). *Creating the ethical school: A book of case studies.* New York, NY: Teachers College Press.

About the Editors

Déirdre Smith is the Manager of the Standards of Practice and Education division of the Ontario College of Teachers. In this capacity, Smith has led the collaborative development, with 10,000 educators and members of the public, of a set of ethical standards and standards of practice for the teaching profession that provide a collective vision of teacher professionalism in Ontario, Canada. These standards or principles of professional practice are a foundational core of teacher education programs in Ontario. Smith has also co-ordinated the policy development of over 300 Additional Qualification courses and programs for teacher and leadership education. As well, she has led the development of provincial multimedia inquiry-based resources for integration into Ontario's teacher education programs.

Smith is co-editor of *Cases for Teacher Development: Preparing for the Classroom*. She has presented nationally and internationally on ethical standards, standards of practice and the relationship of these to teacher education and teacher professionalism. She has been published in the areas of cases, teacher education and ethics. She received the Principal of the Year award in 2000 from the Geneva Centre for Autism. Her experience as a school principal, education consultant, special education administrator, youth counsellor and classroom teacher inform her work in policy development, teacher education and leadership formation.

Patricia F. Goldblatt, a former secondary school teacher of English and art has been published in numerous scholarly journals internationally, provincially and locally on topics that range from women's issues, multicultural teaching, art and education. Through her work as a program officer at the Ontario College of Teachers, she facilitated sessions with principals as well as pre-service and in-service groups at faculties and in schools. Her collaborative research on standards with Déirdre Smith has resulted in presentations at ISATT, AERA, NSDC, CSSE and AACTE as well as a Sage publication based on the stories and commentaries of educators in Ontario, *Cases for Teacher Development: Preparing for the Classroom*.

About the Contributors

Denise E. Armstrong is an assistant professor in Organizational and Administrative Studies in the Faculty of Education at Brock University. Her research and writing focus on personal, professional and organizational change and transitions, ethical leadership and social justice.

Paul Axelrod is a professor in the Faculty of Education at York University and was dean of the faculty from 2001–08. He has written widely on the history and politics of schooling and higher education. He received the 2007 David C. Smith Award from the Council of Ontario Universities for his contributions to scholarship and policy on higher education.

Brenda Beatty is designer and director of the Monash Master in School Leadership and the Human Leadership: Developing People programs, created for the Victoria State School Department of Education. She won the 2002 Thomas B. Greenfield Distinguished Dissertation of the Year Award for *Emotion Matters in Educational Leadership*.

Ulrika Bergmark is a PhD student in the Department of Education, Luleå University of Technology, Sweden. Her research interest lies in the field of ethical issues in schools. Through her research she is connected to a school area in northern Sweden where work is done to develop ethical preschools and schools.

Pam Bishop is an associate professor and Coordinator of Educational Leadership in the Graduate Division of Educational Research, Faculty of Education, University of Calgary. She is editor of the *International Electronic Journal for Leadership in Learning* and former director of professional and continuing education in the Faculty of Education, University of Tasmania, Australia.

Elizabeth Campbell is a professor and Associate Chair of Graduate Studies in the Department of Curriculum, Teaching and Learning at the Ontario Institute for Studies in Education at the University of Toronto. Her scholarship is in the areas of professional ethics and moral agency in teaching, the moral and ethical dimensions of teaching and schooling, and teacher education.

Jean Clandinin is a professor and Director of the Centre for Research for Teacher Education and Development at the University of Alberta. She is a former teacher, counsellor and psychologist. She was awarded the University of Alberta's 2001 Kaplan Research Achievement Award, a 2004 Killam, and the 2008 Beauchamp Award.

A. Rae Clementz is a doctoral candidate at the University of Illinois in the Educational Psychology Department. Her work in education program evaluation encompasses education policy, principal leadership programs, induction and mentoring for new teachers, math and science programs for students, and technology integration programs.

Alice Collins is Dean of Education at Memorial University of Newfoundland. She is Chair, GEO Centre Board of Directors, a former president of the Canadian Association of Deans of Education and a former president of the Canadian Society for the Study of Education.

Vivienne Collinson is an associate professor at Michigan State University. She taught elementary and middle school students in Canada for 20 years before teaching tertiary-level education in Canada and the US. She is co-convenor of a European network for continuing professional development for teachers and leaders.

Cheryl J. Craig is a professor at the University of Houston where she serves as Coordinator of the Teaching and Teacher Education Program and Head of Elementary Education. She is a recipient of her college's research, teaching and collaboration awards and co-editor of the Association of Teacher Educators' yearbook.

Lara Doan is an assistant professor of education at the University of Windsor. Her research interests include pedagogies and mediating technologies; social equity and schooling; experiences of schooling as they relate to experiences of alienation and isolation; and learning identities in schooled contexts.

Jeanne Doucet holds a Master's degree in Education and is presently working on a PhD in Leadership. She held vice-principal and principal positions at the secondary level for the Ottawa French Catholic School Board. She also participated as a tutor for the Principal's course at Ottawa University from 1997 to 1999 and held the position of coordinator and principal from 2001 to 2003. Effective change has always been an object of great interest in her leadership roles.

Ellie Drago-Severson is an associate professor of educational leadership at Columbia University's Teachers College. Her teaching and research centre on school leadership for principal and teacher development and supporting adult growth in K–12 schools and university contexts. She was awarded the 2004 National Staff Development Council's Book of the Year Award for *Helping Teachers Learn*.

Patrick Duignan, president of the Australian Council for Educational Leaders, has been a teacher, principal, lecturer, professor and dean in tertiary institutions in Australia and overseas. An international consultant on leadership development, his research and development projects encompass leadership in education, health and welfare.

Lynnette B. Erickson is an associate professor of teacher education in the David O. McKay School of Education at Brigham Young University. Her research concentrates on pre-service teacher education and elementary social studies education, including democracy in the classroom.

Linda Grant, currently an education consultant, has been a teacher, principal, faculty of education instructor and assistant professor, Ontario Ministry of Education officer, professional development coordinator for school and board leadership certification programs, and a member of the senior leadership team at the Ontario College of Teachers.

Steven Jay Gross is an associate professor of educational leadership at Temple University. His interests include initiating and sustaining deep, democratic reform in schools, leadership mentoring, and turbulence theory.

Andy Hargreaves is the Thomas More Brennan Chair in Education at the Lynch School of Education at Boston College. His numerous books on culture, change and leadership in education are available in many languages

Pauline Hargreaves is Assistant Head at The Learning Project Elementary School in Boston. With a career spanning elementary, middle and secondary schools, she was also previously the Vice-Principal of the Lower School at Maclachlan College in Oakville, Ontario.

Felicity Haynes is a former dean of education at the University of Western Australia, the first female dean appointed there. She taught in philosophy of education for over 30 years and has published in the areas of aesthetic education, ethics, gender studies, epistemology, and conceptual change and metaphor.

James Heap is Dean of the Faculty of Education at Brock University and a former dean of the College of Education at Ohio University. He is a former chair of the Department of Sociology in Education and the Department of Theory and Policy Studies at the Ontario Institute for Studies in Education at the University of Toronto.

Rita L. Irwin is a professor of art education and curriculum studies and the Associate Dean of Teacher Education at the University of British Columbia. She is president of the Canadian Society for the Study of Education and President-Elect of the International Society for Education through Art.

Patrick M. Jenlink is a professor of doctoral studies in the Department of Secondary Education and Educational Leadership, and Director of the Educational Research Center at Stephen F. Austin State University. His research interests include the politics of identity, democratic education and leadership, and postmodern inquiry methods.

Craig E. Johnson is a professor of leadership studies and Director of the Doctor of Management Program at George Fox University. He teaches graduate and undergraduate courses in leadership, ethics, management and communication.

Kay Johnston is a professor of educational studies and women's studies at Colgate University. She is Chair of the Educational Studies Department and has directed the Women's Studies Program. She has taught at Lesley University and Boston College. Her interests are in moral development, teaching and learning.

Laura C. Jones is an associate professor in the Language, Literacy and Technology Department at Nazareth College. She is interested in literacy theory and instruction as well as the relationships between literacy leadership and social responsibility.

Lyse Langlois is an associate professor in the Department of Labour Relations at Université Laval, specializing in the fields of human resources and ethics. Her areas of interest include decentralizing the role of leadership and decision making in organizations.

Pauline Leonard is an associate professor and Department Chair of Curriculum, Instruction and Leadership in the College of Education at Louisiana Tech University. She has extensive experience developing educational leadership graduate courses and programs. Her interests centre on professional collaboration, educational leadership, and the influence of values and ethics on decision making in education.

Ben Levin is a professor and Canada Research Chair in the Department of Theory and Policy Studies at the Ontario Institute for Studies in Education at the University of Toronto. He is a former Deputy Minister of Education for the Province of Ontario. He is known for his work in education policy and reform.

Ann Lieberman is an emeritus professor from Teachers College, Columbia University and a senior scholar at the Carnegie Foundation for the Advancement of Teaching. Her unique contribution has been in moving between school and university, embracing the dualities of theory/practice, process/content, intellectual/social-emotional learning, and policy/practice.

John Loughran is the Foundation Chair in Curriculum and Pedagogy in the Faculty of Education, Monash University. His research spans science education and the related fields of professional knowledge, reflective practice and teacher research. He is co-editor of the journal *Studying Teacher Education*.

John Lundy is Director of the Laurentian University (English Language) School of Education. A former education professor at Nipissing University, he received the 2003 Nipissing University Vice-President's Research Achievement Award. He is currently researching equity of access to teacher education by Aboriginal peoples, visible minorities and people with disabilities.

Peter McLaren is an award-winning author, political activist and professor of education at the Graduate School of Education and Information Studies, University of California, Los Angeles. His contribution to the development of critical pedagogy is well-known worldwide with his writings translated into 15 languages.

Katherine Merseth is Director of Teacher Education at the Harvard Graduate School of Education. She is the Founding Executive Director of the Harvard Children's Initiative and a former director of the School Leadership Program. Her areas of research and writing include school reform, charter schools, school leadership, teacher education and case-method instruction.

Dianna Moreno, former public middle school educator and now doctoral student in education at the University of California, Los Angeles, looks at critical spiritual pedagogy to critique schooling practices in a capitalist economy.

Julie Mueller is an assistant professor in the Faculty of Education at Wilfrid Laurier University. She teaches the School and Society and conducts a professional learning seminar on site in Professional Development Schools (PDS). Her research focus is teachers' integration of technology in the classroom and the impact of the PDS structure on the professional practice of associate teachers.

Anthony H. Normore is an associate professor of educational administration in graduate education at California State University, Dominguez Hills. A former K–12 educator in Canadian schools, he has conducted keynote addresses at principal leadership academies and student leadership academies. He currently researches and writes in the area of leadership development with focus on urban school leaders in the context of ethics and social justice.

John M. Novak is a professor of education and former chair of the Department of Graduate and Undergraduate Studies in Education at Brock University. He is a former public school teacher and author of books on invitational education, democratic teacher education and invitational educational leadership.

Margaret Olson is an associate professor at St. Francis Xavier University. She teaches sociology and inclusion courses to elementary and secondary teacher candidates in the BEd program, and curriculum and research courses in the graduate program. Her research revolves around learning to teach and professional development.

Julia O'Sullivan is a professor and Dean of the Faculty of Education at the University of Western Ontario. She is the founding national director of the Centre of Excellence for Children and Adolescents with Special Needs, one of four centres for children's well-being funded by Health Canada.

Anne Phelan is an associate professor in the Department of Curriculum and Pedagogy and a research associate with the Centre for the Study of Teacher Education at the University of British Columbia. Her interests lie in (a) the relationship between language, subjectivity and power in teaching and teacher education, and (b) the dynamic of judgment, responsibility and hospitality in professional life.

Stefinee Pinnegar is a teacher educator in the David O. McKay School of Education at Brigham Young University. She is a founder of the Self-Study in Teacher Education Practices research movement, Acting Dean of the Invisible College for Research on Teaching, and project director for an endorsement program for teaching English-language learners.

Jean Plante is Director of the Department of Educational Fundamentals and Practices at Laval University's Faculty of Education. He teaches at the undergraduate and graduate levels. Together with his colleague, G.-Raymond Laliberté, he created a televised course whose primary objective is to critically analyze the Québec education system.

Jules Rocque teaches graduate courses in school administration at the Collège universitaire de Saint-Boniface in Winnipeg. His administrative experience includes working in French, English, Inuit and minority education contexts in several Canadian provinces.

Pat Rogers is Dean of the Faculty of Education, University of Windsor. Rogers came from York University, where she was professor of mathematics and education since 1981 and founding Academic Director of the Centre for the Support of Teaching (1989-94 and 1998-2001). Dr. Rogers' research and teaching interests lie in mathematics, the influence of culture on mathematics education, and university teaching and learning. She is currently Chair of the Ontario Association of Deans of Education (2005-2009).

A.G. Rud is an associate professor of educational studies at Purdue University. He teaches graduate and undergraduate courses in the cultural foundations of education. He is the editor of *Education and Culture*, the journal of the

John Dewey Society. His research looks at the moral dimensions of teaching, learning and leading in P–12 and higher education.

Tom Russell is a professor in the Faculty of Education at Queen's University, where he holds a chair in teaching and learning. Most of his teaching involves pre-service teachers in secondary science and supervision of the school practicum. His research centres on how people learn to teach and how teachers improve their teaching.

Jean J. Ryoo is a doctoral student in urban schooling at the University of California, Los Angeles. She is a former middle and high school social studies and English teacher with experience teaching in Boston, Los Angeles and Honolulu.

Michel Saint-Germain is a professor of school administration at the University of Ottawa's Faculty of Education. He has taken part in education development projects in Africa and Haiti. His fields of research include the role of French-language school principals outside Québec, well-being and dignity in the workplace, and learning organizations.

Lorraine Savoie-Zajc is Director, Département des sciences de l'éducation, Université du Québec en Outaouais. Her courses focus on the dynamics of change in education and on research methodology. For several years she has been researching student retention, school success and student dropout.

Theresa Shanahan, a former criminal lawyer, is an assistant professor in the Faculties of Education and the Graduate Program in Education at York University and Coordinator of the Graduate Diploma in Postsecondary Education. Her research interests include education law and policy, postsecondary education and university governance.

Joan Poliner Shapiro is a professor of Educational Administration in the Department of Educational Leadership and Policy Studies at Temple University's College of Education. Previously, at Temple, she served as Associate Dean for Research and Development and as chair of her department. In 2008 she received a Lindback Foundation Award for Distinguished Teaching.

Carolyn Shields is a professor of leadership in the Department of Educational Organization and Leadership at the University of Illinois at Urbana Champaign. She teaches in the areas of leadership and ethics, democracy, policy and social justice. Her research relates to how educational leaders can create learning environments that are democratic, socially just, and inclusive of students' lived experiences.

Richard Shields, in addition to teaching at the Hamilton-Wentworth Catholic District School Board, is a sessional lecturer in both education and ethics at the University of St. Michael's College and McMaster University. His research and writing centre on current ethical issues.

Robert Stake is Director of the Center for Instructional Research and Curriculum Evaluation at the University of Illinois at Urbana-Champaign. He teaches courses on program evaluation, case-study research, qualitative data analysis and curriculum evaluation.

Stéphane Thibodeau teaches school administration in the Department of Education at the Université du Québec à Trois-Rivières. His research focuses on organizational behaviour (leadership, self-efficacy, professional isolation) and on human resources management in schools.

Pierre Toussaint teaches in the Department of Education and Pedagogy at the Faculty of Education of the Université du Québec à Montréal. He directs a research group for pre-service/ongoing teacher education. His research interests include the management of education policies, intercultural education and pre-service/ongoing education for education staff.

John Wallace is a professor in the Department of Curriculum, Teaching and Learning at the Ontario Institute for Studies in Education at the University of Toronto. He is active in middle school curriculum integration, including the school and classroom conditions under which integration takes place and the nature of student learning in interdisciplinary settings.

Lindy Zaretsky is Superintendent of Instructional Services, K–12 and Leadership, in the Simcoe County District School Board. She has been a teacher, consultant and administrator in a variety of school settings in the Greater Toronto Area. She is also a sessional instructor in graduate programs at Ryerson University and the Ontario Institute of Studies in Education at the University of Toronto.

Recycled
Supporting responsible use
of forest resources
www.fsc.org Cert no. SGS-COC-003153
© 1996 Forest Stewardship Council

FSC

MARQUIS

Marquis Book Printing inc.

Québec, Canada

2010

100%

BIO GAS
ENERGY

This book has been printed on 100% post-consumer
waste paper, certified Eco-logo and processed chlorine free.